The Failure of Modernism

THE FAILURE
OF MODERNISM

Symptoms of
American Poetry

ANDREW ROSS

Columbia University Press / New York / 1986

Library of Congress Cataloging-in-Publication Data
Ross, Andrew.
The failure of modernism.
Bioliography: p.
Includes index.
1. American poetry—20th century—History and
criticism.   2. Modernism (Literature)   3. Subjectivity
in literature.   4. Eliot, T. S. (Thomas Stearns), 1888–
1965—Criticism and interpretation.   5. Olson, Charles,
1910–1970—Criticism and interpretation.   6. Ashbery,
John—Criticism and interpretation.   I. Title.
PS310.M57R67   1986   811'.5'09   86-9660
ISBN 0-231-06330-X

Book design by Laiying Chong.

Columbia University Press
New York   Guildford, Surrey
Copyright © 1986 Columbia University Press
All rights reserved

Printed in the United States of America

for John McPartlin

CONTENTS

ACKNOWLEDGMENTS

I AM GRATEFUL, firstly, to Michael Grant, whose advice and encouragement over the years has been a steady source of inspiration behind the writing of this book. So too, Stephen Bann and Paul Smith each helped more than they can imagine, both in conversation and in print.

Joel Fineman's timely enthusiasms were always invaluable, and Constance Penley's theoretical affection irradiated the whole project when it was most needed.

Thanks for information, help, and advice are also due to Ben Brewster, Leon Chai, Cairns Craig, David Ellis, Dalia Judovitz, Walter Benn Michaels, Roger Mitchell, Bill Schroeder, Dick Wheeler, Richard Wollheim, and other stalwarts of the Unit for Criticism and Interpretive Theory at Urbana-Champaign.

Jack Ben-Levi helped with proofing and David Diefendorf was the kindest of editors.

I would like to thank the Princeton University Committee on Research in the Humanities and Social Sciences for supporting publication costs. The editors of *Representations* and *SubStance* allowed me to reprint parts of chapter 2 and chapter 6, respectively.

Acknowledgments are made to the following for permitting the use of copyrighted material:

Excerpts from *Collected Poems 1909–1962* by T.S. Eliot, copyright 1936 by Harcourt Brace Jovanovich Inc.; copyright © 1963, 1964 by T.S. Eliot. Reprinted by permission of the publisher and by Faber & Faber.

Excerpts from *Four Quartets* by T.S. Eliot, copyright 1943 by T.S. Eliot; renewed 1971 by Esme Valerie Eliot. Reprinted by permission of Harcourt Brace Jovanovich, Inc., and Faber & Faber.

Excerpts from *The Family Reunion* by T.S. Eliot, copyright 1939 by

T.S. Eliot; renewed 1967 by Esme Valerie Eliot. Reprinted by permission of Harcourt Brace Jovanovich, Inc., and Faber & Faber.

Excerpts from *Murder in the Cathedral* by T.S. Eliot, copyright 1935 by Harcourt Brace Jovanovich, Inc.; renewed 1963 by T.S. Eliot. Reprinted by permission of the publisher and Faber & Faber.

Excerpts from *The Cocktail Party* by T.S. Eliot, copyright 1950 by T.S. Eliot; renewed 1978 by Esme Valerie Eliot. Reprinted by permission of Harcourt Brace Jovanovich, Inc., and Faber & Faber.

Excerpts from *Poems Written in Early Youth* by T.S. Eliot, copyright © 1967 by Valerie Eliot. Reprinted by permission of Farrar Straus and Giroux and Faber & Faber.

Excerpts from the published poetry of Charles Olson, by permission of the University of California Press.

Excerpts from "The Carpenter" by Charles Olson, copyright © 1976 by the University of Connecticut Library. Reprinted by permission of the Library.

Excerpts from *The Tennis Court Oath* by John Ashbery, copyright © 1962 by John Ashbery. Reprinted by permission of Wesleyan University Press.

Excerpts from *The Double Dream of Spring* by John Ashbery, copyright © 1966, 1967, 1968, 1969, 1970 by John Ashbery. Reprinted by permission of Georges Borchardt, Inc., and the author.

Excerpts from *Self-Portrait in a Convex Mirror* by John Ashbery, copyright © 1972, 1973, 1974, 1975 by John Ashbery. Reprinted by permission of Viking Penguin, Inc.

Excerpts from *As We Know* by John Ashbery, copyright © 1979 by John Ashbery. Reprinted by permission of Viking Penguin, Inc.

Excerpts from *Houseboat Days* by John Ashbery, copyright © 1975, 1976, 1977 by John Ashbery. Reprinted by permission of Viking Penguin, Inc.

Excerpts from *Shadow Train* by John Ashbery, copyright © 1980, 1981 by John Ashbery. Reprinted by permission of Viking Penguin, Inc.

Excerpts from *A Wave* by John Ashbery, copyright © 1981, 1982, 1983, 1984 by John Ashbery. Reprinted by permission of Viking Penguin, Inc.

Excerpts from *Selected Letters of Ezra Pound*, ed. by D.D. Paige, copyright 1950 by Ezra Pound. Reprinted by permission of New Directions Publishing Corporation and Faber & Faber.

Quotation from a previously unpublished letter by Ezra Pound, copyright © 1986 by the Trustees of the Ezra Pound Literary Property Trust; used by permission of New Directions Publishing Corporation and Faber & Faber, London, Agents for the Trustees.

Excerpts from *Lunch Poems* copyright © 1964 by Frank O'Hara. Reprinted by permission of City Lights Books.

Excerpts from *The Collected Poems of Frank O'Hara*, ed. by Donald Allen. Reprinted by permission of Alfred A. Knopf, Inc.

Excerpts from *Gunslinger* by Ed Dorn, copyright 1968, 1969, 1971, 1972 and 1975 by Ed Dorn. Reprinted by permission of Wingbow Press.

I would also like to thank the University of California Press and the Literary Archives of the University of Connecticut Library for permission to reproduce the manuscript page of "I have been an ability . . ."; and the Literary Archives of the University of Connecticut Library for permission to reproduce the photograph of Olson in his father's mailbag.

ABBREVIATIONS

Eliot

CPP   *The Complete Poems and Plays of T.S. Eliot* (New York: Harcourt, Brace & Company, 1952)

KE   *Knowledge and Experience in the Philosophy of F. H. Bradley* (London: Faber & Faber, 1964)

OPP   *On Poetry and Poets* (London: Faber & Faber, 1957)

SE   *Selected Essays* (London: Faber & Faber, 1951; 3d ed. enlarged)

UPUC   *The Use of Poetry and the Use of Criticism* (Cambridge: Harvard University Press, 1933)

WL   *The Waste Land: A Facsimile and Transcript*, ed. Valerie Eliot (London: Faber & Faber, 1971)

Olson

AP   *Additional Prose*, ed. George Butterick (Bolinas: Four Seasons Foundation, 1974)

AM   *Archaeologist of Morning* (London: Cape Goliard, 1970)

CMI   *Call Me Ishmael: A Study of Melville* (San Francisco: City Lights, 1947)

FH   *The Fiery Hunt and Other Plays* (Bolinas: Four Seasons Foundation, 1977)

HU   *Human Universe and Other Essays*, ed. Donald Allen (New York: Grove Press, 1967)

LFO   *Letters for Origin: 1950–1956*, ed. Albert Glover (New York: Cape Goliard in association with Grossman Publishers, 1970)

Mu   *Muthologos: Collected Interviews and Lectures*, ed. George Butterick (Bolinas: Four Seasons Foundation, 1971), 2 vols.

M,I   *The Maximus Poems* (New York: Jargon/Corinth Books, 1960)

M,II   *Maximus Poems, IV, V, VI* (London: Cape Goliard, 1968)

M,III   *The Maximus Poems: Volume Three,* ed. Charles Boer and
         George Butterick (New York: Grossman Publishers,
         1975)
         Note: All three volumes are photo-reproduced in *The
         Maximus Poems,* ed. George Butterick (Berkeley: Uni-
         versity of California Press, 1983)
OL   *OLSON: The Journal of the Charles Olson Archives* (Spring
         1974–Fall 1978), 1–10
O&P   *Charles Olson and Ezra Pound: An Encounter at St. Eliz-
         abeth's,* ed. Catherine Seelye (New York: Grossman
         Publishers, 1975)
PO   *The Post Office: A Memoir of his Father* (Bolinas: Grey Fox,
         1975)
SW   *Selected Writings,* ed. Robert Creeley (New York: New
         Directions, 1966)
SVH   *The Special View of History,* ed. Ann Charters (Berkeley:
         Oyez, 1976)

Ashbery
AWK   *As We Know* (New York: Viking, 1979)
DDS   *The Double Dream of Spring* (New York: Dutton, 1970; re-
         printed New York: Ecco Press, 1976)
HD   *Houseboat Days* (New York: Viking, 1977)
RM   *Rivers and Mountains* (New York: Holt, Rinehart &
         Winston, 1966; reprinted New York: Ecco Press, 1977)
SP   *Self-Portrait in a Convex Mirror* (New York: Viking, 1972)
ShT   *Shadow Train* (New York: Viking, 1981)
ST   *Some Trees* (New Haven: Yale University Press, 1956; re-
         printed New York: Ecco Press, 1978)
TCO   *The Tennis Court Oath* (Middletown: Wesleyan University
         Press, 1962)
TP   *Three Poems* (New York: Viking, 1972)
W   *A Wave* (New York: Viking, 1984)

PREFACE

THE FAILURE OF MODERNISM is the result of a confusion between subjectivism and subjectivity. It is a confusion which still plagues our own critical accounts of this period, even those informed by the recent explosion of theoretical interest in the question of subjectivity. Modernism, then, as it is perceived in these pages, equates a philosophical (or theoretical) attack on the epistemological and metaphysical tradition of subjectivism with a literary (or practical) attempt to dispossess or to purge poetic discourse of subjectivity *tout court*. Consequently, modernism saw subjectivity, as a "problem" which could be solved by reforming language itself, just as thinkers had sought to eliminate the subjectivist bias of a post-Kantian philosophical point of view. In the same way, subjectivity was also perceived of as a *contingent* and not at all *necessary* feature or effect of language. For any history of modernist poetry to have a coherent polemical shape, it ought to be addressed, as this book argues, to the whole series of successive modernist attempts to eliminate subjectivity from poetic form and language in order to establish a discourse that is assumed to be more authentic or "true" to our experience of the natural world. Of course, one of the short-term consequences of such a history would be to clear the air, if not the decks, of any further adventurist criticism or interpretation of modernist texts. In the long term, however, the result would be that *poetics* as such could no longer be regarded as the innocent haven for "wild" philosophy or "wild" politics which modernist poets claimed as their special privilege, but rather as a set of different and often conflicting discourses that are ideologically produced and therefore irreducible to any particular author's "vision."

In presenting these arguments, my basic intention is twofold: firstly, to show that there is a direct correspondence or continuity between the philosophical rebuttal of subjectivism and attempts to pursue similar theoretical ends within poetic discourse itself; and secondly, to describe how language, as a medium, resists these theoretical advances, and reaffirms its *irreducible* share of subjectivity. My title also covers two distinct meanings, and so it speaks directly to the double-edged purpose of this book. For not only does the "failure" refer to the modernist confusion between subjectivism and subjectivity, but it also invokes one of the most consistent qualities of modernist writing—the experience of failure (of history, language, form, etc.). So too, the methodological frame of my argument is shaped by two related impulses. The first is theoretical—to examine the failure of the theoretical will of modernism in general—while the second leans upon a practical criticism of the work of particular authors in order to show how and why the experience of failure is written into modernist discourse. However, it is primarily for the sake of polemical expediency that such a clear-cut cut distinction is presented here, for these two impulses feed upon each other in the chapters that follow, making it all but impossible to say where the theoretical ends and the practical begins. Perhaps this strategy only further reflects what I argue is a symptomatic condition for modernist writers: to misjudge the point at which poetics ends and poetry begins. Nonetheless, I would reserve the claim that mine is a strategic "confusion" which *accepts* itself as problematic and therefore refuses the fatal anxiety of the modernist will to see poetic language as a medium in which one can and must resolve theoretical problems.

Having focused very briefly on the general nature of my argument, it seems appropriate to provide a brief breakdown of the structure of the book itself. Chapter 1 contains a detailed study of Eliot's dissertation on the epistemology of F. H. Bradley's attack on traditional subject/object dualism, and shows how Eliot's philosophical thinking is extended into his own critical poetics and the critical practice of those who followed his example. Particular attention is paid to the points of *discontinuity* between the theoretical propositions of philosophy and the practical applicability of these propositions in a literary or linguistic context. A few of the contradictions that emerge from this discontinuity are explored in the last section, which reviews the dualism of Eliot's own critical theory in relation, historically, to the sermons of Lancelot Andrewes and John Donne. The second chapter extends the critique of a poetics of "invisibility" by examining various interpretive approaches to *The Waste Land* and the irreducible problem of subjectivity which the poem nonetheless raises. It also discusses the question of modernism's confrontation with the "failure" of history, and points to some of the ways in which this failure is represented in Eliot's poetry, in particular, through representations of sexual failure. Chapter 3 is devoted to Eliot's postconversion attempt to come to poetic terms with the problem of a Christian subject's allegiance to external authority. It considers Eliot's role in the New Humanist movement in the twenties, and goes on to describe the tensions that exist between structures of "martyrdom" in his work and the acknowledged "mystic" discourse in the later poetry. The last section discusses his Christianized will to purge poetic discourse of all *material* traces of subjectivity.

Chapter 4 is a polemical account of Olson's attack on the subjectivist foundations of Western rationalism, and his proposed "objectist" alternatives: a new, kinetic, or antimimetic discourse, a nonlinear approach to historicity, and a plea for a new *spatial* realism that would incorporate phenomenological models from the physical sciences into poetic discourse. I argue that each of these projects, in turn, appeals directly to a phenomenological ideal of disclosing a more authentic subjectivity through the "process" of nature. In chapter 5, I describe how Olson pursues this radical poetics in *The Maximus Poems*, and how the resistance it encounters there is part of a larger Oedipal fiction constructed both for himself as a writer, and for Maximus within the poems. The poems are read in the light of Olson's failure to establish conscious control over both fictions at the same time.

The last chapter discusses how Ashbery's work internalizes the temporal and spatial problems that are the respective objects of theoretical anxiety for Eliot and Olson, thereby displacing the problem of subjectivity on the reader. I show how this is achieved through the use of a particular subtext, the Renaissance tradition of painting perspective. Ashbery's poetry increasingly tries to incorporate the machinery of illusionistic subjectivity suggested by these codes of perspective, while dismantling it at the same time; subjectivity then becomes a necessary double-edged effect, rather than an undesirable position or point of view. Extending this critique of illusionism to the earlier modernist experimentalism of *The Tennis Court Oath*, I describe how the compositional techniques of that volume relate to two different kinds of "dream logic," the Freudian and the Surrealist.

T. S. ELIOT

1. TYING KNOTS IN THE EAST WIND

1.   The most subtle of the Athenians used to drain bowl after bowl of
     wine without confusing his brain, and would then reason like a god.
     Charles Maurras

        If the public-house is to fall into the hands of the English
        Association and the British Drama League, where, one
        must ask bluntly, is a man to go for a drink?
        T.S. Eliot

TENNYSON was the most successful Poet Laureate, so much so
that his death and funeral in 1892 served, for many contemporary witnesses, as a graphic consummation of all that was both
public and private about the function of the poet; for others, more
apocalyptically inclined, it represented the death of all established
literary practice.[1] For once, the office of Laureate coincided perfectly with an "idea" of poethood, each codetermining the other in
what is still a popular icon for the public imagination of the poet.
This coincidence, however, is not free of contradictions. Far from
being a staid public office, the Laureate acts on a paradoxical privilege—accruing personal repute from writing the "impersonal"
state poem. In Tennyson's case, this paradox is heightened by the
new demand of his age for publicity, an age which valorized, for the
first time, the idea that the poet should present his *anonymity* in
public, as a sop to the new General Reading Public. Of course, the
demand for visibility is nothing new, but it is no longer for a Romantic hero to sport his expressionist wounds, Coriolanus-like, in
the *agora*, nor certainly for the indiscretion of the Neo-Classical
satirist, offering himself as the butt of every poetaster in a society
that interpreted the idea of "civic liberty" to the very letter (which
often meant that the only consequence of high public knowledge

was that nothing was private). On the contrary, the new paradoxical anonymity arises from the obligation to *show* that the poet was hiding something, to show that the poet was, in fact, the hidden.

If we had to point to some symbolic mark of this difference, it would be in the public significance of Tennyson's cloak.[2] Unlike the dramatic mask, the function of the cloak would not be to conceal, or feign, identity, but rather to hide the body of the poet just as it is in danger of being revealed, for the first time, to the medium of a "mass" audience. It hides the body (which is not to deny it altogether), and hence declares it out of bounds, beyond the limits of public interest in the author. All of which, we may be tempted to suggest, is quintessentially Victorian, indeed the very paradigm of prudishness. Beyond that, however, the cloak comes to stand for something the poet is assumed to have, but which is inscrutably other. Thus the price paid by the poet for Laureateship is to consent to be in the public eye *only on condition* that he, or part of him, is perceived to be "somewhere else" at the same time, or on a different plane. He is both present and absent, striking a natural pose while claiming transcendental attention. If that conception of the poet as creative seer carries little popular weight today, its "form" is preserved nonetheless by the official lionizing of the writer's place in a culture which still takes comfort in designating that transcendental place as consecrated public ground. Like the effigies in Poet's Corner, poetry is still honored largely as a result of its author's funerary complement, and honored thus *because* that is the safest place for it, in another world, so to speak, too immortal to cause a stir in this its own. For Eliot, at least, Tennyson could be imagined on the level of "the man who talks to reporters and poses for photographers" (SE,334), and perhaps because of that, shown to be the perfect Virgilian, "the most instinctive rebel against the society in which he was the most perfect conformist" (SE,337). In this way was the poet both constructed and contained by an image, ideologically, or at least beyond the concrete effects of his writing. It was an age, after all, for which Walter Benjamin questioned "whether the very invention of photography had not transformed the entire nature of art," and, we might add, the image, if not the very concept, of the artist himself.[3]

The obvious point to be made here is that this indecipherable "property" of poethood is not one created out of any personal will or choice, but is rather generated out of certain ideological attitudes, and thus obeys a highly structured social necessity. Tennyson's example is useful because it foregrounds this fact much more immediately than does the subsequent modernist concern with "the Image" rather than the poet's image, and might thus serve as a cautionary preface to the following study of Eliot, whimsically ordained by Hugh Kenner as the "invisible poet," whose public credentials nonetheless satisfy most of the demands of Tennysonian laureateship while lacking the office itself.[4] For Eliot spent over forty years in the public eye, earning popular satisfaction *because of,* and not in spite of, his perfect inscrutability. From his poetry readings to Ottoline Morrell's coterie at Garsington Manor to the late American lecture tours which commanded vast audiences, there is no question about his high visibility. As Yeats put it, however, "man is in love, and loves what vanishes"; whether this quality be a character trait like that of Macavity, Old Possum's mystery cat, or else a discreet object of desire like the "obscure impulse" (OPP,98) which germinates into a piece of writing, it will be a guarantee of public interest, and bring its material benefits, as recognized, for example, in Descartes's motto, *bene vixit, bene qui latuit*—he who lives hidden, lives well.[5] Thus when Eliot appears to rail against a modernity in which "everyone *met son coeur à nu*, or pretends to" (SE,272), and when he disapproves of the libelous content of unofficial biographies (OPP,111), or decries the "fantastic excesses" wrought by the "aberrant criticism" of the psychology of a writer's personality (UPUC,17), then we should be alive to the contradictions that inform his public voice of dissent, a voice that is as much spoken as speaking, because it satisfies an ideological demand and thereby transcends its "genetic" expression as a somewhat reactionary personal opinion.

So too, with Eliot's call, in a "London Letter" for *The Dial* in 1922, for the poet to be more "daring" in his thoughts and images, especially those "which render a man least distinguishable from the mob, the respectable mob, the middle class mob."[6] Behind this address looms the larger issue of an extremist modernist politics, phobicly caught between the prospect of an advancing mass culture and the moribund values of the bourgeois mind. Given this, what then could be more "daring" for Eliot than to outdo the masses in their *anonymity*?

Eliot's lifelong attempt to respond to this question is no less contradictory, and perhaps this is why any study of this aspect of his work promises to be richer in its account of the contradictions of modernism than that of the more clearly defined writer ideologues of the period, especially in their respective appeals to Right and Left during the Thirties. My chief interest here, however, is not with the history of the conceptual adjustment of the poet's persona to changing social conditions, nor is it with the overtly political grounds of modernism itself, but rather with the less well defined but essentially related contradictions that arise within the modernist treatment of subjectivity and its relation to language, history, and philosophy. For it is in that more complex area of study that the formal problems of modernist poetics are posed most fully. And it is there, in the failure to treat the "problem" of subjectivity in terms other than that of a *solution*, that we might begin to look for both the cause and effects of the failure of a literary politics so characteristic of the period.7

2.

> Whatever you know, it is all one
> *F.H. Bradley*

There is a specific continuity between the dominant modernist myth of the *exile* and the image of the transcendentalized *vates* of Victorian poethood, whether in Georgic retreat or on the Whitmanesque "open road"; both are committed to a conception of truth wherein truth is displaced and lies elsewhere, *but still within the purview of poetic subjectivity*. For the modernist, however, the logistics of exile has a more immediate resonance because it is manifest as a discontinuity or distance at every level of poetic expression, from problems of reference to the impossibility of an overview or perspective of history. How does modernism attempt to come to terms with this discontinuity, and why does this attempt involve a further appeal to transcendentalizing versions of subjectivity?

One of the most enduring of his critical convictions is Eliot's observation that the poet does not *think*, although he may well employ a formal set of ideas that bears some unique philosophical trademark; if the poet appears to engage in philosophical thought, it is only by way of a suspension of his disbelief. The poet who would also be a philosopher "would be a monster," an inconceivable, impossible object like the "golden mountains" and "square circles" of Meinong's *Annahmen*.[8] If we accept this elision of "thought," then a substantial part of what is habitually regarded as the writer's working identity is evacuated, or displaced, inasmuch as it is held to transcend its empirical states. Eliot's own "philosophy" underwent a matchless exile itself, for it actually vanished for almost forty years. I am referring to his Harvard Ph.D. dissertation, *Knowledge and Experience in the Philosophy of F.H. Bradley*, which was effectively out of critical circulation until its fairy-tale "discovery" by Ann Bolgan in the Houghton Library at Harvard in 1954.[9] The thesis itself, then, occupies a transcendental position in the history of Eliot criticism until its publication in 1964; empirically it is "suspended," but provokes widespread speculation about its content and its influence on his subsequent literary production. As an interpretive work of critical philosophy, it is the most sustained and arguably radical polemic in all of Eliot's writing. As a modernist text, it focuses directly on leading issues of the day—subjective "point of view," and the challenge to a representational account of truth and reality. And as a statement of ideal method, it implies a position on subjectivity that informs not only Eliot's own literary observations, but also those of critics and writers who followed up and extended his account of the creative process, the epistemological status of the work of art, and the larger question of judging the place of language and literature in terms of social experience. Richard Wollheim,[10] Walter Benn Michaels,[11] Lewis Freed,[12] and Ann Bolgan have examined some of these issues inasmuch as they illuminate either the philosophical or the literary contexts respectively. It remains, however, to determine how Eliot's philosophical treatment of subjectivity is both continuous *and* discontinuous with his sense of poetic or critical "voice." It remains to dispose of the *hunch* from which early critics, deprived of the thesis, had taken their cue, namely, that the poetics which championed an "escape from personality" at the expense of an "expression of personality" (SE,21), was an ad hoc construction, an expediency calculated to deflect attention away from the personal details of Eliot's own waking life, and thus ensure his "invisibility." The evidence of Eliot's dissertation does not in itself eradicate the hunch; it does, however, offer a less gratuitous picture of the methodological grounds of Eliot's poetics of "invisibility."

In developing Bradley's skeptical position, Eliot is dealing with a highly strategic and combative temper. The opening gambit of *The Principles of Logic,* for example, is explicitly polemical: "In England, at all events, we have lived too long in the psychological attitude."[13] Eliot's own choice of polemical target in "Tradition and the Individual Talent" is no less strategic, though described in a more typically oblique fashion: "The point of view which I am struggling to attack is perhaps related to the metaphysical theory of the substantial unity of the soul" (SE,19). These are two fundamental though entirely distinct arguments, the first of which, concerning the "psychological attitude," I will deal with later in describing Eliot's account of reference. The second, concerning the attack on the unified subject of metaphysics, is central to Bradley's comprehensive rejection of a whole inventory of philosophical positions that rest upon the presuppositionless foundation of a logical datum like the *ego cogito,* the Cartesian subject of self-knowledge. For Bradley, the most chronic strain of this constitutive subjectivism is to be found in British empiricism, most recently rejuvenated by Mill: Locke's assumption that the eidectic "imprints" of ideas as mental states are the representatives of objects, and thus the basis of our worldly knowledge; and Berkeley's more radical subjective idealism, hold-

dition of rationalist idealism is just as much under fire: Kant's restoration of the "I AM," a rational subjective datum that repeats Descartes's exclusion of the body in its refusal to accept the world of objects as phenomena established independently of its own knowing and constituting powers; and the new school of intentionalist psychologists, including Brentano, Meinong, and James, who treated the activity of object-constituting or willing as descriptive of fundamental subjective properties. The systematic rejection of all of these points of view is the foundation for Bradley's own system-building, and it sets a radically sceptical tone for every aspect of his work, even to the extent that he repeals any statement of subjective authority made in the course of a philosophical claim—hence the frequent waivers of infallibility like the following in the preface to *Appearance and Reality*: "whatever you know, it is all one."[14] But how does Bradley reconcile this negative cast of mind with his positivistic commitment to a metaphysical telos that can only find ultimate satisfaction in an Absolute?

The Bradleyan system, in its formal structure though not its method, broadly agrees with Hegelian doctrine. It begins with an a priori state of pure feeling known as Immediate Experience, an origin from which relations develop in the temporary and fragmentary form of accidents, points of view, contradictions, and deteriorations, all of which are regarded as mere appearance, impure degrees of truth and reality which are finally resolved in the harmony of the Absolute. Immediate Experience is thus given "before distinctions and relations have developed, and where as yet neither subject or object exists."[15] The relational state of *appearance* which emerges from the breakup of Immediate Experience exists only as a necessary and practical convention, collapsing back into the stable uniformity of Absolute experience. It is important to note, however, that Eliot refuses to accept either of Bradley's ideal limits. He argues that Immediate Experience is always extratemporal, and can never be said to exist at any one time, let alone, as Bradley holds, remaining "throughout as the present foundation of my known world."[16] Even more significant is Eliot's rejection of the Absolute, the observance of which he believes to rest finally upon a mere "act of faith" (KE,202). As a result, his study will be confined to the relational world and its practical limits, with the constructed and the given rather than with the willed, and thus with the sphere of ordinary or concrete human practices from which Bradley is so radically estranged. For Eliot (no doubt echoing Hegel's famous dismissal of Schelling's *Identitätsphilosophie* as a "night in which all cows are black"), the prospect of Immediate Experience "at either the beginning or the end of our journey, is annihilation and utter night" (KE,31).

The breakup of pure feeling, then, is "self-transcendent" and is as much an *objective* event in "the history of the external world" as it is a subjective event for the "history of souls" (KE,21). However, Eliot points out that, because of the subject/object prejudice built into language, the results of this self-transcendence tend to be attributed to the side of subjective properties. Eliot's intention is to emphasize the objective side, and so he claims that it is a mistake "at once fundamental and disastrous" to regard any such experience as inalienably subjective: "We have no right, except in the most provisional way, to speak of *my* experience, since the I is a construction out of experience, an abstraction from it" (KE,19). Given his limited, relational concerns, stripped of any guaranteed subject/object identity in the Absolute, we can perhaps begin to see why the case against subjectivism is even more important for Eliot than for Bradley himself, and thus why his argument must rest upon the indefensibility of any a priori essential self as the ground of experience and knowledge. As a result, the concern of his thesis is with a "theory of objects" (KE,154), and with "the precise meaning of the term 'objectivity' " (KE,15). In his pursuit of the *cogitatum*, Eliot will be concerned to limit any discussion of the subject to a consideration of "point of view": "Everything from one point of view is subjective, and everything from another is objective; and there is no absolute point of view." Consequently, his account of the *history* of the simultaneous constitution of subject and object is, by force of necessity, almost wholly taken up with the object, and therefore runs the risk, as I shall try to argue, of neglecting the *special* case of subjectivity.

For Bradley, the existence of a subject lies as much in the extension of its relations to something outside of itself, as in relations internal to its content and thus exhausted by its content; a fluid and shifting subject, its edges are "ragged in such a way as to imply another existence from which it has been torn, and without which it really does not exist."[17] Any unity it has is organized around what Bradley calls "finite centres," each center being "the felt existence of a sensible whole,"[18] which qualifies the Absolute itself as the only stable and coherent whole. This "me" or "this-mine" of the finite center achieves "a passing aspect of undivided singleness" before succeeding to a higher development of concrete internal unity. Of course, the need for unity is the need for the metaphysical principle itself, in which the true *is* the whole, and therefore the question of holism must go unquestioned in Bradley's system; he admits that the fact of fragmentariness exists, but he cannot in any way account for its manifestation unless it can somehow be said that the universe is "richer" for its inclusion of dividedness and variety. Even if Eliot does not subscribe to the act of faith demanded by the Absolute, his readiness to accept that "the real is the organised" and that the world thus tends "to organise itself into an articulate whole" (KE,82) offers no serious challenge to Bradley's general assumption of immanent unity. Committed to the relational, however, Eliot is concerned with the practical application of idealist criteria like coherence, consistency, and inclusiveness inasmuch as they constitute lower entelechial levels of satisfaction. The resultant diet is hardly the ambrosial fare of Bradley's *contemptus mundi*: "the life of a soul does not consist in the contemplation of one consistent world but in the painful task of unifying (to a greater or lesser extent) jarring or incompatible ones, and passing, when possible, from two or more discordant viewpoints to a higher which will somehow include or transmute them" (KE,147). In its appeal to the arduous elements of this process, Eliot's observation evokes the hard school of Hegel's dialectic, and its laborious movement through the contradictions of materiality in the realm of "unhappy consciousness." By contrast, contradictions for Bradley are simply logical relations, a temporary compromise at most, for they exist ultimately as "differences-for-an-identity" or "diversities-for-a-unity."

Without the overriding appeal to an Absolute, Eliot's obligation to account for unity is problematic, since he must proceed in such a way as to avoid any assumption of a unified subject or object as a logical resting-place. Perhaps this precarious course serves to explain, in part, the curiously divided appeal of much of his critical work; on the one hand, its fugitive or cursory cast of mind, and on the other, its rigorous, methodological feel. And certainly it creates a demand for a correspondingly *ideal* reader, who would be party to a mixed subjective/objective point of view, like "those highly-organised beings who are able to objectify their passions and, as passive spectators, to contemplate their joys and torments, [and who] are also those who suffer and enjoy the most keenly" (KE,23). Eliot's critical problem is exactly how to preserve that ideal balance in practical terms, without falling into the more "banal" categories of empirical or transcendental subjectivity, the respective prototypes of a more familiar split in his poetics between "the man who suffers and the mind which creates" (SE,18). In asking whether this problem is resolved in a poetics of "impersonality" or "invisibility," we shall have to take into account this distinction between ideal and practical terms; the distinction, for example, between a logical theory of language without a speaker, and a theory of discourse, or between an ideal, predicating subject, and a divided subject of enunciation. And in asking whether a transcendentalizing principle of unity, in art as in philosophy, can be kept aloof from the categorical proposition of a unified subject, we shall have to bear in mind Lukács's *caveat* about the grounds of Kantian aesthetics, that "the question of totality is the constant centre of the transcendental dialectic. God, the soul, etc., are nothing but mythological expressions to denote the unified subject, or, alternatively, the unified object of the totality of objects of knowledge considered as perfect (and wholly known)."[19] But what was formally insoluble for Kant's rationalism—the helpless dualism of phenomenal contingency and noumenal necessity—was to be reconciled in the *Critique of Judgment* by the activity of the aesthetic principle. Art, then, was a realm which united nature and reason, a privileged medium in which the divided subject of action could be reconstituted through the process of making up reality in the form of an as-if, a new rational totality. The subsequent long reign of this aesthetic, in which art is perceived as a positivity where contradictions are overcome, extends well into Eliot's lifetime (to be challenged finally, perhaps, by Adorno's late "negative dialectics"). In its epistemological relations, it takes the form of a disinterested, contemplative contract between a judging subject and a "purposive" or organically unified art-object which is an end in itself. Eliot's own critical position, I shall argue, is not irreducibly constitutive in the Kantian sense, but in its vestigial embrace of certain features of a transcendental idealism, it prolongs, anticipates, and shapes the more stable neo-Kantian fate of much of later modernist criticism.

The obvious place to begin such an argument, Eliot's inveterate application of the criteria of coherence and unity as the acid test of the judging critic, need hardly be described again, but it stands nonetheless as the most consistently Bradleyan strain of his conceptual approach to criticism. As a standard of assessment it falls into three broad areas: the expressive structure of the work of art, the intentional activity of the work of art, and the role of literary tradition. One example of the first of these is Eliot's fresh appraisal of the Elizabethan drama, in which the old Unities, and especially the Unity of Action, are to be replaced by a new "unity of feeling" or, the preferred term, Unity of Sentiment. In Ben Jonson's plays, it is a "unity of inspiration" which holds together the assemblage of theatrical particulars as something willed or intended, rather than externally imposed (SE,155). So too, "it is Shakespeare, chiefly, that *is* the unity, that unifies so far as they could be unified all the tendencies of a time that lacked unity," and here Eliot has in mind a unity so local as not to be confused with "universality." What matters, however, is not only "the quality and kind of emotions to be unified, and the elaborateness of the pattern of unification," but also the very fact of unity itself as a general imperative that bears the status of "a human law" (UPUC,34). By contrast, the classical Unities are merely "laws of nature, and a law of nature, even when it is a law of human nature, is quite another thing from a human law" (UPUC,37). The most celebrated instance of the author's fidelity to this "human law" is the case of the Metaphysical poets, for whom the "heterogeneity" of their artistic material was to be "compelled into unity by the operation of the poet's mind," wherein "new wholes" were constantly being formed (SE,283). As with Bradley, the fact of fragmentary, or contradictory, experience is significant only insofar as it leads to, and thus qualifies, the superior activity of "amalgamating disparate experience." The third of these categories is bound up with Eliot's understanding of "tradition" as an epiphenomenon of the entire "mind of Europe," an ideal order formed upon the idea of order (SE,15), and only ever articulated in "organic wholes" or finite "systems in relation to which, and only in relation to which, individual works of art and the work of individual authors have their significance" (SE,23). As a particular medium, developing itself through the series of successive wholes that make up "tradition," *language* itself is often described by Eliot in terms redolent of some neo-Hegelian movement toward self-consciousness: it imposes its own "laws and restrictions and permits its own license, dictates its own speech rhythms and sound patterns," and generally exhibits "an ordered though unconscious progress . . . to realise its own potentialities within its own limitations" (OPP, 56).

Clearly, each of these interpretive areas must be regarded as products, finally, of Eliot's highly individual critical apparatus, and as such, they cannot be challenged on any objective ground. My intention, moreover, is not to agree or disagree with any of Eliot's critical assertions. What is more important for my argument is to recognize a distinction between the *descriptive* and the *prescriptive* grounds of Eliot's critical appeal, a distinction marked by a shift from the use of a principle of unity as a means of explication, to its application as an ultimate criterion or imperative of value. This distinction is a further reflection of the difficulties already raised by the difference between ideal and practical terms, between the universal assertions of philosophy and the practical inscrutability of these assertions as literary goals. For in each of the instances set out above, a descriptive observation joins with a universal principle in order to produce an *imperative* condition which has larger consequences for the ideological development of modernist thinking. Thus, the observation about structural unity in the text is taken up as a prerequisite for a criticism given over to fetishizing its object: as a unified organization or "equilibrium" of impulses (I.A. Richards), as a model for harmonizing tensions or oppositions (the New Critics), or as an organic vehicle for moral regeneration (F.R. Leavis). So too with the "dissociation of sensibility" thesis which emerges from the notes on Metaphysical poetry. As a result of Eliot's speculations about the irruption of sociality that resulted in the Civil War and coincided with or determined a corresponding division in the *personality* of English poetry, a hortatory campaign for its "re-integration" is subsequently launched in his critical work. This campaign is distinguished by a call to order for those critics and writers who followed Eliot, both in their formalistic search for intellectual coherence, and in their commitment to an ontological continuity between the resolution of disorder in the work of art and the disciplined organization of the social world. And lastly, the increasing conformity of "tradition" to a principle of *orthodoxy* inspires the activity of critical canon-making over the next forty years. In this way, history is mined in the polemical cause of "elective affinities," an activity which also carries an explicit political coloring; for Hegel, history finds itself in a restored Prussian state, for Eliot, in the elitist class base of a Christian Britain,[20] and for some of his contemporaries, in newer and more perilous forms of sympathy with the Fascist forces of order.

However important it is to chart the development of this "unity" principle from its descriptive to its prescriptive application, it would be wrong to ground the reasons for this change in an assumed *continuity* between Eliot's philosophical and his literary work. On the contrary, we must seek these reasons in a demonstrated *discontinuity*, whereby the windless theoretical forms of philosophy corrode in the busy air of literary discourse. In his dissertation, Eliot acknowledges a related discontinuity between *theory* and *practice*, and develops it not only into a serious qualification, or perceived limitation, of his arguments, but also as a way of further distancing himself from the self-sufficiency of Bradley's system: "Practice, and this is the difficulty, . . . is shot through with theory, and theory with practice. . . . And the distinction between theory and practice can nowhere be positively drawn" (KE,137). As a result, the "hard and fast" distinctions of theoretical philosophy lose their sway where "the real world of practice is essentially vague, unprecise, swarming with what, from a metaphysical point of view, are insoluble contradictions" (KE,136). Eliot's thesis has been an attempt to describe "the hypothetical transition from sensation to subject-object" where subject and object are still momentary distinctions, but he acknowledges that any commitment to such a theory, even if it entertained less stable relations than the precarious "finite centres" admit, would still be a "speculative activity." What would such a theory mean in a world "in which subject and object are not one," a world which depends upon a much more fixed understanding of subject-object relations? "Metaphysics," Eliot answers, would be "condemned to go up like a rocket and come down like a stick" (KE,168).

While evoking the "failure" of metaphysics in this way, Eliot concludes by calling for a *practical metaphysics* to "keep the frontiers open" between theory and practice (KE,169). Clearly, such a position, like serving God and Mammon, is itself ideal, and would demand the same kind of indeterminacy as that associated with the finite center! It is at this point, however, that the "problem" of subjectivity becomes a real issue, the point where "our theories make all the difference in the world, because the truth has to be *my* truth before it can be true at all" (KE,169). Subjectivity, then, in a lived and not a formulaic sense, is what *links* theory to practice, and endows metaphysics with a pragmatic value that goes beyond formalism, on the one hand, and empiricism, on the other. The "problem" of subjectivity is that it threatens to capsize Eliot's fragile indeterminacy just as much as it threatens to disturb, on the one hand, the rigidity of the classical subject-object dualism, and, on the other, the tranquil fusion of (Absolute) identity theory. Why is this "problem" so important to Eliot's own poetics? To answer this question we must examine the complex discussion of reference that gives rise to his skepticism about the adequacy of theoretical metaphysics.

In attacking the assumptions about knowledge that lead respectively to formalism and empiricism—the literary extremes of the "arid *pièce à thèse*" and the "photographic novel"—Eliot firstly engages the psychologistic tradition of perceiving "ideas" or mental states as the medium of all experience, and secondly, the epistemological question of knowing a world of discrete objectivity that preexists conscious attention. If, he claims, we try to distinguish between ideality and reality, then the world resolves itself into either of two specious forms—a world of ideas, or a world of reals. However, just as subject and object are only practical distinctions, so too the distinction between ideal and real is only an appearance, "and ideality and reality turn out to be the same" (KE,57). In arguing that the idea is *identical* with the real, Eliot then goes on to conclude that psychology has virtually nothing left to study as subject matter. Its subjective fallacy, or *chimera*, of mental states as "meanings torn from their reference" (KE,74) is as imperfect as the assumption that the idea is an imperfect presentation of the object, as in a representational theory of knowledge. For Eliot, however, the most serious problem of traditional psychology lies in its exclusive attention to the effect of sensations upon the experiencing subject. As we have seen, his concern is to deflect attention toward the character of objectivity, and so he is led to account for a theory of reference in which the idea *qualifies* reality, but only inasmuch as it subtends a relation of *identity* as opposed to reflection or representation: "every idea means itself, its ideality consists in its 'pointing towards' its realisation" (KE,56). This insistence on identity is Eliot's ground for disagreeing with Bradley's "treacherous" notion that an idea has a partial role to play in the act of reference, and that it behaves like a sign in the course of producing meaning. The sign, however, can be "misinterpreted" or else mistaken for something else. Its "essential heterogeneity" is what distinguishes the sign from Eliot's notion of identical reference: Eliot's idea has no existence apart from its object, as the sign does, for it is simply the "fact of reference" itself (KE,63).

If we want to clarify for ourselves the substance of this distinction rather than merely accept a sketchy, conceptual understanding of Eliot's reasons for making such discriminating judgments, then his idiosyncratic use of terms will have to be carefully qualified. Otherwise, this terminological problem will become an obstacle to appreciating his flat application of these terms to critical propositions about literature. In writing about Flaubert's *Education Sentimentale*, for example, Eliot notes that the idea of the petty bourgeoisie has become "so identified with the reality that you can no longer say what the idea is."[21] Whatever we might think of this, it both derives directly and means something entirely different from what Eliot asserts in his dissertation about the identical relation between ideality and reality. Even there, he warns us that his use of "idea" does not correspond with "that of any author with whom [he is] acquainted" (KE,56); having successively denied that the idea can be compared with the *concept*, the *image*, and the *presentation*, he goes on to claim that his "idea" is inseparable from the *act* of identical reference. Clearly, this differs from any understanding of the referential structure of the *sign*, in which the signifier, or perceptible aspect, is arbitrarily related to the signified, the absent aspect or concept. Eliot's identity relation is closer to the *motivated* association that inheres between the sign and its referent, the object itself, a relationship of *denotation* that commentators on the sign ever since the Stoics have distinguished from the less stable relation internal to signification itself: for example, "fox," the sign, is necessarily linked to the real fox, but not to the concept of fox. A denotative relation can also be identified within the more homogeneous set of associations suggested by the *symbol*, in which a special resemblance obtains between two signifiers or two signifieds: "fox" and "cunning," for example. What Eliot intends, however, is even more intimate yet: "there is, properly speaking, no relation between the symbol and that which it symbolises, because they are continuous" (KE,104). And yet when he goes on to assert that the symbol must not be "arbitrarily amputated from the object which it symbolises" (KE,132), then it is clear that it is the conceptual object and not the real object that is meant, as in Frege's distinction between *Sinn* (meaning) and *Bedeutung* (referent). By symbol, Eliot claims that he means to conflate two of Peirce's three categories of signification, the *icon*, a near identical (photographic) image of its conceptual object, and the *symbol*, which preserves an arbitrary association with its conceptual object, while he excludes the *index*, Peirce's description of a sign placed in causal contiguity with its denoted object (like a weathervane or a traffic sign). And so we can conclude that the relation to the denoted object is not relevant to Eliot's description after all. Indeed, he insists that the assumption of real objects is, of course, the false epistemological assumption of realism—"that there is one world of external reality which is consistent and complete" (KE,112). Objects are real inasmuch as they are "denoted" but they are not real in themselves.

These two related questions, the identity of reference and the "ideal reality" of objects, form the basis of Eliot's attack on an epistemological theory of knowledge in which he inveighs against the false objectivity of "knowledge without a knower" (KE,46) by contending that such a theory rests upon the same separation of ideality from reality as did the false subjectivity of psychologism. In this, he concentrates on those instances of objectivity which concretely problematize the ideal/real distinction: hallucinated objects, imaginary objects, and unreal objects. It is to the third of these categories, the impossible, nonexistent object which is yet "real" by dint of denotation, that Eliot finds the example of linguistic reference intrinsically relevant:

Idea and phrase both denote realities, but the realities which they denote are so far as idea or phrase denotes, identical with the idea or the phrase. It is a mistake, I think, to treat the word as something which barely points to the object, a signpost which you leave behind on the road. The word "chimera" or the idea "chimera" is the beginning of the reality chimera and is absolutely continuous with it, and the "present King of France" is already partially real. The phrase directs your attention to an object but the object is an object because it is also that object, because the mere hypothetical moment of objectivity is qualified by the characters of the phrase, which are real properties at once of the phrase and of the object. Just as the idea refers to itself, so the denoting phrase denotes itself. But just as an idea is not a thing, and our difficulties arise from trying to treat it as a thing, so a denoting phrase is not a thing. It is not simply *that*, for a mere *that* (which is in fact only a theoretical limit) does not refer to something else; reference is a kind of activity, original or delegated. Like an idea, a word or phrase has existence outside of its objectivity, and a denoting phrase in particular resembles an idea in having an existence which straddles so to speak two moments of objectivity; the one moment being simply those marks or sounds which denote, and the other the object denoted.   (KE,129)

This passage is the clearest formulation that we have of Eliot's implied, general view of reference and signification, and it invites direct comparison with a host of critical judgments that fall in line with Eliot's observation in an essay about Swinburne, that "language in a healthy state presents the object, is so close to the object, that the two are identified" (SE,327). We can, I think, ask the same questions of this "symbolic" law as we did about the "human law" of unity. When and where are we to distinguish the role of these statements about reference as *descriptive* insights from their role as *prescriptive* judgments? And if there is such a difference in kind, then what larger social judgments are prescribed along with the stylistic imperative of the latter?

As with Pound, the most reliable touchstone for Eliot's early ideas about language is indeed the case of Swinburne, perceived as being as far out on the purely verbal limb as was possible. If the limits of poetic formalism could be sketched on to an imaginary map, then Swinburne would represent an almost natural frontier, short of which modernist poetry committed itself to searching out a new middle ground. Even as late as 1925, Yeats, at Pound's prompting, was revising his early poetry in an effort to wrench it away from the Swinburnean aesthetic, draining the diction of emotional or sonic "slither" and reconstructing its Imagist "bone." Eliot's critique of Swinburne is fast and sane:

It is, in fact, the word that gives him the thrill, not the object. When you take to pieces any verse of Swinburne, you find always that the object was not there—only the word . . . the object has ceased to exist, because the meaning is merely the hallucination of meaning, because language, uprooted, has adapted itself to an independent life of atmospheric nourishment. In Swinburne, for example, we see the word "weary" flourishing in this way independent of the particular and actual weariness of flesh and spirit. The bad poet dwells partly in a world of objects and partly in a world of words, and he never can get them to fit. Only a man of genius could dwell so exclusively among words as Swinburne.   (SE, 326–27)

Whether or not one wants to abide by the strict polarity of terms like formalism and empiricism, Eliot's diagnosis is a sufficiently clear evocation of his own anxiety about exactly that kind of dualism, and it was the tyranny of this dualism which precipitated the modernist "revolution in idiom" (OPP, 159). Indeed, as we have seen, his dissertation is an attempt to demonstrate the theoretical redundancy of that dualism, and the thesis about reference is its most potent offering. As for the real literary task of reference, however, the task of "[dislocating] language into . . . meaning" (SE, 289), it is not at all easy to say where Eliot views this as a given fact—the "is" of pure reason—and where he views it as an ideal activity—the "ought" of practical reason—which will always fall short of its mark. Theory is shot through with practice, but as Richard Wollheim notes, "that which, in the critical theory, is asserted as a perfection or as something to be aimed at, is asserted in the philosophical theory as a necessary fact."[22] Indeed, the "true critic," Eliot writes, "is a scrupulous avoider of formulae . . . he finds fact nowhere and approximation always" (KE, 164). But Eliot's "formula" of ideal reference appears often enough as a standard rule of thumb in the course of his critical assessments. Milton and Dryden both fail because "at their worst, they have an interest in the *word* and not the "object" (OPP, 200). Milton's language is "foreign," not just because it militates against the Anglo-Saxon bases of English, but because he presents "the maximal, never the minimal, alteration of ordinary language" so that "his every idiosyncracy is a particular act of violence" against the symbolic law of language (OPP, 154). Unlike Massinger, in whom Eliot found only "a perpetual slight alteration of language" so that "sensation became word and word was sensation" (SE, 209–10). Unlike Johnson and Goldsmith, where "every word and epithet goes straight to the mark" (OPP, 181), or Ben

Jonson, in his satire, which succeeds "not by hitting off its object but by creating it" (SE,158). In the genre of romantic comedy, we are offered the delibitating spectacle of a "concatenation of emotions which signifies nothing" (SE,215), while in a critique of Virginia Woolf, Eliot characterizes as inherently "feminine" the kind of writing "that makes its art by feeling, and by contemplating the feeling rather than the object which has excited it, or into which the feeling might be made. . . . Mrs. Woolf gives you the minutest datum, and leads you on to explore, quite consciously, the images and feelings which float away from it."[23]

Increasingly, this point of view about ideal reference assumes the more rigid features of an authoritative position, whenever Eliot is drawn to define the characteristics of a *healthy* speech condition in matters of correct expression, clarity, diction, grammatical precision, and decorous tone. In seventeen years of editorial commentary in *The Criterion,* he conscientiously abides by this regime of speech and all that it assumes for itself as an index of social and political hygiene. Pound's ex officio stance on the same topic—the state of language is a metonym for the state of the nation—is much more strident, and often fanatical. Eliot's own polemical frame of reference is the shadowy moral struggle between Arnold's culture and anarchy, depicted in terms of a model of ordered enlightenment threatened and appalled by the prospect of "civil" degeneracy. However real this struggle, its consequence for Eliot's thinking is an atrophied conception of the world where ideal codes and laws are pitched against their variously real transgressions, the very same conceptual universe he had sought to undo at every turn in his *practical metaphysics.* What was disputed there as a theoretical chimera returns in his social criticism as a fixed sense of cultural idealism. Of course there is a long list of those who have expressed their disillusion with the development in Eliot's thought of a qualified commitment to conservative categories of order. If, as I have suggested, this development is in any way continuous with his theoretical view of reference, then it is because the latter *is* a theoretical view, condemned to practical failure, or to a nonidentical relation with the real. This is a point which Eliot himself makes quite clearly. An ideal state of reference would involve some "mystic marriage" that, in practice, is never achieved, or else misinterpretation would be impossible. As Walter Michaels suggests, Eliot denies the possibility of a "theory of language," but the inability of such a theory "to produce a formal representation of how we understand things . . . is not a sign of its failure but of its truth."[24]

Has Eliot, then, already accounted for one of the "failures" of modernist thinking, a failure to temper theory with practice? In a sense, yes, for he has suggested the crucial difference between a theory of language and the realm of discourse itself, even if he will not effectively absorb this distinction into his own critical work. Where a theory of language fails, the evidence of discourse is to be found—this is one of the hard-won lessons of a modernism which is obliged to mistake one for the other in the course of imposing its theoretical will upon a resistant medium. I have suggested, however, that there is a third term, the construction of spoken subjectivity, that is coeval with this distinction between language and discourse, and without which it would be impossible to give a proper account of reference. In neglecting to attend to this third term, I will argue that Eliot risks losing much of the headway gained in his philosophical attack on subjectivism.

We might begin by examining Eliot's practice of ascribing a *pathology* to those writers whose work exhibits a "dissociative" quality. The "feminine" debility of Woolf we have seen, while the "morbidity" of Swinburne is viewed as the unhappy psychic burden of a genius. In the same way, Eliot feels "tempted to explain a poem of Mallarmé as we explain dreams, as due to some morbid physiological activity" (KE,76). Hamlet's problem belongs to the same symptomatic order: "the intense feeling, ecstatic or terrible, without an object or exceeding its object, is something which every person of sensibility has known; it is doubtless a subject of study to pathologists" (SE,146). And in the case of Ruskin, the excess we detect in his writing is interpreted as a symptom or "deflection of something that was baffled in life" (SE,445). These, and other observations about how the pathology of the signifier is linked to "personality," attest to Eliot's ambivalent recognition of the Freudian critique of subjectivity. The sometime advocate of a poetics that would incorporate those "deeper, unnamed feelings which form the substratum of our being" (UPUC,148), he was generally inclined to ridicule the methodologies advanced by "the orthodox modern faith" of a psychoanalysis bent on revealing "the more horrid secrets of the past" (OPP, 30). What can we learn, then, about Eliot's comments on pathology and language from Freud's account of subjectivity?

Freud's understanding of the psychic topography of the subject is bound up with a term culled from German philosophy, the same *Vorstellung* of Brentano and Meinong which Eliot examines at some length in his thesis, and which bears a close relation to his own idiosyncratic "idea." As a "presentation" of the object to consciousness, Freud's *Vorstellung* is an impression registered in the mnemic systems of the psychic apparatus. As such, it no longer preserves its relation to the object, but establishes itself in relation to other presentations; like Saussure's signifier, it is defined by its place in a system of differences. Freud distinguishes between two types of presentation, the *Dingvorstellung* (thing-presentation), which is derived from the direct registration of the object, and the *Wortvorstellung* (word-presentation), which is associated with a verbal image of the object. This distinction is further qualified by the topographical nature of the psychical apparatus, divided into a conscious-preconscious system that accommodates word-presentations, and an unconscious system that houses thing-presentations. In the latter, the primary process, thing-presentations are constantly shifting their unattached positions, slipping from one grouping of affect to another. The more conscious secondary process binds up this loosely displaced unconscious affect into the "rational" forms of verbalization manifest in our speech patterns. In certain areas of language use, however—schizophrenia, poetry, a dream's employment of the day's verbal residue—word presentations are directly invested with the affect and sensory appeal of the thing-presentations, and are subject to the "rhetorical" laws of psychic organization which normally only operate in the primary process. It is in these instances that the "auditory" secondary process acquires some of the "perceptual" quality of the primary, generating an excessive attention to phonological effects in speech. As a result of these effects, it is possible for Freud to demonstrate the central concept of divided subjectivity. For the linguistic consequence of Freud's "discovery" of the unconscious is that we speak, or are spoken, in two different psychic places, conscious and unconscious. Eliot, we could say, unwittingly acknowledges Freud's "discovery," for he treats those effects described above, as "pathological" whenever they occur in writing: Swinburne's lyricality, Woolf's vagrancy, Mallarmé's aleatory will, and Ruskin's purple prose.

Freud's development of the *Vorstellung* has encouraged Lacanians to link it with Lacan's own refined post-Saussurean critique of the symmetry and equilibrium of the sign, and hence to focus primarily on the discretionary behavior of the signifier and its effects on language.[25] For Eliot, the "idea" or presentation has no such autonomy. Indeed, it appears to lack any descriptive relation, either motivated or unmotivated, with its object. It is *identical* with reality, a point of view sustained by Eliot even in the face of Meinong's distinction between the *Inhalt* and the *Gegenstand* of a *Vorstellung*, or the content of an idea and the conceptual object intended: "I have already protested against amputating the [mental] aspect for the purpose of a 'special science'; but to graft the member on again after it is dead seems to me even more gratuitous" (KE,93). We can recall that Eliot's theoretical description of reference alluded to Peirce's *symbol* and *icon*, and excluded the *index*. It is the *index*, however, that offers a way of linking theory to practice, or in the linguistic context, what Saussure calls *langue* to *parole*. Peirce's insight into subjectivity is that "the word or sign which man uses *is* the man himself,"[26] and therefore that subjectivity, far from being an uninvolved, predicating faculty, has a linguistic existence in common with any other nominal object. The difference between the subject and the nominal object lies in the indexical status of all *deictic* operations, terms like "I" and "you" (as well as "here" and "now," etc.) which "point" directly to an object that is necessarily and not conventionally related, as in the example of symbols or icons. The *index* is therefore a function of an immediate spoken situation, and, as such, is a necessary intermediary of all acts of objective reference. Subjectivity, in short, is the indexical link between language and discourse. In the semiotic tradition that has learned from Peirce's work, directly or otherwise, it is Emile Benveniste who has produced the clearest account of this function of subjectivity:

What then is the reality to which *I* or *you* refers? It is solely a "reality of discourse," and this is a very strange thing. *I* cannot be defined except in terms of "locution," not in terms of objects as a nominal sign is. *I* signifies "the person who is uttering the present instance of the discourse containing *I*". . . . *I* can only be identified by the instance of discourse that contains it and by that alone . . . . the form of *I* has no linguistic existence except in the act of speaking in which it is uttered. There is thus a combined double instance in this process; the instance of *I* as referent and the instance of discourse containing *I* as the referee. The definitions can now be stated precisely as: *I* is "the individual who utters the present instance of discourse containing the linguistic instance *I*."[27]

Benveniste's distinction between a subject of speech and a speaking subject (or subject of enunciation) establishes an irreducible difference between the signifier and the referent, a difference that cannot be mediated by a conventional signified as is the case with ordinary nominal objects. Moreover, any autonomy assumed for the subject of enunciation is further divided by Benveniste's recognition of the "forked" Freudian tongue, and its determination by both conscious and unconscious registers of speech. As a result, the "reality" of the subject of enunciation is open to question; it, too, must be inseparable from the discursivity of language.

Two basic points emerge from the foregoing discussion. Subjectivity, inasmuch as it is a construction made possible by language, *differs* from the linguistic treatment of objectivity because it refers to a real speaking situation. The result is the recognition of a subject of enunciation distinct from the linguistic subject, but one with no more conscious or transcendent unity than the latter. Both of these propositions have an important bearing upon Eliot's account of reference in the dissertation and in his poetics. Although his concern is with the recognition of objectivity rather than subjectivity, he clearly asserts the necessity of language to this process: "I do not believe that this occurs without the beginnings of speech" (KE, 132). Indeed, objects as such are impossible outside of speech:

Our only way of showing that we are attending to an object is to show that it and ourselves are independent entities, and to do this we must have names. . . . I am very far from meaning that it is the act of naming which makes the object, for the activity does not proceed from one side more than from another. Objects cannot arise without names, and names never spring up without objects, ready to be applied to the first objects to which they seem appropriate. Nor do I mean that the object did not exist until it was known, but only that it has not the character of objectivity until it is known as an object.

The name is not the object, certainly. We may say more truly that it is a category through which one grasps the object (if anyone has a taste for categories), but even this will not state the case correctly, if the category is conceived as something subjective, contrasted with the object. I should prefer to speak of the name as the moment of denotation; it is not that which is denoted, obviously, or merely a convenient means for denoting something which exists in complete independence of the name. In denotes an object which is not itself, and yet, when we ask just what this object is which is denoted, we have nothing to point to but the name.   (KE,133–34)

Insofar as this holds for Eliot's "theory of objectivity," and supports his explanation of unreal or nonexistent objects, it cannot fully account for what I have described as the subjective instance of speech. "Without words, no objects," and also, *no subjects*, but we have seen how this latter case is much less straightforward. If Eliot were to attempt to present a similar description of the relation between "name" and "subject," the "denoting act" would be shown to be irreducible to an identity-relation, for it would be an unfinished act if it were confined to the subject of speech alone, and did not point, deictically, outside of speech. To assert this, then, would be to lose sight of the fact of enunciation altogether, and to deny that language involves any *real* source of production. In many ways, this has been the direction of Eliot's thought in the dissertation, for he is concerned with ensuring the *symmetry* of subject-object relations, at any cost whatsoever. The instance of language (spoken discourse) suggests that such a homology is impossible to maintain, and that subjectivity is a multiple linguistic construction, differing *in kind* from the case of linguistic object-constitution. Eliot tries to match up these two "moments," leveling "point of view" against "point of attention," each acceding to a "self-transcendence" that affects, pari passu, subject and object alike. The poetics of impersonality rests upon the same desire for balance, for it aims to reduce the traditional subjectivist privilege of expressionism to a limited and perfunctory act of passive creativity, in which any record of enunciation is kept to a minimum.

In Eliot's argument, the act of "denotation" is not only the event that constitutes the object, but is also, by implication, the constitutive moment of subjectivity. Each, we could say, are constituted within a *thetic* operation; thetic, in Husserl's sense, because it involves a momentary thesis about the world, or more correctly, a change or transcendence of a thesis about the natural world.[28] Following Husserl, Benveniste emphasizes the movement of transcendence implied by the denoting act, both in the "setting up" of the subject as the linguistic category of "person," and in the relative position of the speaking subject with respect to the addressee. Thus the "person" is defined as "the psychic unity that transcends the totality of the actual experiences it assembles," a psychic unity that is consequently divided by unconscious effects. So too, in the polarity between speakers that has neither "equality nor symmetry: 'ego' always has a position of transcendence with regard to you."[29] What is important here is the operation or activity that accompanies the fact of transcendence, an operation brought about by evacuating all personal or empirical experience. Eliot's creative model of "depersonalization" matches this description, Husserl's and Benveniste's, in the way in which "the progress of an artist is a continual self-sacrifice, a continual extinction of personality" (SE,17). The notorious chemical analogy in "Tradition and the Individual Talent" demonstrates the capacity of such an operation to *reduce* empirical experience in the service of a higher form of production: "the more perfect the artist the more completely separate in him will be the man who suffers and the mind which creates; the more perfectly will the mind digest and transmute the passions which are its material" (SE,18). In Eliot's analogy, it is not the nature or quality of the materials that counts, but the "intensity" of the operation itself in its unification of experience. Husserl's own sense of *reduction* is particularly relevant to Eliot's creativity model. As committed an opponent of psychologism and empiricism as Bradley or Eliot, Husserl is concerned with the "pure" practice of disconnecting any given or naturalistic attitudes about the objective world that might arise from an empirical consciousness. Statements drawn from this "natural attitude" must be suspended, along with belief in practical, empirical existence. Like Eliot, he argues against the sharp differentiation of subject-object, pledging the science of phenomenology to the study of *intentionality*, those pure properties intrinsic to the subjective processes active in the organization of knowledge.

Intentionality involves the clarification of "essences" or ideal meanings through which the object comes to be immanent in consciousness. To implement this science of pure consciousness, Husserl proposes a method which consists of a series of *reductions*. Each reduction is like an abstracting act of purification, whereby experience is emptied of its empirical content by stripping away evidence of naturalistic objectivity and personality alike. Each reduction is both a proof and a successively constitutive origin of the transcendental subject, which is the product or *residuum* of the operation, like Eliot's poet/catalyst in the chemical chamber. In effect, Husserl's attention to objectivity (*Zu den Sachen Selbst*—to the things themselves!) actually involves an attempt to produce a philosophy of "pure" subjectivity, precisely by *eliminating the problems of subjectivity altogether.*

The comparison of Husserl's thought with some of the features of Eliot's poetics is, of course, not one that will bear very close examination, even if it is strikingly resonant at points.[30] Eliot's metaphysical account of self-transcendence—"to realise that a point of view is a point of view is already to have transcended it" (KE,148)— does not profess to share anything like the same systematic rigor as Husserl's reduction, nor does it aim at the ultimate disclosure of a pure, intending subjectivity. Nevertheless, Eliot's "process of realising a world" does involve a series of "moments of objectivity" to which a subject "attends" in successively superior ways. Similarly, the escape from personality involves a forfeiture of the empirical marks of subjectivity; transcending the natural ("the self recovered is never the same as the self before it was given")[31] is clearly an enhancing act because it incorporates "a very great number of experiences which to the practical and active person would not seem to be experiences at all" (SE,21).[32] If we are to acknowledge that this "process of transfusion of personality" is a transcendental activity, then it must, nonetheless, be distinguished from the Romantic process of what Eliot calls "orthodox creation in one's own image" (SE,157). There is no place for a constituting consciousness of this sort in Eliot's poetics. His abstraction of subjectivity from the actual moment of *poesis* or criticism is a simultaneous *effect* of that constitutive moment, and not its aprioristic cause. In balancing this abstraction against his important critical emphasis on the text itself as a unified *object* worthy of attention in itself, Eliot is concerned to effect a shift in critical emphasis away from the vicissitudes and niceties of self-expression. For the critics who followed Eliot, however, his meticulous qualification of the subjective/objective properties of the critical moment proved too discriminating to maintain. Under the New Criticism, the text becomes a fetishized object of cognition (even when it "expresses" the larger and otherwise impossible totality of the "world's body"), while the abstractable subject becomes entirely disconnected, a discrete, external agent intent on demonstrating the rational organization of its object as a neo-Kantian exercise in contemplative self-unification.[33]

The conditions, then, for this kind of hierarchical separation are implicit, though undeveloped, in a poetics of invisibility, for poet and critic alike. For Eliot's critic is "constituted" out of the disinterested Arnoldian *activity* of criticism, the result of his satisfactory distance from the text, while his faculty of judgment is no less abstracted from the personal history and prejudices he might bring to bear upon the critical act. The "critical spirit," even in the redemptionary colors in which Arnold conceived it, was *necessarily* an "attitude," or habitual activity, subtending a discipline of knowledge rather than the private expression of a feeling or an opinion (which would be a symptom of the natural attitude). One component of this trained sensibility is that the critic is required to "see" rather than "read." Eliot's rubric, "to see literature steadily and to see it whole," and Hulme's maxim, "to see things as they really are," are metaphoric extensions of Arnold's seeing "the object as in itself it really is."[34] Of the two, reading is the concrete activity, since it is troubled by contingent factors such as personal associations that fall outside of the purview of immediacy demanded of critical judgment. "Seeing," however, suggests the ideal guarantee of transcendental critical disinterest, since it reestablishes the impression of perfect continuity between the critical eye and the text, and at a distance unbroken by empirical details. Pater's intervention, for example, in Arnold's line of sight, destroys that continuity: "the first step towards seeing one's object as it really is, is to know one's impression as it really is."[35] Eliot takes Valéry to task for proposing a similar thing, namely, that the writer's job is to work up a "state" for the reader, "et de porter cet état exceptionnel au point d'une jouissance parfaite."[36] Again, this would be a function of the natural attitude, especially prone to the kind of psychologizing impressionism practiced by the aesthetes. Eliot goes on, however, to praise the "visual imagination" of Dante, who succeeds in absorbing the philosophy of his contemporaries because he views it not "as a theory (in the modern and not the Greek sense of the word) but in terms of something perceived."[37] *Theoria*, the Greek sense of "looking at" the world systematically, means that "we are not studying the philosophy, we see it." Thus, when we learn from Eliot that Swinburne "has not his eye on a particular place" (SE,324), or that the "eye" and "tongue" of Massinger are not in "co-operation" (SE,209), then we know that they are writing in that diffracted exteriority which is a perversion of the visual imagination. Dante exercised that imagination like a "psychological habit," a habit Eliot claims is now regarded as degenerate, but which was once "a more significant, interested and disciplined kind of dreaming": Dante's intention, then, "is to make us see what he saw," for although "speech varies . . . all our eyes are the same" (SE,243). In the case of Joyce and Milton, the "great blind musicians," (OPP,157) the feeling of being "there" and "then," in "a particular place at a particular time" is, of course, missing. The result is a "foreign idiom" giving on to "acts of lawlessness," in which the range of auditory association is "abnormally sharpened" to the detriment of poetic insight: "a dislocation takes place, through the hypertrophy of the auditory imagination at the expense of the visual and the tactile, so that the inner meaning is separated from the surface and tends to become something occult" (OPP,143).[38]

What is at stake here is not a language of "vision" (a visionary language), but a language modeled on the lucid intelligibility of perceptual experience. Husserl's ultimate description of intentional acts was a "seeing of essences" (*Wesenschau*), or ideal meanings immanent to transcendental consciousness, a privileged estimation of the perceptual which overrides his attention to the complexity of acts of signification. This same homage to specularity becomes an increasingly prominent feature of later developments in phenomenology: Sartre's structured account of the "gaze," and Merleau-Ponty's utter perceptual fusion of subject and object in the "flesh" of the world. Eliot's valorization of sight owes a lot to this new philosophical conscientiousness about doing justice to the object, and it stands up well in the light of the phenomologists' obsession with the ideally unmediated. This is no less an obsession in other modernist poets: the presentational "hardness" of the Imagist sketch, Williams's practical accuracy for local detail, and the optical models of the Objectivists. Wherever it is evoked, the eye is regarded as an unimpeachable source of authenticity.

Eliot's technical approach to this question points beyond poetics. The oppositions he sets up, centered on the primacy of the eye over the ear, are not recognizable terms of reference within the text. On the contrary, they are personifications of the way in which the text is enunciated by the writer and interpreted by the critical reader. Without inquiring at length into the relative worth of these oppositions, let alone the ultimate worth of the opposition itself, it is clear that this contest between the eye and ear, like the other critical antagonisms I have discussed (unity/fragmentation, identity/pathological difference), cedes its descriptives uses in the interests of a prescriptive judgment on Eliot's part, in this case, on the side of the persuasiveness of the visual. This is the paradigm of critical activity in Eliot's writing, and it reflects what Derrida has argued is the dominant paradigm of idealist metaphysics—to establish a set of polemical oppositions and then to enjoin the universal value of one over the other. As a formal method, this procedure is highly regular, and carries no special distinction in itself. Its consequences, however, for the recommendatory tone of Eliot's later thinking, and as a contribution to the generally *imperative* tone of the thirties, cannot be overstated, for they form an important part of any account of modernism as a "movement" in search of final solutions to the "problems" responsible for its very formation.

In approaching the "problem" of subjectivity in his work on Bradley, I have argued that Eliot neither presumed nor encouraged any such solution. Indeed, his immediate aims were to attack the subjectivism current in the philosophy of the day, and inasmuch as his critique rejected what it saw as positivistic assumptions about subject-object relations, it went so far as to question its own theoretical premises. Theory, Eliot concluded, is like "tying knots in the east wind," but when properly spliced with practice, would effectively undercut the need to produce alternative positions or solutions for subjectivity. This meant,however, that if subjectivity no longer required a theoretical explanation, then it no longer presented a problem. It is at this point, then, that Eliot's rigorous polemic falls back into a comfortable plea for contextualism, as part of a more pragmatic approach toward "moments" of subjectivity and objectivity. In examining more closely the arguments about reference with which Eliot supports his plea, I have suggested that it is in relation to language that subjectivity is posed as a concrete issue. The meeting of a theory of language with its practice, far from marking the disappearance of the "problem" of subjectivity, is its terminus a quo, because such a meeting posits one level of discourse, the spoken, against another, the speaking, and demonstrates that they are irreducible. Eliot does not confront this issue directly. I have suggested that it is because he fails to confront it directly that his poetics of invisibility encounters no practical friction in its dealings with the contradictions of subjectivity.

3.   *Seeke* not to be saved by *Synechdoche*
                                            Lancelot Andrewes

Lancelot Andrewes's Twelfth Sermon of the Nativity, preached on Christmas Day, 1618, takes as its subject the medium by which we come to recognize the meaning of the Incarnation, and his text offers an explanatory account of the sign-system by which the shepherds and the Wise Men came to know that they had found the birthplace of Christ. The point of the sermon, then, is "*invenietis,* to find *Christ,*" on a double level, but it will all come to nothing if we do not heed the signs: "*Signes* never come amisse; but are (then) so necessarie, as we cannot misse them, when we should misse without them: when, no *Signe,* no *invenietis*; As heer. For if a *Signe*; if this *Signe* had not been given; no *invenietis: Christ* had not been *found.*"[39] Andrewes invokes a tradition of semiotic interpretation long established within the Christian-Platonic hermeneutic. For Augustine, God is the only nonsign, transcendentally signified by all worldly signs; too much attention to the signs themselves is a Hebraic practice, it misses the revelatory point of the Word's origin. It is this very lesson that Andrewes takes pains to demonstrate, both in the attitude of the shepherds and in the cognitive design of his audience as they are invited to reenact the search for the divine object. Thus there is a mimetic strategy at work within the sermon itself, and it can be read as a commentary upon the exegetical method with which Andrewes reads the Scriptures. The Word seeks refuge in absence, it is always already dissimulated, but it can be "found" through the sign, both sensibly and intelligibly—which is a "wonder": "*Verbum* infans, the *Word* without a *word*; the *aeternall word* not hable to speak a *word*; 1. A Wonder sure." It is this double origin, both there and yet something else, that makes it possible to interpret the signs in a trustworthy and conclusive manner. Without this origin, present and absent, there would be no signification; the Nativity was "borne" for the sake of signification, just as it is for the sign that "He was *borne*." Andrewes demonstrates this necessity:

First, goe to the nature of a *Signe*, if *Christ* had come in excellencie, that had been no *signe*, no more than the Sunne in the Firmanent shining in his full strength; *Hoc non erit Signum*. Contrarie to the course of Nature, it would be, els it is no *Signe*, the *Sunn* eclipsed; the *Sunn* in sackcloth: that is *Signum in sole*, the Signe indeed.

The sign is important because Christ would never have been discovered without it, and we would have lost our way. For the sign is not only "*Signum*," it is also "*Signum vobis*"; it is for us that it was given. To presume, however, to do with the sign whatever we liked, would be to renounce it, because, as with the shepherds, the sign is useless if, once given, it "troubles [us] worse." Its *proper* meaning overrides all else:

Make of the *Signe* what ye will; it skills not what it be; never so meane: In the nature of a *Signe* there is nothing, but it may be such; All is, in the thing *signified*. So it carrie us to a rich *Signatum*, and worth the finding, what makes it a matter, how meane the *Signe* be? We are sent to a *Crib*; Not to an empty *Crib*; Christ is in it. Be the *Signe* never so simple, the *Signatum* it carries us to, makes *amends*. Any *Signe* with such a *Signatum*. . . . And so, *Signo Dato*, this *Signe* given, the Sermon ends. For to find *Christ* is all. *All* in all.

We are reminded of Derrida's observation that the "sign and divinity have the same place and time of birth. The age of the sign is essentially theological,"[40] for it is the Word which both fulfills and transcends signification. As Andrewes points out, "in the mind of *Christ,* there is no odds at all. Ye may strike a tally between the *Signe* and the *Signatum."* His sermon is predicated upon that fact, and the purposivenes of his textual pursuit of it is unequivocal. For all their concrete substance and figural materiality, the Scripture, the signs, and the doubts of the shepherds and audience alike, dissolve as the commentator "sees" through them.

In his praise of Andrewes's interpretive skills, Eliot describes the preacher as being "wholly in his subject, unaware of anything else," his emotion growing "as he penetrates more deeply into his subject" until "he is finally 'alone with the Alone,' with the mystery which he is seeking to grasp more and more firmly" (SE,351). In his famous sermon, *Death's Duel,* Donne appears to be at variance with this point of view when he claims that "the *Mysteries* of our *Religion* are not the *objects* of *our reason."* Clearly, there is much to be gained by opposing and comparing the respective interpretive styles of Andrewes and Donne. Indeed, the comparison is one of the more pellucid examples of Eliot's critical dualism: Andrewes's positivistic conceits and Donne's skeptical wit, the "closed" and the "open" hand of Christian preaching, the contemplative and the personal point of view, the literal and the literary, type and trope. Each of these oppositions, and the list is not inclusive, qualifies a set of critical ethics which I have tried to sketch out in Eliot's work. The Andrewes/Donne comparison, however, has more to offer, for it touches a "live" historical nerve in the ancestral body of Eliot's own subjectivity, one origin of which dates from the theological schisms of the seventeenth century. The more immediate occasion, however, is Eliot's first leader article for *The Times Literary Supplement* in 1926, in which he is writing at the epicenter of the English literary establishment for the first time, and where he takes the opportunity to canonize the relatively unsung Andrewes at the expense of Donne. The article is given a more central place yet, in *For Lancelot Andrewes,* a 1928 collection of essays which marks the end of his three-hundred-year old ancestral exile from the Anglican Church. Symptomatically, the preface announces a further displacement of his authorial subjectivity by articulating a set of ideological interests, defined, in Bradleyan style, as a "point of view": classicist, royalist, and Anglo-Catholic.[42]

Scriptural interpretation, as Derrida has suggested, is intrinsically associated with the idea of exile, irreversible for the Hebraic, if not for the Christian, tradition.[43] Even within the Hellenized Christian tradition, however, there is still an insistent historical antinomy between the *letter* and the *spirit*, and Eliot need only assume this historical conflict in order to manufacture his own dual object. Generally speaking, the early doyens of High Anglicanism preached in the metaphysical style of highly wrought wit quite typical of the rhetorically cavalier strain of *lettered* Scriptural exegesis. Origen was the chief patristic exponent of this pluralistic approach to the holy texts, and his heretical opposition to the literal, his extravagant attention to ambiguity and the narratively scandalous, gave rise to the conservative check of the school at Antioch under Basil, Cyril of Jerusalem, Eusebius, and Chrysostom, which emphasized the historicity and literality of the text. The conflict between Alexandria and Antioch is internalized for those who follow: Augustine, torn between text and Word, and even Luther, confessing to a lifelong regret for his youthful Origenic zeal.[44] So too, the story of the early Puritan settlement turns upon a prolonged difference of opinion over the dominance of the plain style, an issue which divided the soul of New England at every level, from the congregational covenant to the politics of everyday life.[45]

Eliot's youthful saturation in "Puritan" thinking has been well documented, Andrewes's less so. Born to parents of the virulently anti-Catholic mercantile class, he learned his theology at Pembroke College, Cambridge, at that time a Puritan stronghold, and more often than not found himself "at the heart of Puritan society."[46] It is not difficult to find traces in Andrewes's style of the clash between the structural form of the plain style and the epidemic of verbal luxuriance that had come to exact a stylistic hegemony over Elizabethan rhetoric. Eliot's interest is in the former, for his attention is given over to the precision, clarity, and "ordonannce" which marks Andrewes's grasp of the textual process as it tracks down and isolates its object. He is particularly fond of Andrewes's disingenuous way of simulating stasis and yet "proceeding in the most orderly and deliberate manner" (SE,346), a model for his own later poetic style. This Andrewes achieves through the strategic use of short sentences that are not pockets of fugitive meaning, but rather, good currency: "It fareth with sentences as with *coynes*; in coines, they

that in smallest compasse, conteine greatest value, are best es-
teemed, and in sentences, those that in fewest words comprise
most matter, are most praised."[47] Ironically, Eliot chooses the most
remarkably long sentence in all of his writing to emphasize his
solidarity with Andrewes's stylistic "determination to stick to essentials" in the matter of dogma:

To persons whose minds are habituated to feed on the vague jargon of our
time, when we have a vocabulary for everything and exact ideas about
nothing—when a word half-understood, torn from its place in some alien or
half-formed science, as of psychology, conceals from both writer and reader
the meaninglessness of a statement, when all dogma is in doubt except the
dogmas of science of which we have read in the newspapers, when the
language of theology itself, under the influence of an undisciplined mysticism of popular philosophy, tends to become a language of tergiversation—
Andrewes may seem pedantic and verbal.   (SE,347)

Like Eliot's sentence, Andrewes will resort to any logical skull-
duggery to get to his point—"what matter the *Signe* if it lead to a
rich *Signatum*"—while his rhetorical skills are directed toward rein-
forcing what we already know, or at least suspect. The result is a
professional performance, and a circumspect anonymity that is
shared, in principle, by the orthodox Puritan preacher, trained
to be serviceable, rather than instructive or self-intrusive. As the
sermon moves toward its mark, the self-effacement of the speaker
reaches the correct level of "invisibility" demanded by Eliot's
poetics.

   Donne, by comparison, appeals to "a certain wantonness of the
spirit" (SE,353), an observation which indicates Eliot's attitude to
his wayward handling of the text, the capricious self-indulgence of
an author who will not guarantee transcendental truths but rather
try to outdo the tropes and figures of classical rhetoric. Eliot's demands for "ordonnance" and precision are scarcely met at all in
Donne's fitful commitment to expository prose; Donne's logic-for-
the-object is always being sidetracked, seduced by contextual
events, unlike the Magi in Eliot's poem and Andrewes's sermon,
who resist "the silken girls bringing sherbet" and follow the signs
to their proper conclusion. As Stanley Fish remarks, Donne may
serve us by failing rather than succeeding, for his negative theology

works through demonstrating our inadequacy to elucidate the divine in a rational, linear manner: "the distinctions and divisions that were to have marked our understanding, mark, instead, the extent of our entrapment."[48]

Fish's observation throws us back upon the contradictory spectacle of a subjectivity, in the preacher and listener, which is both a cause and an effect of this concrete failure to communicate or apprehend the divine object. Neither subject nor object is transcendentalized, because Donne's way is to expose the full heterogeneity of the various levels of enunciation at work in his text. It is Eliot himself who provides an example of this in quoting the bulk of this extraordinary passage from Donne:

I am not all here. I am here now preaching upon this text, and I am at home in my library, considering whether *S. Gregory* or *Hierome* have said best of this text, before. I am here speaking to you, and yet I consider by the way, in the same instant, what it is likely you will say to one another, when I have done, and you are not all here neither; you are here now, hearing me, and yet you are thinking that you have heard a better sermon somewhere else of this text before; you are here, and yet you think you could have heard some other doctrine of downright *Predestination* and *Reprobation* roundly delivered somewhere else with more edification to you; you are here, and you remember yourselves that now ye think of it: This had been the fittest time, now, when everybody else is at church, to have made such and such a private visit; and because you would be there, you are there.   (SE,350–51)

For Eliot, there is an "impure motive" behind such a rhetorical strategy, perhaps even a lack of "spiritual discipline" (SE,345). Donne's intention, nonetheless, is to foreground the fact that his text is *spoken* in the knowledge of the contingency of *mortality*. The result of this is the funereal code that is so important in his writing; his celebrated taste for the *thanatographical* is much more than a *memento mori* when it stages the "impossibility" of the life-mask as a speaking role, in contrast to Eliot's own whimsical fondness for "playing Possum." When Donne offers his own weakness as a textual example, Eliot interprets this as "self-expression," a symptom of the obsession with personality. And his "impure motive" is finally a "dangerous" thing for Eliot, because it confronts the *abject* side of the sacred—"the sin, the leprosie, the pestilence, the ordure of the soul."[49] To lose one's way in Donne's pollutant underworld is a far cry from losing oneself in a transcendental mystery like Browne's *O Altitudo*.

Beyond Eliot's distaste for self-indulgence or verbal vaudeville, it is Donne's recognition of the fractured condition of our subjective continuity in history that counts against him. As a "sign of his times," his ratio is that of a broken intensity, unlike the *Signe* of Andrewes, which is intact, and if followed in good faith, will restore a particular genealogical history to Eliot after three centuries. In his essay, Eliot suggests, by way of Lord Clarendon (himself an exile and also an agent of "restoration"), that had Andrewes been appointed Archbishop of Canterbury, the political history of England might well have taken a different course entirely. First Abbot and then Laud would not have had the opportunity to be incompetent, and hence the Civil War might never have taken place. Nor, perhaps, would the cultural wound which necessitated the sailing of the *Mayflower*, and the subsequent exile of Eliot's ancestors. Eliot's desire is to mend that fracture by whatever cultural means it takes to reconcile the "dissociation of sensibility," and one consequence is that this leads him to play down his Puritan heritage whenever possible. The English Puritans, for example, "who supported the Commonwealth, were not all of the flock of Zeal-of-the-land-Busy or the United Grand Junction Ebenezer Temperance Society," but were merely political dissenters who believed "that government by a Parliament of gentlemen was better than government by a Stuart" (SE,294).

Excommunicated thrice: once, genealogically, from England; again, corporeally, from America; and yet again, linguistically, from ideal objectivity—the testament of Eliot's desire is to put an end to these multiple separations. In another essay in *For Lancelot Andrewes*, he describes the plight of Machiavelli watching his Italy being "torn and ravaged by foreign invaders," and suggests that "the humiliation of Italy was, to Machiavelli, a personal humiliation and the origin of his thought and writing."[50] For Eliot, who questions whether "the Civil War has not ended" yet (OPP,148), the origin of his own thought and writing may lie as much in the humiliation of these seventeenth-century political dissenters as in the shame he felt for the good people who read the *Boston Evening Transcript*.

2.   "SIGNIFYING MATRIMONIE"

T HE WASTE LAND has commonly been read as an index of the
cultural insolvency of Europe after World War I. One could say
that it is this metaphorical *bankruptcy* that has carried the poem's
reputation through the critical stock market of the last sixty years.
Indeed, the very title of the poem has become a byword for a set of
historically impoverished circumstances, and thus it functions both
as a specific metonym and as a general sign of those postwar times;
the proper name, *The Waste Land*, coexists with the metaphor of
"the Waste Land" that has now become a familiar part of everyday
cultured speech.

Partly because of this semantico-historical development, it has
become increasingly difficult to critically account for the particular
textual conditions under which the "metaphor" was produced in
1921. The result of decades of New Criticism (itself inextricably
associated, as I shall argue, with the canonical ascendancy of Eliot's
poem) was, of course, to generalize the metaphor within the
shrunken confines of the poem's "world," and thereby abstract it
from any living or concretely differentiated context. Even if this
kind of critical "anaesthetizing" of the poem has been largely su-
perseded in recent years, there is no way now of going back beyond
that period to the twenties in order to present a *fresh* socio-histor-
ical reading of the poem's conditions of production. Not only have
the intervening years of criticism become a conceptual element of
the poem itself, but we have also learned the fundamental lesson of
reading History as a text, rather than as an objective account of facts
and events. Eliot's poem has itself contributed to the "text" of twentieth-century history, and that is as high a literary distinction as
any writer can hope to earn. The irony of this contribution, however, invites further examination, for the literary distinction of *The
Waste Land*, above that of all other modernist classics, is that it

articulates the "failure" of History, or at least the failure of an established conceptual view of history. One of the major challenges faced by today's critic is to account for the ways in which that failure is articulated in the poem, and in doing so, perhaps account for the ways in which history has also become impossible to "safely" or comfortably incorporate within the activity of critical interpretation itself.

Despite our time-honored acceptance of the Waste Land metaphor, then, it remains to be shown how the insolvency of postwar history is in fact written into Eliot's poem. Is this bankrupt condition transcribed in an unmediated way through the author's selection of a set of discursive or allusive contents, or is it somehow "reflected," or held in "solution," in accordance with the orthodox Marxist view of ideology? Is it articulated by way of what Yvor Winters called the "imitative fallacy," whereby the formal disorder of the poem directly evokes social or cultural disarray, or is it filtered, as I shall speculatively argue, through the complex medium of enunciation that involves the author's body itself, a way partly charted in Eliot's record of physical and psychical default over the postwar period? Aside from the necessity of forging some common ground between the social and the psychic, this latter perspective will involve the effort to go beyond the traditional psychoanalytical contributions to the relation between authorship and textuality, loosely ranged, as their critical conjectures have been, somewhere in the free bargaining zone between sexual stereotype and biography, and thus in an area of critical interest that has been designated as Eliot's "personal waste land."[1]

1.   The problem before the writer in our time is ££££££
                                                        Pound

Whether in good faith or not, Pound was always willing to support and invest in another man's career, but in London after World War I, he made it plain that he had "not the least interest in the fortunes of any writer in England save" those of Eliot.[2] His concern, however, cuts both ways, because Eliot's own business interests were being shuttled back and forth between his stake in building a literary reputation, and the more routine concern of securing a livelihood that would not entirely consume either his time or his faculties. As an employee in the Foreign Department of Lloyds Bank between 1917 and 1925, he is also a frontline witness to a larger economic debacle, the fickle circulation of capital in a Europe stricken with catastrophic munitions bills and national deficits beyond its reckoning. Many years later, and months before the next war was to break out, he was to regret the hollow complicity displayed by British appeasement of Hitler, and to reflect that the society he had adopted was ultimately "assembled around [nothing] more than a congeries of banks, insurance companies and industries" since it had little more to defend than a "belief in compound interest and the maintenance of dividends."[3] Counting the cost of the World War I, as Eliot discovered, was as much a financial transaction as a moral one, and it found its poetic justice in the reparations debt imposed upon Germany at Versailles, in the same Hall of Mirrors where the French had paid for their loss of national pride in 1871. By 1921, Eliot had been "put in charge" not only of "settling all the pre-War Debts between the Bank and Germans," but also, and increasingly so, of the problems raised by "that appalling document the Peace Treaty" (WL,xviii). This kind of work, then, which is Eliot's job at Lloyds, involved several codes of exchange: linguistic (since it required multilingual translations), a word for a word; monetary, a coin for a coin; and symbolic, a nation's "soul" for the Allied demand for its pound of flesh, the toll of the battlefields. All of these exchanges reflect the kind of economy that abhors a debt, one that must always balance the budget. Any account of Eliot's relation to this rule of exchange should, however, take into its reckoning the fact that Eliot's own "balance" was regularly upset by a long history of personal crises of "exchange," both bodily and financial. Indeed, it is in the three months paid sick leave he took in the fall of 1921, the only period of the eight years in which his services as a Lloyds employee are not good currency, that Eliot, like Phlebas, forgot the "profit and the loss" and put together *The Waste Land*. In this sense, the poem might be thought of as a sheer "waste," an example of what Georges Bataille called the *spendthrift* text (*dépense*), and thus offered somewhat gratuitiously rather than as an explicit token of its author's intentions. Finding itself in the red, *The Waste Land*, for Eliot, would then be an "expense of spirit" purchased at the cost of the "waste of shame" that accompanies all debtors.

In her introduction to a facsimile edition of the original manuscripts (1971), Valerie Eliot has written an exhaustive account of Eliot's circumstances, which reads like a balance-sheet of anxiety, as expense after expense is weighed against the physical limits of the body. His marriage, described to Pound in terms of a bargain discount—"she has everything to give that I want, and she gives it. I owe her everything"[4]—had almost immediately become a liability as soon as he assumed financial responsibility for the upkeep of his wife's pricey health in addition to his own, while the long suspected sexual debt (of nonconsummation) may well have been annulled, as Tom Matthews scurrilously suggests, in Vivienne's brief fling with Bertrand Russell, a rendezvous set up in exchange for the philosopher's monetary aid.[5] Otherwise, however, and in spite of Pound and others' benevolent attempts to enable him to retire from the bank, Eliot generally refuses to take up the debtor's position (unlike Joyce, the other great literary bank clerk of the century, who ran up scores willy-nilly). In this context, perhaps it is relevant that the story of *The Waste Land*'s publication follows the course of a successful financial speculation; its initial evaluation as a mercantile object fixed by the price of its "real" worth against the return in cash payment to its author; its proposed worth to various publishers outbid finally by the offer of *The Dial*'s $2000 annual prize award; the sale of the manuscripts to New York art patron John Quinn; the conditions of market necessity under which the "Notes" were appended to meet a publisher's demand for space; and lastly, its first British appearance in Eliot's own publishing venture, *The Criterion*, underwritten at first by the aristocratic money of Lady Rothermere, and later by Faber & Faber business. This run of events appears to reach completion in 1925 when Eliot signed his own contract of employment with Faber, placing him at what was, quite literally, the central site of the economic production of the literary word.

Apart from these material benefits, what was there to gain from being the "author" of *The Waste Land*? In a number of declamatory statements made over the years, Eliot had eschewed responsibility for the poem (just a piece of "rhythmical grumbling," as he put it), itself a text which, because of its highly allusive nature, seems to eschew of its own accord any exchangist notion of authorship based upon the "originality" of copyrighted material. Did "Eliot" write it or not? And what could he have meant, to suggest that the poem was "unauthorized" in some way, as if History had spoken up for itself? These questions touch upon the problems of literary owner-ship and literary authority, problems particularly relevant to *The Waste Land* if we recall the very extensive and tight editing job that Pound performed on the original with a shrewd eye for the market in 1922. Works of art are usually classified under a single name, or fixed identity—for legal and copyright as much as for artistic rea-sons. Accordingly, if *The Waste Land* made Eliot's "name," then this was surely a result of the fortunes which a more general cultural discourse invests in the necessity of a unified subjectivity which stands as the guarantee of authorial identity. For the critics, how-ever, who, next to the publishers, have the biggest stake in promot-ing the claims of such a cultural discourse, *The Waste Land* was indeed to become a professional *cause célèbre*, but precisely because Eliot was so willing to resign or disavow his rights of authorship. For it was that waiver, or gesture of "invisibility," on his part, which played directly into the hands of a New Criticism that came to swear by the idea of the authorless text. Perhaps this helps to ex-plain why the uncivilized appearance of *The Waste Land* in the twen-ties marked it as *the* text which was unthinkable within the conceptual limits of critical understanding, and precisely for this reason, became instrumental in defining, by dint of its own default, those very limits as ones which circumscribed the traditional, but subsequently outmoded, domain of the "authorized" text. If so, then it certainly helps to explain why the poem's subsequent do-mestication was seen as the definitive and founding fortune of the New Criticism and, by extension, a justification for the new Eng-lish faculties in search of a respectable academic birthright.

I have been trying to suggest that *The Waste Land* and its effects— its metaphor of bankruptcy, and the bankruptcy of its "author"— can be placed within a larger and less restricted "economy" than the New Criticism could afford to acknowledge (ironically, or per-haps symptomatically, the original manuscripts were found to include three bills from the Albemarle Hotel, Cliftonville, Margate). Thus the "meaning" of *The Waste Land* for us, here and now, is more likely to include some of the elements of these larger "economic" conditions than at any other time since Eliot published his text in 1922. Indeed, more than for any other poem, this "meaning" seems, like the metaphor of its title, to have become an epiphenomenon of its 434-line text: the eccentric focus of its allusions; the *esprit de l'escalier* of its "Notes"; its conditions of reception by perplexed reviewers; the tortuous history of its interpretation; and the appendical pressure of the ur-*Waste Land*, lost for fifty years.

For Eliot himself, however, the writing of this poem came to be bound up in what appears to be a complicated, and certainly contradictory, relation to his father's death. For in 1919, he wrote to Quinn: "my father has died, but this does not weaken the need for a book at all—it really reinforces it—my mother is still alive" (WL,xvi). The event of his father's death only served to aggravate the long-standing material source of Eliot's troubles, for it was his father who had stopped his financial support as a response to the marriage, and cut both Eliot and his wife out of the will. As a result of this action, one could say that Eliot was, quite literally, no longer in his father's debt, a fact that could but take on an added resonance on account of the death. To say more than this, however, in terms of Eliot's personal role in the genesis of the poem, would be to enter a realm of conjecture, one to which a certain kind of traditional psychoanalytic critique would nevertheless deliver us. It would be easy to imagine the shape of such conjecture: a sudden acceptance of the death somehow loosened Eliot's neurotically blocked creativity, and fortified his ego, thus "authorizing" him to take on and complete the hitherto resistant task of writing, and so on. In isolating some of the components, sexual, historical, and political, of a personal and individual economy, what I have outlined could justly form the basis of a conventional psycho-biographical reading. Such a reading, however, would be restricted, ultimately, to making the most out of the empirical evidence at hand, in short, those few facts about Eliot's relation to his father which are critically available. To avoid such leaps in the critical dark, I want, therefore, to turn to another way of considering how the significance of paternal death and debt has an effect upon the writing of *The Waste Land*, treating these not as contingent empirical facts, but rather as necessary symbolic effects inscribed within the poem itself.

By understanding Eliot's debt to the father as a symbolic bond, we can propose a different kind of economy of personal exchange. This economy makes it possible to discuss both the literal Eliot and the literary "Eliot," who is, psychoanalytically speaking, the "subject" of *The Waste Land*. Unlike the individual (Eliot) who is assumed to have some consistent identity over and above any relations of exchange into which he enters, the subject ("Eliot") is an effect of the relations of linguistic exchange. Understood in this way, in terms of a purely linguistic economy, "Eliot" becomes a subjectivity *proper* to language.

The idea of a *symbolic debt* is a Lacanian one.[6] It describes the conditions under which the subject gains access to social relations by and through the agency of language, fixing the castration threat as the final "cause" of that accession (the *caption* of subjectivity, both in the sense of a capture, and a proper title). For Lacan, castration is a general term for all bodily disorders which involve loss or violent deprivation. This would refer to both pre-oedipal (including the shock of birth) and post-oedipal losses (the way the subject responds, for example, to the insistence of the death drives). Castration is a crucial term for Lacan because it emphasizes the idea that subjectivity is initially constituted, and repeatedly reconstituted, out of a sense of *lack*. In the oedipal formation, a decisive instance of this for the (male) child occurs when he recognizes the absence of a maternal penis. The child understands this lack in the mother in terms of castration, and, fearing the same fate at his father's hands, renounces his desire for the mother. This opens up a break in the imaginary link between mother and child, which is explained, but also mediated by, the father's intervention as a third person, in possession of the phallus. However, having established the evidence of lack, not even the father's assumed privilege is secure, and thus the child's hope that the father can transcend lack altogether is dashed and must be modified into an acceptance of the parent's "normal" state of privation. This acceptance of privation is effected by the castration threat, confirmed now by a knowledge of the father's equally "lacking" condition, and it explains why the child acts henceforth, not in emulation of the real father, but in the *name* of the father, under the sentence of the castration threat. This also explains why the child's submission to language is conducted under what Lacan calls the Name-of-the-Father, and not as an attempt to follow the real father's example. The same distinction is pointed up in the fact that language enables real anatomical difference (absence/presence of the penis) to be replaced by linguistic differences (linguistic mastery over phenomenal absence/presence). Similarly, it enables subjectivity (absence/presence of self) to be represented for the first time, but only on condition that it be honored as a linguistic status; not as a fixed term, but one which is constantly being circulated in language, in exchange for other signifiers.

Thus understood, subjectivity is the effect of an exchange. It is offered in the form of a "gift" of language, but as a gift for which one pays. The child represents himself in language but this deprives him of his body, which is given up in exchange for the new power to signify. This loss of the body is the largest loss of all, but it is a small price to pay for what the child gains: in effect, legal and social recognition as an identifiable element in the world of symbolic exchange. This identity, as we have seen, is inherited in the name of the father, and therefore, in language, quite literally through the paternal signifier called the Name-of-the-Father. The subject's body is "mortgaged" as part of an unequal exchange for the Name-of-the-Father, while the "contractual" debt between the two, the subject's body and the Name-of-the-Father, has consequences which are played out in language from then onward. Because of its close association with the experience of loss or lack, accession to language is also the point at which the child's demands and needs, both of which could be satisfied hitherto (if only through hallucination), are transformed into the more general Lacanian concept of desire, a permanently lacking condition for which there is no such palliative. The burden of this desire is linguistically assumed at the same time as the name is inherited, and its effects are generated symbolically as a kind of insufficiency, a debt which can never be paid off, except in death. Consider the exemplary fate of the Cumaean Sybil, whose predicament, the result of her linguistic predication, is sealed in the epigraph to *The Waste Land*:

For I have seen with my own eyes, the Cumaean Sybil hanging inside a jar, and whenever boys ask her, "What do you wish, O Sybil?" she would reply, "I wish to die."

Granted the gift of long life by Apollo at her own request, she forgets to ask for eternal youth and is thereby condemned, not only to the loss of her own body, but also to be forever spoken, prophetically, from elsewhere. Every message, oracle, or answer she offers to her visitors is, by her own sentence, and pari passu, the sentence of another. And so, in wishing for death, she calls for the cessation of all desire, since desire is nothing but a hapless condition imposed upon her; because it is the desire of another, or the Other, it is a "foreign" language to her, and thus unstoppable.

In the brief interpretation of Eliot's symbolic debt which follows, my concern will thus be to move away from consideration of the real father (the same father who suggested in a letter that, if a cure were not to be found for syphilis, it might be necessary "to emasculate our children to keep them clean").[7] Instead, it will be an absent father who only functions as a symbolic agent of authority which shall carry the weight of my discussion.

2.   Love is the unfamiliar Name
                                              Eliot

In *The Principles of Logic*, Bradley takes issue with Mill's assumption that proper names have no meaning, that they denote but do not connote. If we agree with Bradley that the name is a sign, and not a simple utilitarian index, then all names, including the Name-of-the-Father, become objects to decipher and anatomize.[8] Eliot is as celebrated as Dickens for the connoting of names: Mrs. Phlaccus, Mr. Apollinax, Madame de Tornquist, Grishkin, Burbank, Mr. Eugenides, Phlebas, Mrs. Equitone, Madame Sosostris, Sweeney, Fresca, etc., while *Old Possum's Book of Practical Cats* is formally posed as a problem in guessing the "name that you will never guess," for it is both "effable" and "ineffable," the result of a long meditation upon the kind of "deep and inscrutable singular Name" which is not to be taken lightly:

> The naming of Cats is a different matter,
> It isn't just one of your holiday games.   (CPP, 149)

So too, the last poem in this volume reveals that the problem all along has been one of "AD-DRESS," a masquerade under other names rather than simply calling the cat "by his NAME" (CPP, 171). Listen, however, to the most plaintive address of *The Waste Land*, the traumatized Philomel's attempt to name her rapist and mutilater:

> The change of Philomel, by the barbarous king
> So rudely forced; yet there the nightingale
> Filled all the desert with inviolable voice
> And still she cried, and still the world pursues,
> "Jug Jug" to dirty ears.
> And other withered stumps of time   (CPP, 40)

> Twit twit twit
> Jug jug jug jug jug jug
> So rudely forc'd.
> Tereu   (CPP, 43)

Here, the naming of Tereus is clipped short by the elision of an *s*. This forms the Latin vocative, the case in which the subject is first named or "called" in language. In the course of the Latin declension, then, the difference between the nominative and the vocative is marked by the reduction of the name, almost as a mutilation to match the violent "change of Philomel." In the discussion of Lacan, I showed how the act of nomination is bound up in the relation of the given name, the Name-of-the-Father, to the castration threat. Castration is experienced as a premature recognition of death, and so if the name is already associated with a threat of mutilation, it can be interpreted in the wider context of a death sentence, an act not only of corporal, but also of capital punishment. The capital letter which distinguishes the proper name from the other ordinary language terms is a sign of the fact that there is a price on the subject's head. These, then, are the terms of the symbolic debt: to accept identity at that price, and under the pain of that death sentence.

Perhaps within the folds of Eliot's poetry we can see how an attempt is made to save the subject's neck by escaping from the *captivity* of an imposed identity. This involves the attempt to "pay back" some of the symbolic debt, or at least to reduce the capital sentence to something less. One of the ways in which this is done is through leveling the capital letter in the proper name, and submitting the identity of the name itself to a process of "naturalization," by assimilating the proper name into the realm of common nouns so as to make it "mean." In this naturalizing process, the name would be torn up, rearranged, anagrammatized, stripped down, rebuilt, and disseminated into more common appellations or forms of designation. As a result, subjective identity would become less "proper," and more of a common part of speech as it is increasingly traded in for a more objective commodity. A whole range of new images—animal, vegetable, mineral—would then become available to the subject as a substitute for, or gloss of, his proper name, offering him a chance to reappropriate the wholeness of his lost body under another name, a nick-name, and thus imagined as anterior (*eke-name*—from the Middle English) to both castration and the captive identity announced in the act of nomination.⁹ As Possum warns, this "isn't just one of your holiday games." On the contrary, it internalizes what, on the one hand, is seen, symbolically, as a matter of life and death, and, on the other, what we recognize as the familiar filial struggle—the dialectic of submission to, and contravention of, the paternal will.

Of all the subterfuges worked into Eliot's "naturalized" name, the doubled monogram of *tsetse* (his Harvard nickname and his identity in Conrad Aiken's novel *Ushant*) is the longest standing. A displacement of the *s* gives us *testes*, which alludes directly to the castratory effect, while the elision of the *s* brings forth Monsieur *Teste*, Valéry's narcissist poet-cum-metaphysician whom we saw Eliot describe as a "monster." *Stetson*, however, creeps into *The Waste Land*, spelling out the difficulties of filial conduct by its counterpaternal suggestions (stepson, and thus begotten elsewhere, by another father). A more complex anagram of the authorial signature is *litotes*, "a figure of speech in which an affirmative is expressed by a negation of a contrary" (OED), a consummate rhetorical costume or ad-dress for the "invisible poet," only present when he cannot be negated. As here in the early and whimsically autobiographical "Mélange Adultère de Tout":

> J'erre toujours de-ci de-là
> A divers coups de tra là là
> De Damas jusqú à Omaha.
> Je célébrai mon jour de fête
> Dans une oasis d'Afrique
> Vetue d'une peau de girafe.
>
> On montrera mon cénotaphe
> Aux côtes brulantes de Mozambique.   (CPP,29)

An "adulterous medley," as its title suggests, the poem dramatizes the dissimulations of the poet's identity, and the colorful strategems of his various incognitos. His "jour de fête"—the celebration of the day of a saint who shares his name—is a joke at the father's expense. Resigned to the bondage of a paternally imposed identity, the subject seems to occupy the name with a grandeur which is, nonetheless, funerary, as if in a *cenotaph*: "an empty tomb, a sepulchral monument raised in honour of a deceased person whose body is elsewhere" (OED) ("On montrera mon cénotaphe"). Here, the capital sentence of the name is already an empty title, prematurely acting out the subject's death. In capitulating to the loss of this title, however, by dissimulating the name, the final act of execution is put off, and the sovereign head saved from the block. Thus, in an earlier part of the same poem, the French nomination *tête*, with its circumflex left as a scar by which to remember the shorn *s*, asserts its immunity in defiant headlines:

> A Londres, un peu banquier,
> Vous me paierez bien la tête.

This alludes directly to the banking circuit of debt, but because of its punning (*se payer la tête*), it also draws attention to an economy of decapitation and recapitation by which the proper name is broken up and restored. The Hanged Man of *The Waste Land* is likewise cut down and revived. The Hollow Men, "headpiece filled with straw," are offered a new bodily accompaniment, a more substantial target

than Gerontion's "dull head among windy spaces." And here, in
Coriolan's address to his mother, the subject can barely stand up for
a head count:

O mother (not among these busts, all correctly inscribed)
I a tired head among these heads
Necks strong to bear them
Noses strong to break the wind
Mother
May we not be some time, almost now, together,
If the mactations,immolations, oblations, impetrations,
Are now observed
May we not be
O hidden
Hidden in the stillness of noon, in the silent croaking night.
Come with the sweep of the little bat's wing, with the small flare
    of the firefly, or lightning bug   (CPP,88)

Perhaps the associations of these "busts" rightly point up the
maternal provenance of such name play in its hankering after the
precastratory comfort of the breast, and the bodily wholeness enjoyed there. The "bat's wing" and the "firefly," however, belong to
an image-repertoire which crops up throughout Eliot's writing, one
in which the anxiety of bodily deprivation is graphically evoked.
For one who suffered lifelong from an anemic condition, the image
of the *tsetse* fly, the bloodsucking parasite of tropical and southern
Africa ("aux côtes brulantes de Mozambique") is an appropriate
foreign body for "Eliot" to occupy. Stephen Spender recalled Eliot
boasting to Stravinsky that a certain doctor had told him that he had
"the thinnest blood [the doctor] had ever tested,"[10] while the Bells
and the Sitwells were among those of his acquaintances in the thirties who noticed that Eliot had taken to using makeup in order to
appear more cadaverous than ever. Unlike the straightforward disavowal suggested by the better known Possum (or *I can* nonetheless,
in spite of my castration), the tsetse vampire is also capable of
evoking the fallible penis (as opposed to the permanent phallus—
which suggests the refusal to accept castration and lack), since the
tsetse is active in both its blood-engorged and its detumescent

states. As a parasite, then, the tsetse lives off the body in which it resides, in this case the name itself, and thus comes to represent the claim to something from which it cannot be separated, and hence something it needs to complete itself.[11] By contrast, the other winged occupants of Eliot's imaginary menagerie stand or fall by their respective mutilations: "my thoughts tonight have tails but no wings" (WL,105); "I should like to be in a crowd of beaks without words" (WL,105); "The white wings still fly seaward, seaward flying/ Unbroken wings" (CPP,66): "Why should the agèd eagle spread his wings?" (CPP,60). A number of Eliot's reviews for *The Egoist* in 1918 were signed "Apteryx" or *wingless,* and in an unpublished poem of 1914 (in the Berg collection of the New York Public Library), entitled "The Burnt Dancer," a moth's wings are singed by a fire in a minor catastrophe which is compared to the burning of a name, and one with expressly tropical connotations. The same violent loss is taken up in a bridegroom's postcoital discontent in the suppressed hymeneal "Ode on Independence Day, July 1914": "Indignant/ At the cheap extinction of his taking-off/ Now lies he there/ Tip to tip washed beneath Charles Wagon."[12] The groom's wings are folded up against the body of a bride who has already been revealed as "succuba eviscerate," one of the castrating demons of feminine folklore.

Among the many metamorphoses of *The Waste Land* (and Ovid is as much its tutelary genius as Frazer), we have seen Philomel transformed into a nightingale, her clipped tongue metonymically associated with the act of de-winging. Her truncated speech resembles the plight of both Echo and the Sybil, whom Ovid describes in turn as being deprived of their bodies, and thereby reduced to nothing more than speech, a mere "tail-end" of the full body of human faculties. And a common Latin designation for the nightingale is *vox et praeterea nihil,* a phrase which suggests the disembodied condition of the signifier.[13] Indeed, in the original version of this passage from *The Waste Land* drafts, it is this "voice and nothing else" which acts out the mutilation of the signifier in Philomel's fractured attempt at speech, the cut-off *s* bringing on a further reduction of the name Tereus to "Ter" as if in search of the poet's own initials.

There is a classic psychoanalytical parallel to all of this. The Wolf Man of Freud's case history, who lives in terror of the beating wings of butterflies and the like, recounts a dream in which a wasp's wings are clipped off, but he takes care to call it an *Espe* (from *Wespe*, wasp in German); the displacement of the *w* as his signifier of castration allows his initials (S.P.) to stand out, and imply his own named identity in the scene of castration.[14] In a remarkable reading of this case, Serge Leclaire gives an account of the process through which a signifier comes to be fixed by a specific letter of the alphabet which is associated, bodily, with the traumatic castration memory. As a somatic record, this fixed signifier is repeated palpably from then on in the form of a bodily tension whenever that letter is repeated within a recurring configuration of signifiers.[15] In following some of the adventures of a displaced *s* in Eliot's writing, we have seen a similar kind of signifying behavior acted out, an emblem for which might be chosen from the earlier "Sweeney Among the Nightingales." There, the birds provide a choral accompaniment for an act of parricide. Agamemnon has been "struck deep with a mortal blow," and the nightingales drop a shower of *s*'s upon the phallic corpse:

> And let their liquid siftings fall
> To stain the stiff dishonoured shroud.   (CPP, 36)

2.   What is courtly love? It is an utterly refined way of making up for
the absence of the sexual relation by pretending that we are the
source of the obstacle. This is really the most preposterous thing
that has ever been tried. But how do we show that it is a hoax?
Lacan

In 1926, I.A. Richards wrote about Eliot's "persistent context with sex," and suggested that it was "the problem of our generation as religion was the problem of the last."[16] Eliot himself may well have been concerned about sex, but his writing is concerned with something more specific—the sexual relation, or rather, the impossibility of a complementary or consummated sexual relation. The critical interest in this sexual relation is that it throws light upon the troubled construction of sexuality in language, rather than upon the tired issue of Eliot's body itself, and the sexual insouciance of that body.

In his earliest poetry, Eliot pays lip-service to traditional gender stereotypes, adopting Laforgue's foppish tone of indifferent repose in the face of a represented threat of loss of control or self-possession. The constant source of the threat is characteristically feminine, a typical range of stock "feminine" images cast as the origin of disorder, falsification, and incantatory desire which will "Dissolve the floors of memory/ And all its clear relations/ Its divisions and precisions" (CPP, 14). Throughout *Prufrock and Other Observations*, this "female principle" is represented as the functional opponent of the "masculine principle" of self-definition. In the benign and ironically mannered tone of these poems, there is no real loss of control, only the psychology of a stereotype, and we are aware of the author's detached success in producing a dramatic posture— "when I am pinned and wriggling on the wall"—at his own "invisible" disposition. This languorous, manipulative mode of writing is checked, tightened, and compressed into the formula drawn up by Eliot and Pound in a famous cafe meeting of 1917:

Two authors, neither engaged in picking the other's pocket, decided that the dilutation of *vers libre,* Amygism, Lee Masterism, general floppiness had gone too far and that some counter current must be set going. Parallel situation centuries ago in China. Remedy prescribed. *"Emaux et Camées"* (or the Bay State Hymn Book). Rhyme and regular strophes.[17]

The result of this curious nostrum was the stringently organized *Hugh Selwyn Mauberley* and the quatrain poems of *Ara Vos Prec.* With its shipshape stanzas, its ostentatious show of diction and syntax, and its offer of narrative complacency, the quatrain is the only formal model in Eliot's work which suggests a set of fixed relations between poet, reader, and language. A suitable emblem for these relations would be the *Views of Oxford Colleges* on Pipit's desk in "A Cooking Egg," its engravured pages promising an *authorized,* transcendental point of view. Unlike Pound, however, Eliot could not combine the twin feats of controlling the rigid quatrain form and producing effective social satire, for his attempts to do so either verge on overkill, or else succumb, as here, to a banal, laconic rhythm beneath the level of excitation demanded by the stanzaic structure:

> She and the lady in the cape
> Are suspect, thought to be in league;
> Therefore the man with heavy eyes
> Declines the gambit, shows fatigue (CPP, 35–6)

Eliot's failure, however, is more interesting than Pound's success. The worked-up Latinate tenor threatens to crack and break away from its encratic functions: "polyphiloprogenitive," the overly fertile, or prodigiously productive: "superfetation," the multiple impregnation of an ovary: "anfractuous," tortuously winding or circuitous. Subterranean sound effects challenge the established measure of the stanza: "Defunctive music under sea/ Passed seaward with the passing bell/ Slowly" (CPP, 24). More importantly, the poem no longer speaks *about* history; history is spoken *through* the novel body of the poem. Here, for example, in "Burbank with a Baedeker: Bleistein with a Cigar," Americans arrive in Europe after the War, and in the poem, a cutting edge opens up, under the cover of an enjambment, across the tight rhythms of a classically strophed quatrain:

> The smoky candle end of time
>
> Declines. On the Rialto once.
>   The rats are underneath the piles.
> The jew is underneath the lot.
>   Money in furs. The boatman smiles,
>
> Princess Volupine extends
>   A meagre, blue-nailed phthisic hand
> To climb the waterstair. Lights lights,
>   She entertains Sir Ferdinand
>
> Klein. . . . . (CPP, 24)

Here what is important is the way in which the de-Kleining of Klein is an event that is seen to materialize on the level of the signifier. The suggestion of a symbolic castration is acted out in the register of language itself, both in the "shortening" pun on *Klein*, and in the separation of a surname which simulates the mutilatory act. These events transcend even the boatman's knowing smile and Volupine's carnal attentions, for they imply another kind of knowledge, borne out in language itself, which escapes the detection and intention of the text. If this knowledge belittles Klein, then it also cuts the assumed "poetic consciousness" down to size, while it surcharges another name with the castratory significance of *"Volupine"* or "Penis-thief." Both of these frights serve to raise the larger question of the historical de-Klein of Venice, and Eliot is closer here than anywhere else in his writing to conjuring up the collective guilt of Pound's trio of untouchables, the Jew, the usurer, and the eunuch. The concluding question of the poem must then appear as somewhat more than rhetorical, while it supplies us at the same time with a winged familiar:

> . . . . . . .Who clipped the lion's wings
> And flea'd his rump and pared his claws?
> Thought Burbank, meditating on
> Time's ruins, and the seven laws.

The answer, to be honest, would be Napoleon, who put an end to the vaulting ambition of Venetian trade, but Eliot clearly intends it to be "Jewish" greed. The rhetoric, however, is tinged with the kind of showy, historicized pathos that is the subtext for the prevailing discourse of the Baedeker. Because that discourse is his only guide to Venice, both past and present, it means that the question can only be rhetorical for Burbank, since that language and nothing else is what situates him in regard to "time's ruins." As a discourse of an other, then, the Baedeker rhetoric proposes a knowledge which is always beyond him, exposing his position of lack in time, space, and language.

In spite of Eliot's critical and theoretical will to resolve the problems of history and sexual difference, they are to be found, spliced together, throughout his poetry in the shape of a textual failure, and one which repeatedly falls short of its prospective meaning. Here in "Gerontion," for example, Europe's "decayed house" is occupied by a tenant whose desire is unpredictable, perhaps illegal, but at any rate insufficient:

> History has many cunning passages, contrived corridors
> And issues, deceives with whispering ambitions,

Guides us by vanities. Think now
She gives when our attention is distracted
And what she gives, gives with such supple confusions
That the giving famishes the craving. Gives too late
What's not believed in, or if still believed
In memory only, reconsidered passion. Gives too soon
Into weaks hands, what's thought can be dispensed with
Till the refusal propagates a fear . . .   (CPP,22)

In this abstract vignette, the encounter with history is represented as a sexual engagement with a prostitute. In coming "too late" or else "too soon," "she" counteracts the phallic dictum that sex (or history) must be *meaningful,* an act of significant emotion which records the union of partners independently of the fictions of passion, fear, and memory. This urge for consummation, which is the *meaning* of the myth of sexual complementarity, is, however, seen to be defeated at every turn in Eliot's work. Gerontion himself is not tempted by these echoes of completion, lures which "multiply variety/ In a wilderness of mirrors." Senile and impotent, he is deprived of the paternal license of produce meaning in a lawful contract with history—"Unnatural vices/ Are fathered by our heroism"—and if his attempts to do so are consistently thwarted, then desire can only be an indifferent burden for him, and subjectivity, as in the Sybil's lament, certainly not worth having if it is to be bound to an imperfect and unstable desire: "I have lost my passion: why should I need to keep it/ Since what is kept must be adulterated?" (CPP,23).

The Waste Land itself mourns the fallibility of identity, and reproduces the same failures—"I can connect/ Nothing with nothing"—within all of the sexual relations it depicts. The "typist home at teatime" has a date with "the young man carbuncular" who has already been likened to a "Bradford millionaire." As an arriviste in class, style, and manner, one might expect that in this instance it is he and not the typist who will come too early:

The time is now propitious, as he guesses,
The meal is ended, she is bored and tired,
Endeavours to engage her in caresses

Which still are unreproved, if undesired.
Flushed and decided, he assaults at once;
Exploring hands encounter no defence;
His vanity requires no response,
And makes a welcome of indifference.   (CPP,44)

Like the encounter with History's harlot in "Gerontion," it is the woman who appears to give in too soon, and thus loses the struggle too easily for the male peace of mind. It is she, however, who puts on the gramophone record after he has left, revealing, with her hand on the stylus, that she has been calling the tune all along; in an earlier draft, the man's shortcoming is further remarked when he is caught short and has to urinate on the stairwell. In the course of this asymmetry—the symbolic failure of the mutual orgasm—any sexual relation is represented as either aborted or lacking at the level of desire and its fugitive condition. Elsewhere in a French article on Dante and Donne, Eliot takes issue with the venerating of ideal sexual union, which he takes to be the "basic theme of modern literature": as for the pursuit of an absolute coupling, "whether it be in adultery, promiscuity, or wedlock; it is not to be found there."[18] He goes on to contrast this with the *trecentisti* vision which demanded that its "jouissance de Dieu" proceed from an intellectual contemplation of the Word.

Both the medieval love of the Word and the modern erotic relation to the body testify to an irreducible distance between, on the one hand, the soul and God, and on the other, the body and its object; there is an obstacle which mediates the lover's discourse. The middle period of Eliot's writing, including *The Waste Land*, confronts that obstacle more or less directly, representing it in terms of a failure of the sexual relation, as an acknowledgment that man and woman are not complementary, and thus cannot be simply joined in mystical union. It would be unnecessarily reductive to attribute the source of this representation of sexual failure to the longstanding charge against Eliot of misogyny and even prudery, just as it is insufficient to confine any discussion of this "failure" to the realm of textual meaning alone. Indeed, we might see it as an effect of, *and* a response to, many factors, not least of which would be the modernist errand of coming to terms with the exhaustion of an Idea of history. Sexual complementarity, or rather its failure, is therefore overdetermined as *the* privileged representation of other forms of ideological crisis. In the later revisionary phase of the modernist critique, this crisis is resolved by plundering history again for secure images of sexual and cultural finitude. Here, for example, are Eliot's ancestral voices in "East Coker," reinstating the ideological harmony of Merrie England:

> The association of man and woman
> In daunsinge, signifying matrimonie—
> A dignified and commodious sacrament.
> Two and two, necessarye coniunction,
> Holding eche other by the hand or the arm
> Which betokeneth concorde . . . .   (CPP, 124)

For Eliot, the problem of History, by this time, had been recontained and rewritten as "tradition," an ideal, self-sufficient, historical fantasy which had gone beyond the need to question or account for its source of articulation. "Tradition" simply is, ideally, and as an "ideal order" it need never be called to justify its readiness to serve as a means to an ideological end. By the end of the twenties, Eliot's critical maintenance of the "tradition" had indeed assumed the hardened contours of an orthodoxy: the recruitment of an ideal memory which housed the power of excluding an historical Other, while selecting an ancestral Same. It was Leavis, however, who became the bread-and-butter keeper of the tradition, responsible for morally screening all of its textual occupants. In deciding who was in and who was out, Leavis's selection process went under the aegis of an "ideal and impersonal living memory" in exercising its authority, while his "great tradition" employed the Nietzschean trick of *active forgetfulness* to win itself an ideal past and a unified present. There can be no doubt now that the task of canon-making, for both Eliot and Leavis, was a directly ideological activity, aimed at inculcating the pastoral values of a classical conservatism which both writers revere—Merrie England and all of its effects.

At the moment in literary history when the very idea of literary history is in question, this overriding interest in "tradition" comes as a placebo, a way of sublimating the traumatic knowledge that history is not rational. Eliot's literary career straddles this moment, which bisects the history of high modernism itself. The primary formation of high modernism, even as late as the mid-twenties, evolves around a recognition that the past can no longer be success-fully produced or articulated as a rational whole. History no longer worked. To consistently meet this challenge, however, would in-volve consistently challenging or accounting for the place of enunci-ation of history in the present. In the face of such an indeterminate fate, it is a *secondary* phase of high modernism which posits "tradit-ion" as a solution, and thus rejects the challenge of enunciation, choosing instead to manufacture new voices, new forms, and new languages for the rejuvenated purpose of unifying the past. By that time, history, even for Joyce, had become a "nightmare" to shake off, and for Pound, a "rag-bag" to take to the cleaners. Both Eliot and Leavis recognize it as a lost cause which they are commis-sioned to retrieve, and if there remains no secure subjective ground from which to speak about their historical construction of the world, then History itself assumes that office, voicing the ideal ancestral accents of "tradition." History articulates itself.

The early radical experience of modernism had perceived history as something outside of the reliable "coniunction" of facts, forces, and ideas which it had been for so long. If history had stopped working, then it was a *waste* of time, excluded like waste matter, and thus in a state of irreversible decay—"rocks, moss, stonecrop, iron, merds" (CPP,21). *The Waste Land* gathers up this historical "stuff" as its discontents, or bodily lining, into a noxious panorama which was just as surely to offend Pound's anality when he came to edit the original drafts. Never slow to establish the sexual stakes of any issue (of Eliot's judge of sexual difference, Tiresias, he wrote, "you, Tiresias, if you know, know damn well" (WL,47)), Pound describes his professional skills appropriately in a letter to Eliot which in-cludes some verses entitled "Sage Homme" (male midwife). In these, his editing role is compared to the performing of a Caesarian operation:

> These are the poems of Eliot
> By the Uranian Muse begot
> A man their Mother was,
> A Muse their Sire.

How did the printed Infancies result
From nuptials thus doubly difficult?

If you must needs enquire,
Know, diligent Reader,
That on each occasion
Ezra performed the Caesarian operation.[19]

Here Eliot is accredited as a maternal father, while his Uranian Muse—"your anian"—is sexually unorthodox. The normal reproductive model of artistic production has been inverted, suggesting a homosexual bias which Pound then sets out to correct. This he does, as Alan Durant points out, by posing as a male midwife in order to neutralize the sexual imbalance.[20] For Pound, Eliot has not been man enough to put things in their proper order, and so the poem needs to be thoroughly reorganized. Hence, the problem is represented in clearcut sexual terms: there is a male and a female position of enunciation, one active and one passive, and thus reversible or complementary to one another. Pound would have sexuality fall back into the kind of simple opposition between male and female principle which we have seen dominate Eliot's early poetry. But the lesson we learn from the middle period is that there is no such ideal commutative test of sexuality and that the sexual relation never achieves any consummate form. This is the lesson of sexual *difference* and not gender *opposition*, a difference that is manifest whenever Eliot's text shows its reluctance to represent sexual contact in complementary terms.

In drawing attention to Pound's editing, the publication of *The Waste Land* drafts have, in a sense, only served to deepen our inability to unify the various levels of enunciation at work in Eliot's poem. Moreover, they show that Pound's attempt to prevent this miscarriage of critical justice is indeed appropriately suggested by the image of his successful midwife, delivering a "full" body from Eliot's drafts in accordance with his *incorporative* editing style: a typical comment from his correspondence with Eliot—"the song has only two lines which you can use in the body of the poem."[21] Similarly, it is his "howling to high heaven" which prevents *The Waste Land* from being split up into its constituent parts on its first American appearance in *The Dial*.[22] Despite Pound's efforts, however, to vouchsafe its bodily coherence, the open-faced, excavatory appearance of Eliot's poem is still very striking. In trying to describe this porous form, Stephen Spender cites Freud's archaeological comparison of the individual unconscious with the simultaneous coexistence of all of the historical strata of Rome's ruins, and suggests that history fills the "poetic consciousness" of *The Waste Land* in the same manner.[23] What Spender means by "poetic consciousness," however, is very close not only to what Leavis means when he says that it is the "inclusive consciousness" of the whole poem that is its source of enunciation,[24] but also to Peter Ackroyd's more formalistic suggestion that "it is language which speaks and becomes the hidden subject."[25] Each of these claims, Spender's, Leavis's, and Ackroyd's, proposes ways of *solving* the problem of enunciation in Eliot's poem, by displacing it onto the level of the enounced, and away from its problematic subjective origin. Eliot himself invited even more reductive readings by including his note directing attention to the centrality of Tiresias: "what he *sees*, in fact, is the substance of the poem." Even if Tiresias, as a sightless castrato, is hardly the most trustworthy example of human judgment, his *centrality* has offered many critics a stable point of view around which the poem, or their reading of the poem, can be organized. Grover Smith, for one, notoriously constructs a complex pictorial narrative based around Tiresias's "comprehensive" perspective.[26]

Such readings do scant justice to a poem which militates against this kind of voyeuristic control; there is very little *seeing* at all in *The Waste Land* (even the clairvoyance of Madame Sosostris is deficient). If anything, we tend to *follow* sounds and voices that issue from elsewhere. Unlike much of Eliot's work, there is no direct address— "Let us go then you and I," or "Here I am, an old man in a dry month"—but rather, an insistence on shifting levels of interpellation. And far from subscribing to the kind of hermetic self-reflexive activity which characterizes the modernist sublime of Symboliste poetry, Eliot's text draws attention to, and questions, its mode of enunciation:

> "Speak to me. Why do you never speak. Speak.
> "What are you thinking of? What thinking? What?
> "I never know what you are thinking. Think?"   (CPP, 40)

Who is the third that walks always beside you?
When I count, there are only you and I together
But when I look ahead up the white road
There is always another one walking beside you
Gliding wrapt in a brown mantle, hooded
I do not know whether a man or a woman
—But who is that on the other side of you?   (CPP, 48)

Whatever we know in *The Waste Land*, it is not enough, for it always lacks some consistent point of view. Even after sixty years of critical activity spent in filling out and smoothing over its gaps, *The Waste Land* still foregrounds the same questions—"Who is speaking?" and "Who is seeing or hearing this?" These questions are *different in kind* from those addressed to purely exegetical interests—"What does this mean?" and "Why is this here?" The questions about enunciation point to a failure in the attempt to establish a speaking identity for the poem, whereas the questions about meaning and structure either take that identity for granted or else seek to resolve any uncertainty about it by inviting a unified response at the level of the organization of the poem. It is likely that Eliot felt more comfortable with the second set of questions, if only because they do more justice to the idea that *The Waste Land*—in providing the spectacle of history articulating itself—presents a solution to a problem of identity. I have argued, on the contrary, that Eliot's poem *identifies* this problem, articulates it through representations of failures of sexuality and history, and in a way that is resonant with his other work of the period. These failures may be construed at the level of enunciation; they are inherent not only in the poem's meaning, but in how the meaning is produced, and more important, in the fact that these two processes are irreconcilable. Perhaps the only result of this is that we can better come to terms with the *success of Eliot's failure* in *The Wasteland*, a success, however, which incriminates the notion of the "invisible poet" just as much as it vindicates the scrupulous will of the modernist text to examine its historical, if not its social, conscience.

3.   EGO DOMINUS TUUS

1.

I am the man with unclean lips
(Isaiah,VI,5)

Lips that would kiss
Form prayers to broken stone
Eliot

IN CONTRAST to his earlier work, Eliot's postconversion writing is
addressed to more self-conscious ways of dealing with subjectivity. The question which it submits for consideration is no longer
the one asked in *The Waste Land*—Who is speaking?—but one
which appeals to a different register of authority—*In the name of
whom* or *in the name of what* is this being spoken? The result is more
complex than the sacrifice of *personality* demanded in Eliot's critical
formulae. For not only is that sacrifice itself taken up and
thematized in these later poems, where the right to be able to speak
in one's own name, in one's own body, and in one's own language,
is regarded as a luxury to be consistently and abjectly denied, but
we are also drawn to ask how and why Eliot's own strongly can-
vassed case for "martyrdom" in the face of social and political authority should find its correlative in the literariness of such a
sacrifice of subjectivity. The answer to this last question points as
much away from the poetry as toward it. In either case, however,
what is at issue is a "problem" of subjectivity, construed by Eliot in
terms of a set of indeterminate relations between authority and
language that must be made secure if the polity is to maintain its
health.

One of the most concrete signs that this "problem" has been
evaded is the way in which the critical reception and exegesis of

these poems has consistently been divided over the headache of doctrine; as Allen Tate put it in 1931, critics are "a little less able each year to see the poetry for Westminster Abbey; the wood is all trees."[1] While amused to note that the issue of orthodox religious faith was "at last relieved from its burden of respectability" (SE, 325), Eliot was more than aware of his own ironic role in the critical Passion staged around these poems, as he increasingly became the object of a kind of religious persecution, and for the Left at any rate, the sacrificial victim of the political tribalism of the thirties. George Orwell, for example, railed againt the "gloomy Pétainism" of *Four Quartets*, a resentful allusion to the spectacle of a colonized poetic voice, stripped of its sovereign powers and acting only vestigially in the name of some foreign overlord.[2] And for Edmund Wilson, the "low blue flame" of Eliot's later writing was an act of political cowardice, a "fundamentally dishonest" act which threatened to lower the moral temperature of all other contemporary literature.[3] Such judgments, of course, are drawn from the same dualistic logical order as the banal pleasure of the Anglican reader, for whom the poetry is little more than a pellucid affirmation of an articled faith; that same logical order, founded upon a demarcation between the subject and his beliefs, which is challenged by these poems. And it is this same dualism which runs its course through three decades of modernist politics, from the early drawing up of ranks for and against Romanticism, to the espousal of the great transnational causes of Communism and Fascism in the thirties, in what Spender called "the war of light against darkness,"[4] to which Eliot's own contribution, of course, was to propose a third militant alternative in the shape of theocratic ideology. But to what extent does his role in the development of this spirited polarity arise out of a debate about subjectivity itself?

One very relevant case history here would be Eliot's own relation to and association with, the American vanguard of the New Humanist movement. An outspoken literary and philosophical coterie during the twenties, the New Humanists had replaced the "genteel tradition" of the neomonastic Brahmins with a brand of "imaginative conservatism" that was fighting the old reactionary battle of Ancients against Moderns in the universities. Although they never quite achieved their promised transition from an inner circle of "angry professors" to a political cause of educational and social reform, this would have been an ingenuous transition on anyone's terms, since their platform was little more than a leisurely polemical haven for deeply conservative men of letters and, indeed, little less than academic sleight of hand when placed alongside the turbulent social spirits uncorked in the subsequent Depression. Nonetheless, the debate which engaged the minds and reputations of its most prominent figures, Irving Babbitt, Eliot's Harvard mentor (the direct source of many of Eliot's published observations, early and late, about literature, society, and politics), and Paul Elmer More, turned upon a contemporary issue which was real enough: the problem of the post-Christian place of authority, whether internal, as the Humanists believed, or, as Eliot himself argued, "anterior, exterior or superior to the individual" (SE,478). The debate reached its high point in 1930 with the publication of two books, *Humanism and America: Essays on the Outlook of Modern Civilization*, edited by Norman Foerster, and *The Critique of Humanism: A Symposium*, edited by C. Hartley Grattan. In his contribution to *Humanism and America* (luridly advertised on its dust jackets as "the challenge of culture to the anarchy of our times"), Babbitt recapitulated his central ideas about the decadent and subversive impulse of Romantic individualism and then addressed the relation of humanism to religion, noting that humanism brought together the best of each religion while dispensing with the ecclesiastical dogmas which make up their respective differences. The issue of religion was already a point of disagreement for at least two of the other contributors: More, who had begun his exploration of Platonism and Christian mysticism, and Eliot himself.

In the absence of any ultimate appeal to external authority, the New Humanism was seen by its critics to be based upon the assertion that the free will of each individual to choose his own mechanism of self-control is sufficient to provide a code of ethical action distinct from and superior to that of naturalism. For Eliot, the suggestion that humanism could not only provide an alternative but also act as a substitute for religious dogma was unacceptable, and he came to characterize Babbitt's emphasis on the "inner check" (or *frein vital*, to offset Bergson's *élan vital*) as a dangerous obsession with control for control's sake. So too, in his contribution to *The*

Critique of Humanism, Allen Tate argued that the Humanists' values were worthless without "a definite and living religious background," and added that their idea of self-imposed restraint actually courted a kind of "external control" which he equated with "moral Fascism."[5] For those young liberals who contributed to *The Critique of Humanism*, Malcolm Cowley, Kenneth Burke, R.P. Blackmur, Yvor Winters, and Lewis Mumford, and for others like Edmund Wilson who added their dissenting voices elsewhere, a more immediate point of contention was the assumption that classical literature was the exclusive repository of value in a modern, democratic culture. The New Humanists championed a traditional canon of literature at the cost of neglecting and derogating virtually all modern writing and art, especially the kind of novelistic literature which the liberals increasingly saw as a possible agent of social redemption. Indeed, the impatient polemical mood of the anti-Humanists was symptomatic of the burgeoning demand among American critics for social relevance. Cowley pointed out that it is "almost impossible to be either human or Humanist on ten or twelve dollars a week," and went on to pose the celebrated question that, for better or worse, became the vulgar obituary for the New Humanist movement: what possible validity could a "communion" of "angry professors" have for the "mill hands of New Bedford and Gastonia, for the beet-toppers of Colorado, for the men who tighten a single screw in the automobiles that march along Mr. Ford's assembly belt?"[6]

Much of Eliot's own social thought runs parallel to this debate if not in its mainstream: the Romanticism/Classicism dispute, for example, positing Intuition, and what Middleton Murry called the Inner Voice (Eliot called it the root of Whiggery), against Intelligence, and the appeal to Tradition. What was at stake was the place of authority, and thus for Eliot, a *remedy* for "that meanness of spirit, that egotism of motive, that incapacity for surrender or allegiance to something outside of oneself, which is a frequent symptom of the soul of man under democracy.[7] This search for a *solution* to the problem of authority is of course a sign of the times, and it radically informs the hundreds of pages given over in *The Criterion*, by Eliot and others, to the respective social claims of Fascism and Communism. Indeed, the serious attention which Eliot devotes to the Soviet experiment in his monthly commentaries indicates the extent to which his idea of an institutionalized version of "scientific socialism" came close, in its formal demands, to the disciplined self-sacrifice reflected in Eliot's own Christian mirror-image of a "militant" Church. The difference, however, lay in the *voluntary* extinction prized by the latter—"a *training*, of the soul as severe and as ascetic as the training of the body of a runner,"[8] as opposed to what he saw as an easy relief from the burden of having to think for oneself which arose out of a socially imposed individuality (hence the appeal to Eliot of Jacques Maritain's Catholic *praxis* of a politics of love, enshrined in an "open" humanism based upon the Thomist ethic of personality and the democratic rights of the person: theocratic rather than anthropocentric, its watchword—an end to subjectivism!).[9] Beyond these doctrinal differences, however, the advantage of recognizing a stable external authority was that it promised deliverance from questioning subjectivity itself. In other words, Eliot's question—Is authority internal or external to the individual?—already assumes a prior understanding of the "individual" as a conceptual fixity which is as much immune to the *determining* functions of authority as to the responsibility delegated these functions in the construction of subjectivity. The "final solution" offered by formations of external authority in the thirties, whether political or religious, is, in more ways than one, a solution to the burdensome problem of having to account for this construction of subjectivity.

Whether or not the New Humanism came close to seriously contemplating such large-scale solutions, its influence and destiny, by 1932, had fallen, in Eliot's view, from respectable heights into the hands of "John Dewey and a committee of the Unitarian clergy."[10] What is interesting, however, is the way in which its debate about authority had progressively become internalized into a debate about language and subject positions with respect to language. The Humanists saw themselves as employing one kind of language, marked by a visible commitment to the high Socratic mode of precise definition, while their "opponents" were accused of promoting a stylistic fluidity and indeterminacy which called forth the Bergsonian stream of consciousness, a style which Julien Benda described as a "form of aphasia."[11] Thus, by 1930, when Gorham

Munson is called upon to register Eliot's dissociation from the movement, it is enough for him to point to Eliot's "non-Humanist" style, and to suggest that his writing is no longer "a full-bodied prose, the weight of the whole man concentrated on the pen, but the prose of a judge, conscious of the weight of authority behind, not in, him."[12] If this signals an ideological split, then it is enough that it be made manifest in terms of an "alien" writing habit which, in a sense, acts out, stylistically, what it believes in. Understood in this way, the discourse of authority is that which *bespeaks* the individual, or, more specifically, provides it with subject positions— from the ideological clubbishness of "you are who/where you are," to the unkenneled coercion of "you are who/where I say you are." Language, then, and its interpellating discourse of address, are always as much determining features of authoritarian practice as they are its instruments of power. As we will now see, however, it is this perception—that language is a potentially ambivalent form of mediation between authority and subjectivity—which explains the partial failure of Eliot's attempts to translate his ideas about authority into literary practice.

2. Perhaps the whole of it had not slipped out of our memory; but a
    part of it was retained by which the other lost part was sought for,
    because the memory realized that it was not operating as smoothly
    as usual and was being held up by the crippling of its habitual
    working; hence it demanded the restoration of what was lacking.
    St. Augustine

If we are to take seriously Eliot's words about a "voluntary extinction" or self-sacrifice in the name of an external authority, then we must look at how this carries over into displacements of subjectivity in his writing. Enough is known about the displacements of "Mr. Eliot," the dapper city gent who, from time to time, renounces all evidence of earthly identity; from St. Louis and a "gray" Unitarian childhood, to Russell Square and the adoption of a significant voice within the Anglican Church, he is consistently where he should not be, and speaks where one least expects him (that is, where he has least authority) to speak. But what of the displacements in his poetry? And how successfully do they "martyrize" our reading of the conversion experience they take as their general theme? Perhaps, over the years, the illicit nature of these displacements has lost some of its effective irony. We may be largely immunized, for example, to the contagious breed of scandal which a poem like *Ash Wednesday* harbors in its mediation of the sacred with the profane. Unlike the writing of Dylan Thomas, or even the later Auden, where religious symbolism is sublimated or else accepted as continuous with the expressive grain of the voice, there is no attempt here to graft the liturgical discourse onto the skin of a secular body of speech. On the contrary, we find it foregrounded, and precisely because it is formulated outside of its functional context in order to register a new *ostranenie*, or strangeness. *Ash Wednesday* is punctuated by broken fragments of litany: *The Mass, The Litany of the Virgin, Ave Maria, Salve Regina*, and the *Anima Christi*. As if stranded on foreign ground, they are no longer ex cathedra pronouncements; the pronouns no longer provide a reference to a fixed time and place, as a way of guaranteeing that their performative function is being observed. This displacement from a sanctified locus is important inasmuch as the sacred depends upon its place, its ritual function being one which maintains an exclusive order of purity only by keeping the impure at bay, outside of its limits. From *Ash Wednesday* onwards, Eliot's poetry expresses its disregard for those rules of quarantine which serve to regulate the separation of sacred and profane. Here a purified, hygienic speech is made to socialize with the contaminating traces of Sweeney's unholy trinity of "birth, copulation, and death," and in the tension generated by that encounter, we shall see later how the poetic subject is projected as if caught "turning," "wavering," "between," miming the mystical condition of an abeyance, abject before God.

As a constant subtext of Eliot's later writing, this mystical way asserts that an affirmation is only possible through the negation of a negation, and thus it might be read as a more exorbitant form of the figure of *litotes* which I have suggested can be bound up in the named identity of Eliot himself: fertility, masculinity, and innocence, for example, are normally taken to be connoted by the not-barren, the not-feminine, or the not-corrupt. A willing instrument of the apophatic temper, then, *litotes* involves a shuffling of identity in the various reversals of the relation between subject/object or

active/passive positions. In certain psychoanalytical configurations, these reversals are quite integral, and in a poem of 1914,
"The Death of Saint Narcissus," one of those—the sadomasochistic
circuit of inversion—is reproduced in a very orthodox way:

> He walked once between the sea and the high cliffs
> When the wind made him aware of his limbs smoothly passing
>   each other
> And of his arms crossed over his breast.
> When he walked over the meadows
> He was stifled and soothed by his own rhythm.
> By the river
> His eyes were aware of the pointed corners of his eyes
> And his hands aware of the pointed tips of his fingers.

In "Instincts and their Vicissitudes" (1915), Freud describes the
inversions in the subject/object relation by which the instincts produce first a sadistic and then a masochistic point of view. Primary
masochism is the stage in which the aggressive will to master,
originally directed at objects, is turned around upon the self: "there
is a turning around upon the subject's self *without* an attitude of
passivity towards another person,"[13] in other words, an autoerotic
relation. The "active voice" is changed into what Freud calls the
"reflexive middle voice." This reflexive phase, described here in the
first part of Eliot's poem, serves as a prototype for that transformation of the active into the fully passive in which the subject takes up
the position of the object, and is thus acted upon. It is in this
secondary masochism that the sexual tension of pleasure/pain is
born:

> Then he knew that he had been a fish
> With slippery white belly held tight in his own fingers,
> Writhing in his own clutch, his ancient beauty
> Caught fast in the pink tips of his new beauty
>
> Then he had been a young girl
> Caught in the woods by a drunken old man
> Knowing at the end the taste of his own whiteness
> The horror of his own smoothness,
> And he felt drunken and old.

Here, the confusion between subject and object fuses together the "middle" and the "passive" voice, rendering the swift alternation of sense and identity almost impossible to follow. In the final movement of the poem, a more "stable" relation of passivity is asserted, bringing with it the full genesis of the sexual which Freud isolates as its conditions:

> So he became a dancer to God
> Because his flesh was in love with the burning arrows
> He danced on the hot sand
> Until the arrows came.
> And he embraced them his white skin surrendered itself
>   to the redness of the blood, and satisfied him.[14]

The body is accepted as an object, which acts passively. Freud goes on, moreover, to note a similar structure in the development of the scopophilic drive. The reflexive phase is also a narcissistic one in which the sexual pleasure derived from looking at oneself is transformed in the search for an extraneous other who will act as the subject in the ensuing *exhibitionistic* scenario, where the real subject is looked at as an object.[15]

A corresponding sequence can be found in an unpublished poem, "The Love Song of Saint Sebastian," written at the same time as "Saint Narcissus." The protagonist flagellates himself in a display of abjection before his female lover with whom he subsequently spends the night. In the morning, however, he is transformed into the active agent, and in another turn of the subject (which in the Freudian schema initiates the sadistic position), he strangles the woman with a towel.[16] Lyndall Gordon suggests that these poems were written after Eliot had seen paintings of Sebastian's martyrdom in Italy and Belgium (by Mantegna, Antonella da Messina, and Hans Memling), and in a letter to Conrad Aiken he had noted that in view of the obvious eroticism of the spectacle of youth exposed to penetrant arrows, "a female saint would have been more appropriate."[17] It is the "feminine position," then, the implication of the body as object, and its passive relation to an other, which Eliot notes, and which bears out the consequences of a passion that culminates the "masochism" of martyr, saint and mystic. From the narcissistic wound of love to the beatitude, this "feminization" has run its historical course; from St. John of the Cross's spousal offering to the limits of masculine paranoia in Judge Schreber's love affair with God—his desire to be woman to all men, to beget all men (here, and elsewhere, "masculine" and "feminine" are to be understood as a purely conventional set of terms, regretted by Freud for their social connotations, but acknowledged anyway as standing for constructed sexual positions, not as indices of a fixed sexuality intrinsic to Eliot's own sexual makeup, or as natural expressions of gender).

The same "burning arrows" figure again in "Little Gidding" where, during an air raid, a Stuka dive bomber reenacts the fertilizing agency of the Word, and brings on a "timeless" moment:

> After the dark dove with a flickering tongue
> Had passed below the horizon of his homing
>
> (CPP, 140)

and, in the more explicit form of the anal penis:

> The dove descending breaks the air
> With flame of incandescent terror   (CPP, 143)

Ernest Jones has argued for the significance of a "homosexual" economy in the Christian doctrine of the Word (and the Breath—the ambivalent "poetic afflatus"), and suggested its provenance in the fantasy of anal impregnation, the conception by the fart in which the anus is identified with and displaces the vagina. Similarly, the phallic height of the dove/Stuka, and the pentecostal heat still redolent of the warmth of the bowels gives rise to a rereading of the Stoic *logos spermatikos* in terms of his sublimated homosexual circuit.[18]

Classically speaking, the distinction between active and passive does indeed belong to the anal phase. Turning around upon the subject, however, in the earlier oral phase, and for Melanie Klein at least, involves an actual interiorization in the sense of an oral incorporation of the object. As an inverse form of the oral drive, the fantasy of being devoured or gobbled up is a displacement of subjectivity, played out here in Eliot's description of the anxiety of the hysteric:

As she laughed I was aware of becoming involved in her laughter and being part of it, until her teeth were only accidental stars with a talent for squad drill. I was drawn in by short gasps, inhaled at each momentary recovery, lost finally in the dark caverns of her throat, bruised by the ripple of unseen muscles.   (CPP, 19)

Here, the syntactical passivity is similar in structure to the inversions which Freud explored in "A Child is Being Beaten": the subject objectified, and then acted upon, the narrator thus being twice removed. In Eliot's passage, it is the metaphor of the subject's own open mouth which confronts, threatens, and devours him. A position which is common enough in the poetry, from Mr. Apollinax's "dry and passionate talk" which "devoured the afternoon" (CPP, 18), and the curious conflation of Sweeney's desire to convert Doris into a "nice little, white little, missionary stew" on his "cannibal isle" (CPP, 80), to Celia's violent end at the hands and mouths of a cannibalistic tribe in *The Cocktail Party;* "Christ the tiger" who is "eaten," "divided," and then "drunk" in "Gerontion," returns the compliment—"Us he devours" (CPP, 22)—while the three white leopards of *Ash Wednesday* feed upon "my legs my heart my liver and that which had been contained/ In the hollow round of my skull" (CPP, 61). Such an alternating economy is predicated upon the important bodily distinction between *inside* and *outside,* that which is introjected and that which is projected, a distinction borne out, for example, by the counterpoint of watery coordinates which navigate us through "The Dry Salvages"; "The river is within us, the sea is all about us" (CPP, 130): "Also pray for those who were in ships, and/ Ended their voyage on the sand, in the sea's lips/ Or in the dark throat which will not reject them" (CPP, 135). In "Little Gidding," where any action is a "step to the block, to the fire, down the sea's throat," the genital, the anal, and the oral are all passively projected. So too with the passivity of the scopic throughout Eliot's writing, the sense of being looked at or gazed upon which is most pronounced in *The Family Reunion,* where Harry is everywhere pursued by the look of Eumenides until he passed under "the judicial sun/ Of the final eye" in the desert (CPP, 277).

In the plays generally, this objectification of identity becomes a dominant thematic as well as a structural element, because their plots often turn upon cases of lost, mistaken, or regained identity, thereby exploiting the simplest of all the ambivalencies of theatrical form and its basic prop, the mask. Like the dramatic monologues of the *Prufrock* volume, however ("when I am pinned and wriggling on the wall"), this crisis of identity is harmlessly manipulated into a staged event, especially in moments like this, when Henry Harcourt-Reilly suggests "that you're suddenly reduced to the status of an object":

> You have the experience of being an object
> At the mercy of a malevolent staircase.
> Or, take a surgical operation.
> In consultation with the doctor and the surgeon,
> In going to bed in the nursing home,
> In talking to the matron, you are still the subject,
> The centre of reality. But, stretched on the table,
> You are a piece of furniture in a repair shop
> For those who surround you, the masked actors;
> All there is of you is your body
> And the "you" is withdrawn. . . . . (CPP, 307)

As I suggested in the case of Eliot's early monologues, this thematization of the loss of self-control is actually a way of affirming authorial control. When Eliot comes to address the *failure* of the "sexual relation" in his middle period, a much less stable construction of identity comes into play, because troubled by the evidence of sexual difference. How much, then, of the later poetry attempts to make up for this *failure* by positioning itself beyond desire altogether? For whether or not it is useful to talk about sublimation in any general sense, it is clear that Eliot's attention to mystical love harbors the promise of *success* on a level of desire which is hitherto lacking: "When the tongues of flame are in-folded/ Into the crowned knot of fire/ And the fire and the rose are one" (CPP, 145). One of the marks of this *success* would be the relative stabilization of the body-as-object, wholly subject to an external authority. In this way, Eliot would replace the problem of Woman with the problem of God, for it is a fantasy of Woman as complete, unified, and homogeneous which stands behind and supports the finitude of divine adoration. The fantasy of Woman, moreover, is wholly conventional; she is either a criminal or a saint, a luscious adept like Grishkin, or else the Lady of *Ash Wednesday,* a holy mother and thus sexually off-limits—like Beatrice, a guide or bodyguard who will guarantee safe conduct beyond the restlessness of carnal failures. If the Lady and the Whore are the only women in Eliot's writing then they are clearly siblings because their exclusive domains, respectively, are that of the sacred proper and the profane proper.[19] (Ironically enough, Vivienne Eliot was summarily described by Bertrand Russell as "a person who lives on a knife edge," and who will "end a criminal or a saint . . . with a perfect capacity for both."[20] There is no taboo or obstacle in the world of the criminal or saint because the taboo is a Christian absolute; in transgressing it, as Bataille argues, one discovers that the holy and the forbidden are exactly the same thing, and that something only becomes sacred *when* and *because* it is put beyond our reach.[21] Eliot's poetry testifies to this, both in its fantasmatic qualifications of "femininity" as an unapproachable other, and in the later attempt to valorize the passive "feminine position" as a workable one. Nonetheless, when either of these desires fails to stabilize its object, then we are aware of desire itself, and its constant displacement of subjectivity. Eliot need not resort to theology to recognize this, namely, that the libertine is closer to the saint than the man without desire, for it is implicit even in his preconversion poetry. From the late twenties onwards, however, this fact can be seen as the uncertain ground of his move to come to terms with the vicissitudes of conversion. Thus even "Satanism" is acknowledged, in his essay on Baudelaire, as a territorial claim on the sacred, for it is "an attempt to get into Christianity by the back door. Genuine blasphemy, genuine in spirit, and not purely verbal, is the product of partial belief, and is as impossible to the complete atheist as to the perfect Christian. It is a way of affirming belief" (SE,421).[22]

Affirming belief in these poems goes by way of a powerful negativity. The result is a vertiginous display of turning (troping, or more properly, *verse*) around a logic of uncertainty:

> Because I do not hope to turn again
> Because I do not hope
> Because I do not hope to turn
>
> . . . .

> Because I do not hope to know again
> The infirm glory of the positive hour
> Because I do not think
> Because I know I shall not know   (CPP,60)

Clearly, the "I" here is in no position to hope or know or think or strive. In fact, it advertises that it is as commutable as any of the other words that keep it company. The lines create a sense of studied dereliction which serves to amputate the rhetorical assertiveness of the speech. The acrobatic metaphor—reverting, inverting, converting, averting—is common enough in the more fragile passages of Eliot's writing, while it has a special resonance within the classical mystic tradition which underlies the meditative practice of these later poems.[23] *Ash Wednesday* attempts to duplicate some of the subjective disequilibrium characteristic of the Mystic Way of St. John of the Cross: as Evelyn Underhill describes it, a series of turbulent oscillations in which "an intense and progressive affirmation . . . is paid for by a negation; a swing-back of the whole consciousness, a stagnation of the intellect, a reaction of the emotions or an inhibition of the will."[24] This sudden asset-stripping plunge into the poverty of mortification, a negation where the full extent of deprivation is held in check only by the last limit of death itself, is matched by a recovery of control as unballasted as its counterpart, restoring the "ancient rhyme" of bodily memory just as "the weak spirit quickens to rebel" (CPP,66). In this ever-transitory process, the mystic is never a person, always a *subject*, because she or he is entirely at or in the service of an other. So too in these poems do we have something like an evacuation of personality, radical for a poet with such a strong feel for the dramatic, at least, perhaps, until he came to write drama himself.

Alongside this precarious subjective presence, a condition of temporal displacement is evoked through the activity of memory. To rejoice or to mourn "the vanished power of the usual reign" is a challenge which memory presents either as a luxury or a scourge, in the form of the stigmata of what happened in another time and place, and, in a way which is far from figurative, to another body— almost like someone else entirely. Forgetfulness, on the other hand, can be the same as purgation, and it is this counterpoint between "the Rose of forgetfulness" and "the Rose of memory" which runs through *Four Quartets*. These poems are almost spoken by a center of forgetfulness, always the consequence of a lack and never the witness of Being: "As I am forgotten/ And would be forgotten, so would I forget" (CPP,62). In the *Confessions,* Augustine begins his self-analysis by posing the same question about memory. How can I remember forgetfulness? If forgetfulness was once present, "when it was present, how did it write its image on the memory, since forgetfulness, by its presence blots out even what it finds already there?"²⁴ Even in the final sublation of knowledge, this *paradox* of memory remains, and for Augustine it becomes the very sign by which he recognizes divinity, through its vexed logic and not some other, more transparent act of grace. His questioning along the way leads into a complex meditation on time:

How is it that there are two times, past and future, when even the past is now no longer and the future is now not yet? But if the present were always present, and did not pass into past time, it would obviously not be time but eternity. If then, time present—if it be time—comes into existence only because it passes into past time, how can we say that even this *is,* since the cause of its being is that it will cease to be? Thus can we not truly say that time *is* only as it tends towards non-being?²⁶

Eliot's formulation of the same topic in "Little Gidding" is no less involved:

> Time present and time past
> Are both perhaps present in time future,
> And time future contained in time past.
> If all time is eternally present
> All time is unredeemable.
> . . . .
> Time past and time future
> What might have been and what has been
> Point to one end, which is always present.
>
> (CPP,117–18)

This holy trinity of time is not God's conjugation of the verb *to be,* because it is only ever enunciated in a human, speaking present (not the *nunc stans*), the only tense of linguistic time for the speaking object. Other, past times, however, are held like hostages within memory, and thus wholly in the present, where they do not belong: "destroyer, reminder/ Of what men choose to forget" (CPP,130), where they bear witness to "the enchainment of past and future/ Woven in a weakness of a changing body" (CPP,119).

For Eliot, this contradictory position is both a source of discomfort and an object of fascination. His attention, for example, to the image of the mute infant Christ, *verbum infans*, the Word within a word and yet unable as yet to speak, "the still, unspeaking and unspoken Word" (CPP,65), evokes the aphasic dividedness of Christ's heterogeneous body; for such a body, which is unable to speak and yet is already possessed of a full speech, memory is a redundancy already. For the human present, however, memory is an uncomfortable construction of several different times, and thus a disturbing resurrection of several different bodies. The equally disturbing question of impossible identity is then raised—How can I be myself when I remember? I am no longer what I was, and yet when I remember, I have to be where I was. I speak and am spoken in different places when I remember; and there is no stable language for this:

> The knowledge imposes a pattern, and falsifies,
> For the pattern is new in every moment
> And every moment is a new and shocking
> Evaluation of all we have been . . .   (CPP,125)

What was truly barbaric about this moment had already been addressed in *The Waste Land*, with its resurrected corpses and poisonous mix of "memory and desire," and its original, open preface to Kurtz's "horror" of reliving the past in its concrete entirety. *Four Quartets* aims to account for the reconciliatory excess of that moment, beyond the "rending pain and reenactment/ Of all that you have done, and been" (CPP,142), and to turn this excess to the service of a communication of divine will. The otherness of that moment is thus accepted as simply God's place in time, just as Augustine seeks out God within the practice of memory itself— "Where do I call to thee, when I am already in thee? Or from whence wouldst thou come into me?"[27] Hence, what had been memory's terrorist raids on identity in *The Waste Land* become the benign medium of divine communication in *Four Quartets:*

> . . . . This is the use of memory:
> For liberation—not less of love but expanding
> Of love beyond desire, and so liberation
> From the future as well as the past. . . .   (CPP, 142)

When memory "speaks," it introduces a contradictory experience because of what it contains, something which happened elsewhere and then disappeared, but which returns here, both "in time
and out of time." The model for this is the Incarnation, manifest in
the Johannine Word which splits and bisects time only to disappear
again, responsible, however, in its disappearance, for the "symptomatic" capacity of all subsequent language to recall the originary
moment (Christ's resurrection, returning only to leave again, is a
theatrical demonstration of this). In generalizing this model, what
becomes important in *Four Quartets* are those "footfalls" which only
"echo in the memory" and "point down the passage which we did
not take"; memories, as Augustine or even Freud put it, which have
been partially rejected, but which germinate in another time available neither to mnemic recall, nor to the desire to reconstruct the
past. In this sense, they are like symptoms of the Word itself:

> For most of us, there is only the unattended
> Moment, the moment in and out of time,
> The distraction fit, lost in a shaft of sunlight,
> The wild thyme unseen, or the winter lightning
> . . . .
> The hint half guessed, the gift half understood, is
>   Incarnation.   (CPP, 136)

In this "wild thyme [time] unseen," we can, perhaps, read Lacan's
interpretation of the Aristotelian *tuché* as that which is always beyond what is available to us, because nonsymbolized; such moments are encounters with the real, "the real as encounter,
encounter inasmuch as it is missed."[28] This is different in kind from
the epiphany of grace secularized by Joyce in order to collapse the
panreligious dualism of immanence/transcendence. It is not the
basis of a doctrinal system, nor does it support any "authentic"
Buberian dialogue of I/Thou. On the contrary, what *Four Quartets*
addresses is the praxis of an experimental time—"old men ought to

be explorers" (CPP,129)—in which the experience of memory serves as the primary signifying material for working at the understanding of Christian subjectivity. Time, hitherto a corrosive and execrable force for Eliot, is now a propitious redeemer sought through the agency of memory.

Again, we can find the same effects thematized in the plays, where Eliot comfortably manipulates the identity crises of his characters. In *The Confidential Clerk*, Colby is given back his entire past along with a set of parents so brand new that he cannot help but feel like another person. Similarly, the appearance of a counterfeit figure from Lord Claverton's past, a man who has changed his name and assumed another identity in the interim, sets off a sequence of remembering which can only end in the death of *The Elder Statesman*, a sequence in which Claverton seems to be "playing a part/ In [his] own obituary, whoever writes it." Everything has been prewritten, and so what is said in the past determines the real to come when that past is remembered. The result is a familiar characterology, set up around the classical drama of internal conflict-as-dislocation. Harry, for example, in *The Family Reunion*, is the son of the house of Wishwood, where childhood memories hold sway. He returns there for a reunion, bringing with him his new past, and suffering

> The degradation of being parted from my self,
> From the self which persisted only as an eye, seeing.
> All this last year, I could not fit myself together:
> When I was inside the old dream, I felt all the same emotion
> Or lack of emotion, as before: the same loathing
> Diffused, I not a person, in a world not of persons
> But only of contaminating presences.
> And then I had no horror of my action,
> I only felt the repetition of it
> Over and over.   (CPP,272)

These "repetitions," which are the source of Harry's affliction throughout the play, are not, however, repetitions with a difference. Elsewhere, internalized as linguistic effects by the anaphoric rhythms of Eliot's poetry, they become locked into a formal pattern of paradox and periphrasis which nonetheless apes the movement of a commentary and yet never gets to its point, because there is no point. What is given in *Four Quartets,* for example, is not of any substantial order, but given in the spare, unpampered diction which has exasperated so many critics and readers. Donald Davie, for example, attacks their "loose and woolly incoherent language," and places them within the tradition of the "faded and shop-soiled locution" of the post-Symboliste poetry which runs counter to Davie's own preferred neoclassical taste for the phrase "new-minted."[29] In a 1938 article, Allen Tate responded to a similar observation—Max Eastman's complaint about the absence of logic in Eliot's "oily puddle of emotional noises"—by suggesting that logic, far from being absent in the later poems, is too much present: there is an excess of logic.[30] Whether or not Tate's observation answers Eastman's or even Davie's objections, it is a useful way of describing the kind of mystical discourse that informs these poems, a discourse, as Eliot suggests, which is bound to have recourse to "diverse and even mutually contradictory images and metaphors to express the inexpressible."[31] For Bertrand Russell, for example, all representational contradictions in language were a problem of logical typing. Following this, we could say that Eliot's language of paradox, embrangled in its own endless commutability, belongs to a different logical type than the discourse of lay communication. Indeed, much of the later verse is aimed at the evacuation of such a system of linguistic exchange in which "shop-soiled" forms of meaning like the cliché help to foster the illusion of living in a language world full of shared meanings and exchangeable values. In making this a language which can no longer be *inhabited,* Eliot's verse (in spite of Davie) seems to work toward a different end from that of Symboliste discourse, where the reader is offered universal access, in any time and any place. Eliot's language is concretely bound up in the rigorous logic which militates against any such vanity of localization:

> To arrive where you are, to get from where you are not,
>   You must go by a way wherein there is no ecstasy.
> In order to arrive at what you do not know
>   You must go by a way which is the way of ignorance.
> In order to possess what you do not possess
>   You must go by a way which is the way of dispossession.

In order to arrive at what you are not
    You must go through the way in which you are not.
And what you do not know is the only thing you know
And what you own is what you do not own
And where you are is where you are not.   (CPP, 127)

This kind of paradox, heterogeneous to the cliché, belongs to the maverick, apophatic structure of negative logic, culled, on Eliot's part, from St. John of the Cross, and the fourteenth-century English mystics like Dame Julian of Norwich. In the sense in which it juggles with and inverts subjective and objective positions, however, it is just as much pre-Socratic. A Heraclitean quality, for example, may turn into its opposite without any change occuring through the judging agency of some Artistotelian third. Thus the Heraclitean fragment which prefaces "Burnt Norton"—"the way up is the same as the way down"—is a mature example of the pre-Socratic logic of both/and, as opposed to the digital either/or of classical logic, with its laws of excluded middle and contradiction. If such a paradox is of a higher logical type, then it is because it contains within itself a metacommunication, a message about itself: in other words, how to read it. There is no subjective respite outside of this kind of circuit, because every successive message about the message forces us into an increasingly tighter double-bind. The more one reads into the paradox, the more its economic efficiency as a medium of exchange is demolished.

A similar kind of conflation, of the metaphor with its literal meaning, is a common feature of schizophrenic discourse, where Freud suggests that "word-presentations" were being treated by the patient as if they were "thing-presentations."[32] And clearly this corresponds to a familiar modernist aim—to treat the word as if it were a material thing. Eliot's concern is to produce the same kind of displaced effect but in a way which is quite different from asserting the materiality of the word: he opts for a logically circuitous route that runs the risk of driving its wordy repetitions into meaninglessness. Gregory Bateson, whose work on the behavioral patterns of schizophrenics led to the formulation of the term *double-bind*, describes how the "victim" of a paradoxical injunction responds to a paternal command of the logical type both/and—you must and you must not: it is "not only safer for the victim of a double-bind to shift to a metaphorical order of message, but is an impossible situation, it is better to shift and become someone else, or shift and insist that he is somewhere else."[33] It is this shift to the a-topic or non-topic which is thematized throughout *Four Quartets* and practiced in the mystics' writing generally. To be *in place* is the authoritative, noncontradictory position of divine enunciation, God's voice being the only one that can speak "I am that I am." To think that this place is inhabitable, on the other hand, is the humanist fancy of self-definition, as Thomas points out in *Murder in the Cathedral:*

> . . . . Only
> The fool, fixed in his folly, may think
> He can turn the wheel on which he turns.   (CPP, 184)

Bateson goes on to observe that the advanced schizophrenic reacts to further double-binds by attempting not to communicate at all, or to speak as if he or she were silent by effacing any memory of what has just been spoken. This aim, to speak as if one were silent, is the ultimate vocation of mystic discourse, and it is the best promise that Eliot has of delivering the disembodied voice approved by a poetics of invisibility. God's enunciation, however, though perfectly lucid itself, is no guarantee of sublunary stability, for the human corollary of the Word, the "still point of the turning world," is a place which generates such confusion in the ranks of memory that it is better that it be effaced altogether: "I can only say, *there* we have been: but I cannot say where./ And I cannot say, how long, for that is to place it in time" (CPP, 119).

3.   It's the words, the words we need to get
             back to, words washed clean.
                         William Carlos Williams

I have been suggesting that there is a structural *negativity* in Eliot's later poetry which both supports and thwarts his desire to manage and stabilize a subjective relation to an external authority. It is important to distinguish this negativity from the digital negations and oppositions studied, for example, by Anthony Johnson in his book, *Sign and Structure in the Poetry of T.S. Eliot*. In analyzing the conflict in the poems between two sets of paradigmatic elements—the positive and the negative, the male principle and the female principle, spiritually and carnality—Johnson suggests that when Eliot tries "to eliminate negatives from his writing . . . its quality . . . suffered an immediate and striking decline; without conflict poetry cannot exist," and he concludes that those critics "who wish to defend [the later work] as *poetry* should set about digging up new paradigmatic oppositions."[34] Johnson's terms of analysis, however, are drawn from a structuralist model of oppositions (the pure semiotic categories of Greimas), and the logic which governs this kind of closed and static interpretive system lacks the conceptual apparatus for dealing with the question of subjectivity and enunciation. Indeed, we could say that the negativity implied by the paradox or extended contradiction belongs to a different logical type from that implied by negation. Johnson himself describes this kind of logical problem as a movement characterized by its "perpetual evasiveness," thereby recognizing its resistance to the hermetic dualism of a theoretical taxonomy which only sees what it wants to see in terms of neat oppositions.[35]

Johnson's obloquy on the tendency of *elimination* in Eliot's work is a crucial response, nonetheless, to a poetry that is increasingly exclusive rather than inclusive, as it submits to the ascetic thirst for a utopian body, stripped of its qualities and properties, and projected beyond the wearisome aphanisis of desire. I am referring to the purgative vein of Eliot's work, which, if it is especially evident in his case, need not be passed off as a "pathological" development, nor even as a dynamic peculiar to one man's literary effort. For Eliot's crusade to "purify the dialect of the tribe" involves a lived subjective relation to the fundamental aim of all Christian discourse—in flushing out of speech the material, translinguistic traces designated as impure because archaically associated with the earliest bodily functions. Bearing their allegiance to a maternal authority which is neither internal nor external, but which confuses that distinction altogether, their "origin of wretchedness" (CPP,273) is not in the turning Copernican universe of the Word, but in a Newtonian environment in which things fall from the body—the class of partial objects, neither subject nor object, which

Kristeva calls the abject: excrement, menstrual blood, sperm, sweat, vomit, etc., expelled or dropped from the body but still its disturbing partial possession.[36] In upsetting the distinction between inner and outer, the abject threatens the maintenance of identity which depends upon the power to exclude. As a category of the profane, it is obsessively supervised by ritual acts of purification like the codes of alimentary taboo in the Old Testament, codes of hygiene that are coextensive with the very maintenance of social order, a fact recognized by the Women of Canterbury in *Murder in the Cathedral,* for example, who know that "these acts marked a limit to our suffering" (CPP,214). It is not, however, the absence of cleanliness in itself which endangers identity, but the return of a remembered series of bodily losses that precede the infantile development of subject/object relations. Language, the principal medium of this development, is thus embedded in the abject, and has its matrix in the impure transubstantiation of the Word made Flesh; both are staggered between innoculation and infection.

In Eliot's writing, the double-bind of abjection, that which both fascinates and repels, promotes a wide range of fear and anxiety. Indeed, there is almost enough material on this topic for another chapter in the account of a constructed sexual identity in the poems, especially in the light it throws upon their often overtly "misogynistic" tone. Any such account, as I have already pointed out, would not be a "wild analysis" of the author himself. To suggest that the poetry is phobic, a suggestion few would care to deny, is not to diagnose a psychosexual condition for Eliot himself. On the contrary, it is to suggest that there is an authorial body *at work* in the writing, as opposed to an author's body *behind* the writing. And this might help us to understand why it is a poetic and not a personal subjectivity that is being "martyred" in the struggle against the abject.

A panorama of partial objects and their contagious effects range from Eliot's earliest writing onward: the "female smells in shuttered rooms" and the "washed-out smallpox" of *mam'zelle la lune* in "Rhapsody on a Windy Night" (CPP,15); the "subtle effluence" and "feline" fetor of Grishkin, which raises Eliot's problematic fascination with cats in general; the punned vaginal odors of Fresca in *The Waste Land* draft, "odours confected by the cunning French," which disguise the "hearty female stench"—Fresca, whose "doorstep is dunged by every dog in town" (WL,23–24); the fecal reminders of the "fetid air" which assaults the protagonist's ascent of the Holy Ladder in *Ash Wednesday*, and the untidy orifice of an "old man's mouth," jammed open, and "drivelling beyond repair" (CPP,63); the congenital "disease" of "Gerontion"'s Jew, abject also because stateless and nomadic, *uncontainable* by national boundaries and thus contaminating, associated everywhere else with the rat, or "red-eyed scavenger" (CPP,27): in short, a contagious trinity of "flesh, fur, and faeces" (CPP,123) which stains almost every page of Eliot's work.

The outermost manageable limit of abjection is, of course, the body itself, which eventually does fall into an object-cadaver (*cadere*, to fall), and it is indeed the corpse that exercises the most ambiguous fascination in Eliot's writing, whether sprouting or decaying, soused in a bathtub full of Lysol, as in *Sweeney Agonistes*, or else suffering the sea-change of Phlebas's corpse in "Death by Water," a corpse which, in the draft version, belongs to Bleistein, and which is being graphically and slowly devoured by crabs. The concluding image of this subterranean last supper suggests that Bleistein's penis is being consumed. The image is arrestingly quiescent, and is pitched in a level tone that almost escapes the animus of the abject and its uneven oscillation between the poles of fascination and repulsion; death, after all, is the only stable object, and thus lies beyond abjection altogether.

Freed from longstanding bourgeois constraints of literary and social comportment, the response to the abject is an important feature of major modernist writing inasmuch as it contributes to the desire to reject old languages and create new ones: Pound, Joyce, Stein, Lawrence (Eliot's own "abject" writer), Williams, Marinetti, Breton, Céline, Bataille, and Mayakovsky, all concerned in some way with the need to confront the body in new ways, and each governed by a formal imperative to "make it new" on behalf of language and humanism. Eliot's determined role in this is tempered by a more mainstream, though still radical, traditionalism, for the Christian renaissance in his work entertains the style of the *novitiate* learning to speak a new language, and coming to terms with the disciplined catharsis of a hitherto lived discourse. The will to purify in Eliot's work is distinct from other libertarian crusades only in its appeal to a familiar external authority: unlike Mallarmé's *pur,* a busy world of impulsive motion, freed from all guilt, Pound's desideratum of Mediterranean clarity and color, Joyce's international cause of the signifier, Celan's desire to alienate the German language forever, and Breton's attempt to modify speech to match the respective contradictions of psychic and social experience.

In the novitiate discourse of the New Testament, for example, the location of the impure shifts away from the old *outside* of the Judaic alimentary taboos, and becomes interiorized. Sin, for the Christian, is something which issues from *inside* and is expelled in speech itself: "not that which goeth into the mouth defileth a man: but that which cometh out of the mouth, this defileth a man" (Matthew,XV,11).[37] The history of Christian purification, then, is one enacted in speech itself, the purgative process institutionalized, for example, in the confession, a partially performative speech act in which sin, the impure or profane, is simply spoken away. In Eliot's later writing, speech is often reified as a polluting presence: in *The Rock,* the "new life, new form, new colour," of the sculptured masonry of the Church is figuratively raised "out of the slimy mud of words, out of the sleet and hail of verbal imprecisions" (CPP,111), an escape prefigured fourteen years earlier in "The Hippopotamus," where the Lamb, "washed white as snow," rises above the Church down below, its noisy ecclesiastical debates "wrapt in the old miasmal mist" (miasma—"infectious or noxious exhalations from putrescent organic matter," OED). Words inherit the weakness of the flesh as carnal accretions, just as the "Word in the desert/ Is most attacked by voices of temptation" (CPP,122). So too, the leopard's meal in *Ash Wednesday* is a consummation devoutly to be wished, since it strips away all bodily accompaniment to the voice, leaving behind the bones to lie "chirping."

In the plays, this conflict between language and purgation is manifest both on a thematic level, as in *The Family Reunion,* and on a structural level, as in *Murder in the Cathedral.* Harry's predicament is to be caught between his old language and the new, and hence between two assumed identities. Because his family still speaks the old language, he allows them the liberty of "necrophily to feed upon that carcase." In seeking to subject himself to the new, however, he is constantly brought up short, menaced by an outside that has now been internalized:

> You can't understand me, it's not being alone
> That is the horror, to be alone with the horror.
> What matters is the filthiness. I can clean my skin,
> Purify my life, void my mind,
> But always the filthiness, that lies a little deeper . . .
>
> (CPP, 269)

To be still "befouled" as Harry is, involves a total identification with the impure in which the subject himself becomes the abject; a part of the body, an impurity, synechdochically assumes the identity of the whole. The limits of this metonymy, which Harry calls the "contagion of putrescent embraces," are reached when its ceaseless movement of "in and out" mechanically falters:

> The chain breaks,
> The wheel stops, and the noise of the machinery,
> And the desert is cleared, under the judicial sun
> Of the final eye, and the awful evacuation
> Cleanses.   (CPP, 277)

Certainly this is no more "awful" than anything to be found in Eliot, and we will probably think it less of a "final" or "judicial" limit than many passages from *The Waste Land*. Indeed, in bringing together the sun, the eye, and the anus in what could be read as one comical constellation, it wants to fart in the reader's face. An intrusive note of surrealist farce threatens the gravity of Eliot's dramatic moment. Bataille's strikingly similar image of the *oeil pinéal*, a kind of solar anus at the crown of the head, captures the serious comedy which is the other, scatological side of horror's coin.[38] Bataille's endlessly excreting eye is no cleanser in Eliot's sense. It does, however, aim to cleanse us of solar ambitions by holding up for ridicule the anal derivation of the mastering drives. The patent effect, then, to teach humility, matches Eliot's dramatic purpose. While for Bataille, however, the abject is often a working medium, Eliot's writing works its end *in spite* of the abject.

As a structural force, however, the abject vision is most prominent in *Murder in the Cathedral*, where the tapestry of pollution, "woven like a pattern of living worms/ In the guts of the women of Canterbury" (CPP,208) depicts the workings of a necessary mechanism of exclusion, geared toward the abjection of Thomas as a dangerous social agent. From the outset, this mechanism writes his death sentence in a bodily legibility across the whole play, like the death machine in Kafka's penal colony. Under pain of death from the first scene, Thomas is killed, however, in the service of life, to preserve a social order that depends upon its own purgation in the form of persecutory blood-letting.[39] Bad blood, the menstrual flow of the women among others, speaks epidemically in the play, forming a "curtain of falling blood" and representing a much larger mimetic contagion which threatens to embrace the whole world in its abominating virus:

> It is not we alone, it is not the house, it is not
>   the city that is defiled,
> But the world that is wholly foul.
> Clear the air! clean the sky! wash the wind! take the stone from
> the stone, take the skin from the arm, take the muscle from the
> bone, and wash them. Wash the stone, wash the bone, wash the
> brain, wash the soul, wash them, wash them!   (CPP,214)

It is important to see the red menace in the play as a *cause* and not the symptom of Thomas's bloody end. This means that the sacrificial reading usually accorded the play might be reversed, for it is one in which the role of the Women is regarded as one of structural passivity, their impure state viewed as a symbolic or sympathetic registration of an issue which is being resolved on a stage external to theirs, and in conformity with an extratemporal decree. It is not, however, a divine blight which is responsible for this pollution, but more like an inversion of this causal logic. By that same inversion, it is a blood lust that bespeaks Thomas's death, one bred out of the fearful prospect of a world of organic matter that should be excluded from the body, but which is here "flowing in at the mouth and the ear and the eye":

> . . . . .I have tasted
> The savour of putrid flesh in the spoon. I have felt

The heaving of the earth at nightfall, restless, absurd. . .
· ·
    I have eaten
Smooth creatures still living, with strong salt taste of living
    things under sea: I have tasted
The living lobster, the crab, the oyster, the whelk and the
    prawn; and they live and spawn in my bowels. . . . .
· ·
Corruption in the dish, incense in the latrine, the sewer in the
    incense, the smell of sweet soap in the woodpath, a hellish
    sweet scent in the woodpath, while the ground heaved.
· ·
In our veins our bowels our skulls as well
As well as in the plottings of potentates
As well as in the consultations of powers.
What is woven on the loom of fate
What is woven in the councils of princes
Is woven also in our veins, our brains,   (CPP, 207–8)

There is no clear division between internal and external here, and
the lack of any such demarcative limit is the concern of peasant and
politician alike. This jeopardizes not only a bodily law of coherence
dependent upon purity, but also the exclusivity of the social order
itself. Set on this larger scale, the final "ecstasy of waste and
shame" acted out in the cathedral becomes a communal event, a
violent social orgasm involving more than Thomas's body alone (in
spite of the Knights' insistence that his phallic status, the fact that
he is "swollen with pride," goes beyond any degree of toleration).
Moreover, if his death is a murder, then it is the cause and not the
consequential sign of his sanctification, for it is only by an act of
exclusion from the social body, that such a person or event acquires
the rank of the sacred or profane.

    The result of this reading is that Thomas's blood can be seen in
terms of an insurance policy for the whole community, a sublimation of other, more risky investments in bad blood. Such a reading
also calls into question the interpretation of Thomas's martyrdom as
a sacrifice in the name of an external authority. Rather, martyrdom
here is acted out as a social solution to the problems posed by an
authority that is much closer to home. It is an authority which

stands or falls by the need to recognize the distinction between internal and external, along with the categories of identity that comfortably proceed from this distinction.

My concern here has been to suggest that Eliot's later writing follows the same sacrificial path in its pursuit of a stable acknowledgment of the extrasubjective place of authority. Such a view of subjection had been theoretically advanced in the social and political criticism which accompanied and followed upon his conversion in the late twenties. The attempt to reproduce this position in poetic discourse, however, meets with a full range of resistance, indeterminate and shifting in its effects. This crusade to match poetic practice with a social polemic based upon the ethic of "voluntary extinction" may or may not transcend Eliot's own "personal" interest in martyrdom, proclaimed by Lyndall Gordon as the master key to the poet's work. The evidence that I have been discussing, however, with respect to structures like the active/passive inversions, the paradoxical abeyance of the "feminine" mystic position, and the negativity bound up with abjection, would suggest that it is a desire to sacrifice poetic and not personal subjectivity that governs Eliot's literary cult of invisibility.

CHARLES OLSON

4. OUT OF TRUE

1.   What shall we do with Papa's shovel?
                                                Olson

CHARLES OLSON, in 1952, is the first American writer to call
himself "post-modern" (LFO,102). Since he came to writing
late, after a career in Washington as a political administrator, he
may well also be "the first writer to produce a major body of work
in full consciousness of the implications of modern totalitarianism."[1]
This is not to say, of course, that one proposition necessarily
implies the other. It would be more fair to say that Olson self-
consciously tries to write himself out of the contradictions of modernism, and the acute dualism that obliged someone like Pound to
be "in language and form . . . as forward, as much the revolutionist
as Lenin," while "in social, economic, and political action . . . as
retrogressive as the Czar" (O&P,53). Olson's challenge is to be read
and acted out in the light of his "post-historical" desire to learn the
lesson, and thus clarify the failure, of the modernist attempt to
match formalism with humanism. As visibly as any other Anglo-
American writer since the war, his literary drive feeds directly into
politically positivist aims—to successfully produce a new cultural
humanism out of novel and radical mutations in language, idiom,
form, and subjectivity. There is no doubt that the vigor and heroic
intensity of this project has been exemplary for poets, readers, and
critics who have been affected by Olson's work. I will argue, however, that Olson's epic cause is taken up in much the same spirit as
that of his poetic fathers, if only because it treats constitutive problems as if they can be isolated, externalized, and punctually resolved. Writing after the high modernist fact, his claim to the "postmodern" is not one that we should seek to challenge; we can, however, explain why it may be premature.

For the sake of polemical efficacy, we might choose one of Olson's metaphors of difference to express the antisystematic impulse of his postmodernity. In his professed role as "archaeologist of morning," it is appropriate that he should be putting to use a paternal signifier like "Papa's shovel," and in the service of a "special view of history" (SVH,58). In the early "A Bibliography on America for Ed Dorn," his injunction is to *"dig one thing or place or man,* until you know more abt that than is possible to any other man" (AP,11), and in a later lecture, to "dig place" until it becomes a conceptual habit (OL,10:103). The methodology—to dig holes—takes precedence over the object. The modernists' labor, on the other hand, had been a counteractive one. What had appeared for them as a hole in time and space, the newly vacated place of a subject which had always known its place, became a lack from which the modernist interrogation of history took its cue—to fill in that hole. In his 1947 account of Pound's monomaniacal meddling with bric-a-brac, or the "rag-bag" of history, Olson barely hides his contempt for the cultural imperalism of *The Cantos*: Pound's Kultur, like the freely circulating dust of Caesar's once perfumed body, is now "so much stuff in a hole to keep the wind away" (O&P,20). Eliot too, by Olson's reading, was reluctant to admit any perforation of his medium. In his annotations of a copy of the *Collected Poems*, Olson suggests of the first ten lines of "Burnt Norton" that they reveal at the "heart of it, in the man . . . a lack of the hole of space & it is that lack which gives Eliot his minority."[2] Where the modernist hole is the site of an obsessional attempt to camouflage its very existence, Olson's hole, by contrast, is one which is dug wilfully and indiscriminately, in a flagrant show of disavowal.

One model for this cognitive distinction can be excavated from two articles written by Freud in 1924, "Neurosis and Psychosis," and "The Loss of Reality in Neurosis and Psychosis." Seeking to define an opposition which would differentiate, firstly, the one process from the other, and secondly, the displacement of each subject, neurotic and psychotic, with respect to the external world, Freud is led to examine the ways in which a piece of reality becomes "scotomised," producing a hole in the subjective makeup: "In a neurosis, the ego, in its dependence on reality, suppresses a piece of the id (of instinctual life), whereas in a psychosis, this same ego, in the service of the id, withdraws from a piece of reality. . . . In a psychosis, a loss of reality would necessarily be present, whereas in a neurosis, it would seem, this loss would be avoided."[3] Both conditions, however, involve an attempt at reconstruction or compensation, in which the neurotic reaction is in the form of a delusion, applied "like a patch over the place where originally a rent had appeared,"[4] while the psychotic subject turns away in an attempt to construct a new reality, a complete remodeling of the world. To review Freud's distinction: the reconstructive campaign on the neurotic's part is like filling in a hole, or repairing a tear in the symbolic fabric; through the psychotic hole, however, the external "traffic of the real" crowds in, replacing in its entirety a universe that has been rejected primordially.

Olson's *push*, as he has monumentalized it, would be in the direction of this "psychotic" space, for his demand for a "re-definition of the real" is accompanied by a massive, willed rejection of the traditional order of symbolic relations which bind us together within a commonly intelligible network of codes and discourses. Olson's oppositionality is like a *foreclosure*, or rejection of the paternal signifier that governs entry into the symbolic order.[5] "Papa's shovel," as it were, is in the wrong pair of hands, and the paternal metaphor it might have suggested is written off, and excluded. If Olson's positivist gamble is correct, however, this will be a small price to pay for putting to rights what he sees as "the inaccurate estimate of reality men have had to go by since the Ionians" (HU,116). (For Olson's disavowal, to furnish it with its full historical scale, coincides with the Athenian "Oedipalization" of Western man, circa 500 B.C., and his *push* will then be an escape from the Socratic orbit of rational man at its very inception.)

As an appropriately foreclosed signifier, the epsilon on the Delphic omphalos which appears in "The Kingfishers" had lost all of its legislative sway long before Plutarch, High Priest at Delphi in his day, came to puzzle over its dispersed meanings in his speculative essay, "The E at Delphi."[6] Of the several possible solutions that Plutarch offers, his Apollonian parti pris for the rationalist cause of identity and self-consciousness finds expression in his choice of "Thou Art" or "Know Thyself." Olson, however, had heard the epsilon "sounded otherwise," and in one of his lectures at Black

Mountain, he proposes another meaning: the loss of identity sung as "Man Rejoicing." Thus, the obscure history of the epsilon mediates the difference between Odysseus's response to Polyphemus's question—"No-man"—and Oedipus's answer to the Sphinx's riddle—"Man" (OL,10:68,69). The epsilon itself is a signifier of the lack upon which the Western cultural order is articulated. To disavow it is not just to scratch the rational surface of things, but to abolish all of the conceptual ways of rationalist cognition in favor of a more "natural" mode. In promoting the will to think outside of that rationalist order, Olson contributes directly to the politics of naturalistic alternatives which surfaces in the various "archaic" poetics of the late fifties and sixties. The most immanent assumption of this *faux-naïf* primitivism (Lawrence is an important precursor) is that the Law, syntactical or otherwise, is an unnecessary and unwanted constraint. A condition like psychosis, then, to follow up our model, becomes a desired style. Like the anti-psychiatrists, R.D. Laing and David Cooper, Gilles Deleuze and Felix Guattari argue for an inversion of the normative bias of the Freudian distinction, in viewing the psychotic loss of reality as a positive response to the forced oedipalization of the repressive neurotic order.[7] Their "schizohero," the psychotic, engages a more continuous and fluid process in which experience is lived "unmediated," an ideology that is dominant among the "open" American poetics of this period. For poets like Olson, who tapped into Whitehead's universe of dynamic events, this process was held to be more "real," or as hip jargon used to put it, and here is the problem—unreal.

For Olson, this lived sense of the "real" is bound up within his ambitious attempt to modify the classical realist position of reflecting or reproducing the world "as it really is." This much the famous "Projective Verse" manifesto seems to promise when it takes stock of the degree "to which the projective involves a stance towards reality outside a poem as well as a new stance towards the reality of the poem itself" (SW,24). The position advanced in "Projective Verse," then, for all its anti-aesthetic bluster, insists on observing two separate cognitive registers, the inside and the outside of the poem. Because of this, the "new stance" it proposes will always be dependent on some kind of identity-relation between these two registers, when the discourse is "equal, that is, to the real itself"

(SW,46). Olson's "realism," I will argue, is his epistemological "last instance," which is brought in to mop up some of the more indiscriminate excesses which his Quixotic disposition gives rise to. When he falls back on realist ideology, his canvassing for an "ALTERNATIVE TO THE EGO POSITION" loses its edge; his desire to write "the real," the "actual structure and character of the real itself" (SW,52), becomes yet another symptom of the Rousseauesque delirium of "first writing," long extant in the American grain of an Emersonian "natural" language, while his "restoration of the human house" (SW,57) repeats the infallibilist Puritan reforming zeal: "the American push to find out an alternative discourse to the inherited one, to the one implicit in the language from Chaucer to Browning, to try, by some other means than 'pattern' and the 'rational' to cause discourse to cover—as it only ever best can—the real" (HU,64).

Olson's speculations on the need to renegotiate reality appear, however, at one level, to approximate Brecht's reflectionist maxim that since "reality alters: to represent it, the means of representation must alter too."[8] In assuming that there is a correspondence between social reality, concrete and lived, and its technical means of representation (a correspondence open to political change), Olson's thinking falls on the side of a politicized formalism that dominates the Marxist debates about modernism.[9] In response to the functionalist view of realism put forward by Lukács—the correspondence theory of a *reflection* of social totality—Brecht emphasizes the investigation of the contradictions which the real articulates when familiar modes of representation are disturbed or adulterated. Both the Russian Formalists' *ostranenie* and Brecht's *Verfremdung* push the subjective response beyond agitprop—to change the world, it is enough to represent it differently—and into a complete loss of belief in a fixed reality available to us in a noncontradictory place.[10]

Despite Olson's commitment to an experimental methodology, he courts an idealist conviction about the ends of a radical realism; a *proper* humanist discourse will rectify the social and cultural injustice whereby "man is estranged from that with which he is most familiar." In effect, he holds out for the messianic return of subjectivity to its *authentic* epistemological space, a naturally ordained position with easy access to the discourses of freedom. Olson's panegyrics against "falsity" stem from his theoretical aversion to mediation; not from the belief that representation and reality have become unhinged, but from the supposition that representation is itself a needless and harmful convention, that it keeps people from the real, and enables them "to have experience by mimesis and therefore their experience then becomes mimetic" (Mu,I,47).

Olson's ceaseless campaign for an *other* discourse incorporates some of his more positivistic claims: that there is, for example, a set of syntactical relations which is more "true" than classical subject/ predicate expressions; that different grammars such as those of certain North American Indian tongues are closer to the premises of an originary "Indo-European space-time"; or that the spatio-temporality invoked in Homeric narrative is somehow more "proper" to our *essential* epistemological needs and concerns (SW,28; AP,52–53). There is, however, no question of any language being more legitimate or authentic than another. Each has different resources and semantic ranges, but all cover entirely their field of significations because there is no object or continuum external to language to which language must be adequate. In this respect Borges's Chinese dictionary is as efficient a calibration of linguistic experience (it can only be that) as Linear B script. Like the Fenellosan Pound, Olson pursues a language of nature beneath the language of convention, tracking down the raw, uncooked real in the tradition of American poetry's obsession with the hieroglyphic and its promise of an archaic, "picturesque" or emblematic, language.[11] Indeed, he writes to Robert Creeley from Mexico that "a Sumer poem or Mayan glyph is more pertinent to our purposes than anything else, because each of these people & their workers had forms which unfolded directly from content (sd content itself a disposition towards reality which understood man as only force in field of force containing multiple other expressions" (SW,113). The attempt to revive this disposition, to replace the "Classical-representational by the primitive-abstract" lures Olson into even more capricious schemes. Here, for example, is his metaphrasis of Yana-Hopi speech: "And past-I-go/ Gloucester-insides/ being Fosterwise of/ Charley-once-boy/ insides" (M,I,144). Edward Sapir, the champion of linguistic relativity, is Olson's authority here. In a famous paper, his student Benjamin Whorf argues for the different organization of Hopi space and time, and claims that "the Hopi language is capable of accounting for and describing correctly . . . all observable phenomena of the universe."[12] Whorf's assumption is that Hopi *appears* to do less violence to the continuity of nature than our own grammatical itinerary of segmenting and classifying reality into three-dimensional space and one-dimensional time. Whorf's point, however, is that Hopi, finally, is one of an infinite number of possible symbolic orderings of experience, and thus its coherence or efficiency cannot be evaluated from outside its own language system. Husserl makes the same "ethnographic" point in *The Origin of Geometry,* where he observes that "every people has its logic" and that everything can be coherently explained in terms of that logic, "whether in Mythical-magical or European-rational terms."[13]

To privilege one set of symbolic relations over another is to assume that there is an *a priori* and empirical field of reality to which language must find a relation of adequacy. That Olson subscribes to this point of view is quite evident in the work he did on the Mayan glyphs while visiting the Yucatán in 1949. The problem he set himself was to determine whether the glyphic system was an alphabet, a syllabary, or a language. His preference for the third category plays to his Adamic interest in figurative rather than phonetic characters, because they suggest more direct and nonabstract relations with the object world, relations which Olson patronizingly believed that the Mayans enjoyed. Such an unfallen language of pure radicals would offer a truer picture of physical things: "the tremendous levy on all objects as they present themselves to human sense, in this glyph-world" (SW,111). The glyphs, then, were to be understood as visual representations and not as phonetic signs, in the same way as Pound supported Fenellosa's willful interpretation of the ideogram as an ideograph.

2.　　where the right is, is, that he goeth by language: this we must do, and do, and do, otherwise we better go into, say, politics.
Olson (of Pound)

Such a "levy" upon the real as the glyph offers would be a powerful recruit in the service of power, the will to truth, and the poet's traditionally prophetic, political office, all of which are revived in

Maximus's design to "write a Republic" (M,III,9). When Olson took the platform at the Berkeley Poetry Conference in 1965, the dominant metaphor was an electoral one, posed in the form of a campaign address to the convention audience of poets: "Ed Sanders, who proposed that I run in '68, has already proved I'm running tonight, and I have my cabinet present, and therefore it's already over" (Mu,I,129). Caucusing those poets whom he had been hailing as "the new leaders of society" since 1956, Olson's high style directly courts the form of the Pre-Socratics, for whom the right to speak was also speaking the right (poet-politicians like Solon spoke "true" because their speech was sanctioned by a "regime" of discourse which empowered it as "true").[14] A discourse like this declares its propinquity to power which is there for the seizing: "How easy it is not to be Nixon, that's all" (Mu,I,146). For Olson, the Berkeley conference was like a talking *junta*, the nearest thing to what he saw exemplified in the Iroquois or Senecan longhouse, where the speech of each participant was properly a social act, a noninstitutional, nonpartisan opportunity to ground the idea of *plebiscite* in the body of the community. Political action would be bound up in a new "kind of discourse which is oral, private, public," private *and* public, a discourse upon which "the establishment of future society depends" (Mu,I,142). The threat which such a speech offered to the complacency of rational public debate was that it would be endlessly *oralizing*. At Berkeley, then, Olson said, "look, I'm going to talk forever tonite," and it took until the arrival of the campus police many hours later for the threat to be withdrawn.

In this respect, the value of Olson's oppositional zeal lies at the level of the production of discourse, and not in the power of its discursive meanings. Unlike many of the essays done in "presentation prose" where one feels the presence, as Barthes put it, of an all too human master making the effort to "speak badly," the more convincing of Olson's texts are transcripts of speech.[15] Outside of the Berkeley reading, perhaps the most successful of these is the *Paris Review* interview with Gerard Malanga, where the interrogatory rules of the interview are bewilderingly displaced and transformed. Since the interviewee is normally subject to a discourse which is putatively his own, but which is elicited and supervised by a master-interviewer, he is caught up in the formal knowledge akin to that of the witness/suspect making a statement to the police; everything he says will be taken down and possibly used in evidence, while everything he did (not) say is read back to him as if it were his own. Throughout his interview, Olson willfully avoids the confessional tone, shifts and shunts the codes of dialogue, and absorbs the questions merely to deflect them back on to the interviewer. The form of *address* becomes wholly internal. In other words, if the subject is on trial, then it is not at the instigation of the interviewer, nor by the questions raised by him, but by the language posed in the course of discussion. Perhaps this is one of Olson's quiet lessons, that mastery and its effects are internalized in the infrastructure of language itself, and that knowledge of this fact is a concrete form of political action (unlike the example of Pound, characterized as the "exterior man," lured onto "retrogressive" political terrain (O&P,20,53): "today, as much as action, the invention, not the invention, but the *discovery* of formal structural means is as legitimate as—*is* for me the form of action. The radical of action lies in finding out how organized things are genuine, are initial . . ." (Mu,I,94). Olson's covert revolution follows on the proposition that "we are, all of us, now, essentially guerrillas— maquis, frontier or sidestreet" (HU,125), because we are all imprisoned in the common cause of language.

One might contrast this to the full frontal tactics of the Beats in their use of language as an instrument of holy war. Ginsberg, for example, wields language like a theurgic weapon, and for him at least, the association with overt phallic display is omnipresent. "Wichita Vortex Sutra" waves the privately political parts of language in the stern face of its adversary, the perpetrator of a linguistic Vietnam: "Poet can dismantle the language consciousness conditioned to war reflexes by setting up (mantra) absolutely contrary field of will as expressed in language. By expressing, manifesting, his DESIRE."[16] Even if he shares some of Ginsberg's prophetic style, Olson is loath to enter into that sort of confrontational mirror-image politics. In a paper published in the year he gave up Washington politics, the metaphor of reflection is still useful, but less straightforward: Yeats addresses the future poets— "You are the antithetical men, and your time is forward, the conflict is more declared, it is you to hold [sic] the mirror up to authority, behind our respect for which lay a disrespect for democracy as we were acquainted with it. A slogan will not suffice" (O&P, 30).

This Yeats article, and the other early pieces collected in *Charles Olson and Ezra Pound,* are different in another respect. Their solid patrician prose stands in marked relief to the "prose putsches" of their successors, written in the famous "Ultima Thule" of discourse which the polemical Olson fashioned for his didactic purposes. Joyce had been concerned with the full lexical dissolution of *parole,* split open at the phonemic level: a "universal language of the unconscious," as Olson saw it, and, following Pound's anal distaste for *Finnegan's Wake,* as so much "mush and shit" (SW, 82). The lexic is too small a space for Olson, whose reorganization of the syntactical surface is intended to take place somewhere between what we would understand as *langue* and *parole.* In fact, we could say that where Olson proposes to reclaim *langue* as *parole,* he is only placing his own "ideolect" above the commonly accepted "sociolect": "there is point now to speak of a syntax which is, ultimately, dependent upon the authority of a completed man, might I say, in this sense, that the syntax is of the man's own making, not something accepted as a canon of language in its history and the society."[17] Olson's attempts, then, to "make English behave" are a way of idealizing a new fully "completed man" with linguistic powers over and above the inherited social codes of communication. These more "authentic" powers are always on the point of being "dis-closed" ("meaning is that which exists thru itself") in a discourse which announces its idiosyncratic superiority at every turn. Cid Corman has described this effect: "Olson's language is thrown back at him as if it were impossible. But the meaning is in the motion of it. And what *is* impossible is to read him consecutively and fail to grasp, or be grasped by, what he is driving at. For the 'end' arrives at every moment and is co-substantive."[18]

Corman is describing the dynamic of "action poetry," and the mode of "presentational immediacy" which Whitehead's philosophy had taught the Black Mountain poets as a "school." This discourse observes no common rules of structural balance since it enforces itself by "spontaneous, irregular, guerrilla forms" (LFO, 10), and obeys only that rhythm which issues from the individual body. Any sudden exercise of constraint acts like the Heideg-gerian dis-closure of a "full" subject, if only because there is no other way of recognizing that a subject is in control. In eschewing the use of subordination, the entire register of relative clause, qualifier, and generally hypotactic usage such as is provided by the most basic causal connectives, Olson denies the possibility of para-phrase and the whole range of alternative expression, not all gram-matical, which we assume that the "I" can fall back upon with any degree of certainty. Ironically enough, we are forced to question this subjectivity on account of its *infallibility*. The subject of normal discourse is accustomed to the routine feint, the circuit of doubt which is walled into every proposition and which leaves room for the Socratic response—the request to repeat, clarify, and expand. There is no *doubt* about Olson's way of saying things, and this in itself would be sufficient grounds for invoking the linguistic experi-ence of the psychotic, for whom every experience of reality is a deadly certitude. Our shared, fallible discourse assumes that the rational subject selects only one of a number of available certitudes, while acknowledging that all of the possible alternatives are being set aside. For Olson's projective subject, however, this is merely one of "the dodges of discourse. . . . For any of us, at any instant, are juxtaposed to any experience, even an overwhelming single one, on several more planes than the arbitrary and discursive we inherit can declare," and so such a project is always "with-it," whatever it is that is "going on" (SW,55). As a result, forgotten and archaic "kinetic" qualities of the preposition are reactivated in terms of their adverbial force, as in the diagnostic "of" which termi-nates so many of Olson's clauses. The dynamism of each gram-matical element is reinvented: a noun is only a "motion which has not yet moved" (OL,10:83).

Whether or not we agree with Geoffrey Thurley's thesis that, in practice, the Imagist movement (Black Mountain included) does nothing more than pay lip-service to this notion of a naturalistic dynamism underlying "artificial" grammar forms,[19] we should ac-knowledge the sirenic appeal of the theoretical claims that lie be-hind Olson's attempts to rewrite the laws of language. For each of his new revisionary measures is taken up in the cause of whittling away at what is assumed to be the accidental or contingent legacy of

subjective bias inscribed in our language by "Greek" thinking. As I shall now argue, the attack on this subjectivism is indeed conceived through the need to attack a linguistic category of subjectivity, as if it too were contingent and not at all necessary.

3. The Greeks . . . could hardly combine the objects in nature into any classes but those which were made for them by the popular phrases of their own country; or at least could not help fancying those classes to be natural and all others as artificial.

John Stuart Mill

It is Whitehead's formulation of an "objectivist" position in *Process and Reality* which provides philosophical support for Olson's mistrust of the inherited classificatory structures of language. As committed as Bradley was to the dissolution of the classical constitutive subject, Whitehead proceeds by turning Kantianism on its head. In place of a subject for whom the world is a theoretical construct, he proposes a subject which is the "superject" of its experiences, an emergent a posteriori position, always in the process of becoming through objectification. The problem with this is in its logical correlate: the Kantian recognition of the prior immanence of objects inasmuch as they are "received" into subjectivity, and thus an objectivist principle which is an exact mirror-image of the subjectivist Cartesian one. Whitehead's solution lies in what he calls "the reformed subjectivist principle," which holds to the claim that all objective process (the busy flux of *organic* experience) necessarily presents itself to the subject in an unmediated way and on common terms. A "natural" egalitarianism is brought to bear on subject and object, for even if the object world preexists the establishment of a perceptual substantiality, "apart from the experience of subjects, there is nothing, nothing, nothing, bare nothingness."[20] The difficulty of translating this position into the terms of a debate about the "hierarchical" makeup of language itself, is all too apparent. For Whitehead complains (as Eliot did in his dissertation) about the long established subject/predicate form of expression in Western languages, arguing that such a taxonomy already presents a morphologically prescribed way of looking at the world: "The result always does violence to that immediate experience which we express in our actions, our hopes, our sympathies, our purposes, and which we enjoy in spite of our lack of phrases for its verbal analysis. We find ourselves in a buzzing world."[21] If language were only in touch with this natural process, if only it did not provide such an arbitrary division of reality, then we could truly mean what we say.

For Olson, committed to a reformed humanism, or "ALTERNATIVE TO THE EGO-POSITION," Whitehead's appeal to unmediated object relations is an attractive one, and he is determined to pursue this ideal in language itself, seeking out practical ways of reducing or abolishing the role of subjectivity. He is prepared, for example, to follow up on Sapir's speculation that the subjective/objective distinction is only a late development in the Indo-European language (AP,30), and one that can therefore be reversed by thinking back to the grammatical force of the "middle voice." The middle voice falls between active and passive inasmuch as the act it represents is one in which "the subject is represented as acting."[22] There is no action involved in this which is exterior to the subject, and thus transitivity only develops historically when the middle voice is displaced by the broader category of the passive. The middle voice, then, seems to offer a partially objectified subject that cannot be easily recuperated into a predicating position. For Olson, this satisfies at least two of his demands for new rules of linguistic conduct: things said are things done, but objectively; and speech acts have access to an unreflecting, *kinetic* mode of discourse to replace the more discrete art of *mimesis*, predicated upon the "false" abstraction of the object world.

It is the Pre-Socratics who present Olson with the most powerful evidence for a nonmimetic discourse that refuses any discontinuity between subjective and objective time and space. In a review of Havelock's *A Preface to Plato*, Olson describes the "antidote" to the periodic sentence:

(1) that [the poetry of Homer and Hesiod was based on] a wholly different syntax, to which Notopoulos (1949) has applied the word *parataxis* in which the words and actions reported are set down side by side in the order of their occurrence in nature, instead of by an order of discourse, or

"grammar," as we have called it, the prior an actual resting on vulgar experience and event:

(2) Zielinski, 1901, and literally therefore almost contemporary with Planck, was saying that "time" in such poets as Homer and Hesiod cannot admit of intervals where nothing happens, that there is no such thing as nothing, and that therefore you cannot leap over, you do therefore necessarily traverse, in writing, and any one event series once narrated fills up the available time space. There is no while back at the farm sequence possible. The epic action is a stream and you are not free to play around, jump as though you was on the bank or the other or in the water—at your choice or privilege or pleasure, that you either is or you isn't, definitely:

(3) Fraenkel's [2d ed., 1960] is another lovely indication of what the difference of Homer is: that Homer is innocent of any *concept* of time, and *chronos*, in the idioms in which he does use it, covers periods of waiting or delay or doing nothing—literally doing nothing, not "nothing"—and that it was through waiting that the experience of time is born, that a day, literally a day, is how it is, the thing itself the business possible and the report whereof thereon thereafter repeats slowly or however you do it, just that swiftly. (AP, 52–53)

This poetics of *transit*, its impatience with discontinuity and abhorrence of the virtual vacuums of time and space, is consistent with the turbulent stir of Olson's high style. Homer may nod, but he never falls asleep. Havelock's description of the Homeric art of concretely articulating concrete events is intended to contrast with the subsequent Athenian *gnome*, an epistemology that assumes a timeless discourse addressing itself to abstracted objects of knowledge. Thus, Plato's complaint with the poets—that they kept man from the real—may have been true of his contemporaries, but could not be applied to the premimetic art of Homer. Mimesis, then, is a "false" discourse, not because intrinsically so, but because it must acknowledge the abstract distinction between true and false, logical distinctions that only begin to take on their meaning toward the end of the sixth century, in Thucydides and Pindar. Indeed, Olson took great pleasure in pointing out that *muthos* and *logos*, the Platonic margin between falsity (myth) and truth, may have meant one and the same thing to Homer—*logos*(*legein*, to speak) and *muthos* (what is said); *muthologos*, the narrative mode of the epic poet, is "to speak of what is said, " or to reenact the old stories. Belief, in this kind of narrative, rests upon a concrete reality presented "in exactly those terms by which a human being experiences reality"

(OL,10:66). Just as clearly, however, belief depends upon an illusory identification with the enounced subject, or as Havelock puts it, "me identifying with Achilles," rather than the abstract conceptualism of "me thinking about Achilles."[23] To think, act, and fight with Achilles will become the standard illusion of classical realism.

Olson's experimental interest in narrative time, then, leads him to reduce all temporal contradictions to an uninterruptible presence: a totally synchronous and conscious attention to the "event." We might also ask whether his "special view of history" is finally an effort to assert a similar freedom, not only from the constraints of linear history, but also from the materiality of historical contradictions: whether his historical practice is a genuinely productive archaeology of the layered complexity of certain historical moments, or whether it reduces itself to a disavowal of historicity; typical of the latter would be his claim, for example, for "a 'literature' (of which Hesiod seems to be a conclusion) which is now for the first time again available" (AP,33). Clearly, the spirit of free enterprise with which he engages in historical speculation is sanctioned by the Romantic ideology of *poetic license*. In other words, anything that the "innately" poetic mind comes up with, even in the way of esoteric knowledge, is worth the effort of understanding. Olson's celebrated status of educator at Black Mountain, Buffalo, and Storrs rests upon that ideology, as does his self-styled stance as an augur: "I'm old-fashioned enough to be—not scared—to *wish* that the earth shall be of another vision and another dispensation" (Mu,I,75). For the professional historian, his pseudoscholarship will be that of the crankish novice, while the mindful poet will shy away from the loud pedantry of his high didactic performance.

Olson sets about doing history as a way of repudiating the modernist fetish of tradition. Recognizing that Pound's methodology is touched, at every turn, by the plundering "beak of his ego" (SW,82), deployed in the vain undertaking of fashioning history into a willfully coherent image, Olson proposes a different kind of history lesson in what methodology *means*: the Herodotean sense of *'istorin*—finding out for oneself. What Olson dug up, as he moved from culture to culture, proves that he was willfully indiscriminate in his selection of material. Outside of the Gloucester material in

The Maximus Poems (and by the second volume, this "local" project is running alongside a much more general interest in "archaic" history), his research makes little sense as an organized field of knowledge, despite the efforts of students and critics to round it off as a "system." There is no doubt about the use-value of this knowledge for his poetry, but it is the digging in itself which is of lasting importance. Olson, then, is an agitprop historian, and most successful when he weighs the Nietzschean inspiration of his method against the pedagogical citation of facts. To fall too heavily on either side would be to violate what he holds sacred in Keats's principle of "negative capability"—"that is, when man is capable of being in uncertainties, mysteries, doubts, without any irritable reaching after fact and reason"—and to revert to the old will to truth. Olson notes that Keats goes on to fault Coleridge's inability to remain "content with half knowledge" (SVH, 14) and thereby show how he comes to represent the "Man of Power," a hunter touched by the "Egotistical Sublime" of history's finitude. In *Call Me Ishmael*, Olson had announced his own opposition to such killer-thinkers, finding in Ahab's "sultanism" and his thirst for "lordship over nature" all the characteristics of a "Roman feeling about the world" which was so busy in the nineteenth century building up an American imperialist ethos (CMI, 13, 73); Ahab's quest for the great white truth is a metaphor for those philosophers of history who, as Michael Serres suggests, pursued their military calling in metaphysics. Negative Capability, by contrast, is the thesis of the "Man of Achievement," who would command nature by obeying it, taking the wind out of the sails of history's linear ship, even that messianic wind of historical materialism which blows Benjamin's anxious angel backwards into its future port: Herodotus, prospecting for evidence and not truth; Heraclitus, always panning in different rivers; Whitehead, in the process of changing his mind but never caught in the act; and Olson, not "knowing" what he is doing, but that history is what one does.

Against this appeal to humility, we must ask what is all too easily abstracted by announcing one's freedom from history, or at least the freedom to engage it at will. In this respect, Olson's restorative claims—"resetting man in his field" is "doing no more than giving him back his 'time'" (SVH, 27)—look to a new prescriptive humanism in which history-making is "the science of the ideal human character" (SVH,46). In doing so, they court the phenomenologist's reduction of all historicity. For Olson's idealist "time" resembles the noncontradictory time of *Dasein* manifest in a Living Present where the past is totalized as a natural dwelling space for subjectivity. In its ultimate quest for "first things," Olson's archaeological method shares the same temper as the phenomenological "return inquiry" into origins, and the nature of ideal objects at those origins, an inquiry that strips away the accretions of history and language which "cover up" or obscure the past.[25] Olson would "not urge anyone back" (M,I,22), for that is the modernist homesickness, "a structure of mnemonics raised on a reed, nostalgia" (O&P,98). His reappropriation of the past is a more utilitarian revenge against time and historicity, for it aims at the original, privileged use of first things: the pristine perceptions of Pleistocene Man; Cro-Magnon artistic objectivity, "Ist stone carved with cuphole, first wall painted, first bracelet worn . . . first clay shaped, first woman statue, first 'signs,' first paint . . . first dance" (OL,10:80); and almost inevitably, the origins of the American experience—"date 7,000 B.C. place circum Mt. Lycaon, Arkadia" (which is where Williams, according to Olson, should have begun *In the American Grain*) (AP,12).

If Olson views his transcendental historicizing as a way of recovering some authentic or primordial consciousness, then how does this contradict his desire to undercut the long tyranny of subjectivism? Since the multiple birth of the human sciences (Olson's date—1875), man has been both "the instrument of discovery and the instrument of definition" (SW,53): in other words, both subject *and* object in what Olson calls the *human universe*. If the dualism of subject/object is, however, in error, then it is an error of logic and classification. For Olson, at least, these categories no longer apply; the classical witness of a perceiving subject is "now inside and down under his own eye as microscopic or probe. He can't get himself out on a glass slide. Therefore he has to assume he is a glass slide" (OL,2:54). This is the rhetoric of objectification, and it comes into full play in the "Projective Verse" manifesto: "Objectism is the getting rid of the lyrical interference of the individual as ego, of the 'subject' and his soul, that peculiar presumption by which western man has interposed himself between what he is as a creature of nature (with certain instructions to carry out) and those other creations of nature which we may, with no derogation, call objects. For a man is himself an object . . . " (SW,24).

Clearly, Olson's "objectism" ought to be distinguished from Zukofsky's "objectivist" focus on "historic and contemporary particulars":[26] it is the difference between a discourse about subjectivity and a discourse about objectivity. For Olson's objectism is a subjectivism turned on its head once more, and therefore every bit as essentialist as the position it sets out to attack. The most literal rendering of such an objectist position might be in the speech act "I object," inasmuch as it signals an intervention on the part of a debater, or a participant in a legal proceeding. An "objection" is only successful if a subject fully "objects," if he can fully affirm his unitary right as a legal subject. Objecting is therefore a powerful affirmation of subjectivism. It is, however, Olson's belief that objectism, as an antidote to subjectivism, can be brought about by changing the codes of discourse; language can be reorganized or modified in order to accommodate this more "democratic" point of view. Purged of the "lyrical interference of the individual as ego," language would then be a more natural expression of man's relations with the object world, because it would no longer mediate these relations, it would dis-close them. Such a language would directly speak what it sees, having discarded all "intervening" subjective effects. Reality would articulate itself, or claim some medium outside of language, like the body, "the skin itself, the meeting edge of man and external reality" (SW,60).

4. Traces of quite remote glottochronology fold into the diorite stone
                                                    J.H. Prynne

Olson's adoption of measures aimed at changing the face of language usage is based upon a response to the dominant subjectivism of humanist epistemology. It is further supported, however, by an *ethical* appeal to the "realism" of his writing practice. Realism, after all, is not just a traditional aesthetic category (like genre); it involves a much wider claim about its relations to a *universal*, whether social, political, or historical.[27] In this respect, it can be distinguished from the case of isolated "realistic" effects produced by a writer who does not necessarily subscribe to a realist tradition. Clearly, Olson's case falls into the former category, and so I shall not be concerned here with evaluating his success or failure as a writer in reproducing the real.

Given its broad imperative to speak to some concrete picture of reality, we might characterize realism as a representative discourse which assigns final authority to the referent alone, while invoking a superior, ethical criterion of truth (the correspondence theory). Of the various forms this definition assumes, Olson rejects outright the mimetic; his claim is to *reenact* reality, not to reproduce it. This "fierceness of realism" excludes itself from the more polite Aristotelian notion of verisimilitude, which draws upon a universally accepted version of possible events and facts. It is equally removed from the resilient form/content dualism; Olson widely propagates Creeley's dictum that "form is never anything more than an extension of content." Even so, a theoretical realism is required to account for the nature of its medium; reality, after all, is articulated, it is not thrust in our face. The correspondence relation which Olson cites is an equation of *quantity* drawn from a physicist discourse in which the means of representation are "equal, that is, to the real itself" (SW,46): a relation of perfect, physical congruence by which the spatial congruence of an object, the "measure" of its phenomenal physicality, is reenacted by mapping out a corresponding counterfeit reality within writing itself. Hence the accomplishments of Melville's geometric "art of space" (for Olson, the first modern use of the nonmimetic imagination) which attempts to reenact the felt presence of an object's sensory presence; Olson's example is "The Tail" in *Moby Dick,* where the phenomenal experience of the object's dimension (the very contours of the tail) is captured in Melville's writing as a kind of photogrammar. Olson's understanding of this "equation" is drawn from his interest in Riemann's post-Euclidean geometry, with its proposition of a nondiscrete network of spatial congruence. This, along with the discoveries of Bolyai and Lobatchewsky, is an event contemporary with Melville's writing:

Congruence was spatial intuition to Kant, and if I am right that Melville did possess its powers, he had them by his birth, from his time of the world, locally America. As it developed in his century, congruence, which had been the measure of the space a solid fills in two of its positions, became a point-by-point mapping power of such flexibility that anything which stays the same, no matter where it goes and into whatever varying conditions (it can suffer deformation), it can be followed, and, if it is art, led, including, what is so important to prose, such physical quantities as velocity, force and field strength." (SW,49)

Representation thus takes on a vectorizing function, in which the metrical dimensions of writing are a measure of what it can *stretch* to, in directly articulating what it sees as a field of reality. In his flight from the *discursive*, Olson wants to recover the capacity of archaic art "to get down the force in the object" (OL,10:90).

This is close to, and has an echo in, Olson's interests in the importance of the cartographical model to the history of American space. In *Call Me Ishmael*, his "book of space," Olson describes Melville's own recognition of the political experience of space as the siren song of American expansionism: "he understood that America completes her West only on the coast of Asia" (CMI,117), the natural Pacific boundary being only a temporary stage in the growth of the political body. For Olson, the clean *fact* of space is already there as "the central fact to man born in America" (CMI,11), and it only needs to be un-covered by the appropriate means of representation. What this empiricist point of view ignores, however, is that it is just as surely the map itself, with its historically innovative representations of space, which makes the fact of space and the idea of expansionism possible. The map, then, *creates* our conventional space, which is why it is indeed the instrument of modern political internment, just as the ethnographic museum and the great exhibitions of exotica were the semiotic tokens of classical European supremacism.

Not all maps subscribe to the representational forms of the Western model; some, notably in Arab and Japanese cultures, are markedly less "objective."[28] It is the means of representation which determines what is represented, and not vice versa, and even the smallest alteration in the scale of a map will serve to illustrate this. It is important, then, to distinguish the *cartographical* from the *mapping* model that underpins Olson's theoretical realism. His equation of "congruence" is one which is mapped, or made to measure, because it assumes that there is a natural a priori space occupied by a particular constituent reality, and that it is the task of language to honor the caliber and proportions of that space. The phenomenon of space uncovers the true nature (*physis*) of man's "homeland," the revelatory form of a lived (not learned) knowledge which bears with it a presence primordially determined, hitherto hidden but now revealed as natural, measurable, and finite—Husserl's "essence implied in its flowing, vital horizon."[29] The Italian neorealist filmmakers grouped around Rossellini claimed to be working under similar theoretical auspices in their attempt to "help man to recognize the actual horizons of his world."[30] The presentation of simple, phenomenal appearances would reveal what was already there, prior to meaning, and while the diegetic world constructed in the film is fictional, it claims to obey the same laws and present the same spatial experience of the object world as does reality.

One of Olson's ambitions in *The Maximus Poems* is to build up the same kind of steady gaze as in those films, a gaze which is consistent only because it is imperfect and thus "humanly" real. The dominant metaphor in this is that of the *landscape*—"a portion of land which the eye can comprehend in a single view" (AP,21), or the more resonant *scope*, in the Greek sense of a privileged vantage point from which to "descry" a horizon of events on a terrain made up of historical and geographical elements. This practice of looking is that of an amateur, and thus real in its apparently random attention to significant and pedestrian detail alike. The "detail" of Gloucester that is presented in *The Maximus Poems* is "the practice of space in time" for its single, heroic consciousness. Olson's *scope*, however, as it moves into what Robert von Hallberg calls the "visionary mode" of the second and third volumes, increasingly comes to refer to the synoptic scrutiny of a fixed point of view, that of Maximus himself. Its final idealism is to call upon the reader to see what Maximus sees, and blunder when he blunders, rendering him or her the bodiless witness to the spectacle of phenomenal man, whose "ascent is its own mirage," as in the transcendental elevation of "Maximus, At the Harbor": "apophainesthai/ got hidden all the years,/ apophainesthai: the soul/ in its progressive rise" (M,II,71).

There is no place in such a phenomenological realism for the empirical check, the classical response to most "true to life" claims of realism. By contrast, its criterion of correspondence belongs ultimately to an esoteric knowledge, the only kind of knowledge which invests the phenomenological model of cognition—appearances dis-close essence—with value. Intuitive rather than utilitarian, it is this esoteric knowledge that governs Olson's interests in myth in his later work, the aim of which is "the re-arising of a primordial reality in narrative form" (OL,10:64). Absorbing the Jungian belief that all myths are archetypal formations which reveal the truly universal structure of human nature, Olson asserts that the rewriting of myths constitutes a self-sufficient realism, privileged in its source, form, and content. Increasingly, the mythologies become more generalized and less recognizable in terms of Maximus's "personal" mythology. The late quest for a mythic "cure" for postmodern civilization is too arcane to describe here.[32] Not only has it left behind the still unconfronted problems of language and subjectivity, but it also bears no trace of any of the problematic experience of contemporary American life.

Elsewhere, we find Olson falling back upon the older and more traditional measures in his proposals for a new humanism. *Measure*, for him, begins to be the "lengthened shadow of man" which Eliot had thrown back at Emerson: the correctly readjusted proportions of a subjective *Lebensraum* in the object world. Olson's late moralizing mode comes to insist more and more upon an *absolute* coefficient of subjectivity, expressed in the form of a perfect measure for the *size* of an individual life/style. The dimensions of this measure appear to differ little, if at all, from those of the classical humanist balance of *hominem quadratum:*

> The old charts
> are not so wrong
> which added Adam
> to the world's directions
>
> which showed any of us
> the center of a circle
> our fingers
> and our toes describe   (M,I,60)

Olson sets out to locate the most appropriate scale for this human "quantity." Hence his interest in "natural" mathematical constants like Hermann Weyl's 1/137 ("one of the two/ pure numbers out/ of which the world/ is constructed"), or the obsession with working out the ideal scale for cartographical mapping: 1,200 inches to the inch, man's most "representative" stereoscopic range.[33] His most consistent ratio, however, is what he calls the Lake Van Measure, whose scale is computed from the structure of an Armenian cruciform church featured in Josef Strzygowski's *Origins of Early Church Art*. The harmonious dimensions and symmetry of this church take on a special significance:

> there is no gerund nor is metonymy possible
> when the material
>   wood   stone   gold   color   blue
>   the rate of ration 1 : 1200
>
> the Lake Van measure [for repro. of
>   cosmic condition]
> is adhered to. Otherwise
> there is NO ACTIVE SUBSTANCE
>   NO CEREMONY   OR
>   SUBSTANTIVE ACTION POSSIBLE   (AP,63)

Olson's proposed cultural ruling is virtually identical in form to Pound's hypothesis about the "economy" of Quattrocento painting, by which the clearness of the figurative outline directly corresponded to the social and political health of the nation. Both poets, moreover, support their choice of a particular, historical measure with an appeal to racial supremacy. As George Butterick points out, the Armenian measure appears to have a distinct racial association for Olson. Just as he looked for evidence of the "Armenoid-Caucasian physical type" among the Mayans (SW,97), so he argues that since Armenia is on the path "of the Indo-European migration, it may even be considered an Indo-European homeland." Perhaps the Caucasian type has "reasserted itself and persists in Armenia today."[34]

Such are the prescriptions which make up the far edge of Olson's new humanist golden mean. Olson's measure may not be the Greek one he speaks so ill of, for it is appropriated from a Northern European or "Gothonic" culture. But this is a mere displacement, for the *measure* is a Greek idea in itself, a rationalist formula for an idealist ethos, and thus, for Olson, a mixture of antidote and poison, the serpent of his private mythology, returning with a singular vengeance to take its tail in its mouth.

5.   I learned
                     the world does not stop
                     for flowers

Beyond the hue and cry of Olson's postlinear, posthistorical campaign, we might pause and take stock of another kind of circularity feeling its way around his writing, a way so clearly plotted that it seems determined to write its way into our critical attention. For despite Olson's theoretical desire to escape the rationalist discourses of authority, there is indeed a stronger "textual" desire to come full circle, and to acknowledge the contradictions that arise out of the necessity of *observing* the symbolic functions of paternity. In describing how this manifests itself as a chain of metaphorical substitutions, I shall be suggesting that Olson's "holes" are either filled in or else form a larger pattern among themselves. At any rate, subjectivity, in this reading, becomes a properly linguistic quality, and refers to the familiar double-bind of the paternal metaphor.

By the time of "Golden Venetian Light . . ." in the third Maximus volume, Maximus had settled into the ritual of sun-worship and its direct (Poundian) invocation of paternal authority:

> I believe in what the Arabs by
> muezzin—that at least once a day
> (& for me it almost has to be sunset) to face the sun directly
> as often as it is out & let its rays or whatever
> . . . .
> . . . . seen
> & felt as the Father Plant & Day-Sun of
> life he Helios / to quote pater

> Helios etc but equally not to quote
> at all, to recognize this moment I too enter
> into that contract. . . . .   (M,III,212)

The terms of that "contract" ("to quote" and also "not to quote"), if they are fixed by "pater Helios," are familiar enough. Freud, for example, quickly recognized the "delusional privilege" of Judge Schreber's willful abuse of paternal authority in his claim to be able to gaze at the sun without being dazzled.[35] Who, then, would look upon the prohibited face? Ahab would, for he "worships fire and dares to strike the sun," and determines to fix the paternal sun with his own "heliotrope glance" (CMI,73, 62). Ahab must find sanction for his own swollen conduct, and so he grudges the sun its natural movement through the sky. The doubloon he nails to the mast of the Pequod is a metaphoric doubling of his resolve, the "fiery hunt" of his ego to "fix" the sun in like coin. Even if the doubloon is offered as a pledge, the prize for sighting the whale first, we always know that Ahab will be the one to claim it back, thus refusing the symbolic debt. Indeed, in Olson's dance-play, *The Fiery Hunt*, this scene marks the beginning of the Quadrant Dance which suggests a heliotropism proper to the filial relation, but then turns on the other side of the coin, and becomes a Black Eucharist Dance which reverses the magically ordained movements of the Quadrant. Ishmael senses that Ahab's purpose contradicts the metaphoric gesture:

> The sun's a coin but he reads it backward
> the sun's our gold but he sees it dark   (FH,18)

Eventually, Ahab will forsake the use of the quadrant altogether, since it represents an addiction to the solar fix. He will follow "line and log" instead, thereby asserting the autonomy of his own navigational power long before the age of power itself.

Ahab's full frontal ambitions, however, are undone by the lack of confrontation in Melville's text, which chooses for the encounter with the whale, to cathect its back parts: "I celebrate a tail . . . how comprehend his face, when face he has none?" The narrative search for Moby Dick fails to face its object head-on, and Ahab has no eye for a tail. In this he resembles a recurring figure in Olson's work, a Yucatán farmer who first appears in *Mayan Letters*, tending his narcissistic wound after a fight with the tail—of a bird, and, as it happens, a "frigate-bird" with the taunting name of *chii-mi*, or, see me!: "And that toc-bird—the one I may have described to you, that picks its own tail away to beautify itself (or so Stromsvik taught me), leaving the end only, which is a peacock's eye—troubles this poor farmer, troubles him so, he stones them because, says he, can't look into the mirror of that tail, it frightens him, so he has to smash it!" (SW,122). Here, Olson summons up the fear of being "eclipsed" by the heliotropism of a brighter eye. The flight of the bird momentarily blocks out the solar ray, flashes a surrogate glance from its tail, which sends the farmer's memory running for cover.

Maximus, unlike Ahab, is not one who "can seize/ as the sun seizes," but his trope, as we saw in "Golden Venetian Light . . ." is one which finally leans toward the West, and the setting sun. Not the Eastern rising for him, the earliness that melts identity with its harsh novelty. Nor Mao's call for action in "The Kingfishers," welcoming the new materialist dawn of 1946:

> I thought of the E on the stone, and of what Mao said
> la lumière"
> > but the kingfisher
> de l'aurore"
> > but the kingfisher flew west
> est devant nous!
> > he got the color of his breast
> > from the heat of the setting sun!
> . . . .
> Mao concluded,
> > nous devons
> > > nous lever
> > > > et agir   (SW, 168)[36]

The heliotrope is acquiescent, it bends toward a greater will. There is, however, a flower in the East, the lotus, which has absorbed and interiorized the solar qualities, and has no need to submit thus. To eat it, as Odysseus's dreamers did, is to forget origin, father, and identity. The lotus's power to cultivate these effects is a metaphor of self-consciousness itself: the sun internalized by man at the end of a bright day, an interiorized solstice which climbs to its zenith as the old one sets:

> The light is in the east. Yes. And we must rise, act. Yet
> in the west, despite the apparent darkness (the whiteness
> which covers all), if you look, if you can bear, if you can,
> > long enough
>
> > as long as it was necessary for him, my guide
> > to look into the yellow of that longest-lasting
> > > rose   (SW, 172)

This is also the lotus of "Burnt Norton," but it invokes no fear or anxiety because it is lit from within, to illuminate even the darkest unreflecting night in the Platonic cave. Olson's early memory of the heliotrope is reinterpreted in the same manner:

When I was a kid, there were Canadian sailors used to come and visit—not my sisters, which I had none—but girls whom I knew and were older than I, and we would be baby sitters for these chicks, and it was the Canadian Navy on station in Gloucester, and I think the first cigarettes I smoked were Heliotropes, which was the most peculiar—no, excuse me, they were from His Majesty's Ship *Heliotrope*, they were Player's, right? And I think—I still have a queer imprint or stamp of believing that the meaning of—like now I can spill it—of tropism in ourselves is the sun.   (Mu, 11, 34)

Here already, in that slip from "Heliotropes" to "Player's" is the mark of the metaphorical displacement which is the heliotropic movement par excellence, a chronic transference from term to term of a circular chain which copies the orbit of the solar revolution. *Tropism* is Olson's term for that interiorized sun as it moves toward completion in a circle: "that we become sure in the dark, that we move wherever we wish in the six directions with *that* light. . . to *light that dark* is to have to come to whatever it is I think any of us seeks" (Mu, II, 35). Inscribed in that "have to come" are the tropic acts of the subject as it is shunted around the signifying chain under the fierce glare of the *Ol' Sun*, the paternal metaphor. In "White Mythology," Derrida argues that, in the course of his inquiry into the philosophical history of metaphor, he has "been constantly drawn, without willing it, by the movement which turns the sun into metaphor, or attracted by that which turns philosophical metaphor towards the sun. Is not the flower of rhetoric (like) a sunflower—that is, though it is not an exact synonym, analagous to the heliotrope?"37 For Derrida, the heliotropic movement is a perpetual metaphorization suggested in the very structure of metaphor itself; it too will turn toward the (good) sense of the sun, its source, but find that most sensible of signifiers turning away, always occluding its presence. Everything, nonetheless, turns upon the sun, and for the subject, the truth of its own sliding inconsistency is one which *dawns*:

> And I twist
> in the early morning, asking
> where
> does it stop
> . . . .
> And if this is true
> How can you avoid the conclusion, how
> can you be otherwise than
> a metaphor   (AM, 104–5)

Olson's title here is "Concerning Exaggeration, or How, Properly, to Heap Up," an appropriate description of the very properties of metaphorizing. To pursue this description further, we might follow some of that metaphorical activity and the resistance it meets with in a few of its displacements in Olson's writing. "The Twist," for example, eponymously associated with the reflex action of the heliotrope, describes the fishermen's annual memorial at the Cut, flowers strewn from the bridge, "coming/ to this pin-point/ to turn/ in this day's sun" (I,85). The embodied stigma of the "twist" is blazoned across the face of Maximus's rivals, the "poet who read at Gloucester," his nose out of line with the cleft in his chin (OL,4:7), and the sexual challenger of "The Librarian," a former intimate of his wife: "He/ (not my father/ by name himself/ with his face/ twisted/ at birth" (SW, 218). The twist is the colophon of the father, a sun brand embossed on that part of the body which wears itself. In "Tyrian Businesses," the nose-twist flowers into a nasturtium, from *nasua*—nose + *torquere*. The nasturtium is presented as the "trophy" of Maximus; it belongs to the genus *tropaeolum*, itself derived from the same Greek root as trophy, *tropaion*. It is an emblem, and is worn like a badge, or the escutcheon on a shield: "if the nasturtium/ is my shield,/ and my song/ a cantus firmus" (M,I,93). The nasturtium is not a heliotrope, but its leaves are like a shield, and its flowers resemble a helmet; it is so well equipped to ward off the corrosive rays of the solar attack that it can boast an autonomous "cantus firmus" of its own. Written in what Olson calls "logography," with words and not ideas, "Tyrian Businesses" reads across the dictionary instead of using it as a reference book. On the same page as *tropaeolum* is the entry for the tropic bird, the same one we saw in *Mayan Letters*, here called the "toc." Section Five of the poem offers another tropic flight in its account of the voyage of an Essex schooner which ends just short of disaster. The master is an Ahab, and, greedy to pick up driftwood for his onshore use, he seriously damages the screw propeller of his ship, putting his crew in unnecessary peril. Since the navigational will to power has already been linked to the heliotrope, the propeller is seen as a mere extension of that hubris, for it turns on its own steam in disregard for the movement proper to the sun. The poem ends with a recapitulation of that movement in the image of the "fylfot," or *swastika*, the ancient solar symbol which describes the moral properties of heliotropism. In *Themis,* her classic study of Greek religion, Jane Harrison reproduces the surfaces of two Syracusan coins (antique protohistories of Ahab's doubloon): one with three winged legs revolving counterclockwise around a face, the other clockwise around a nonspecific stump. To follow the course of the sun in the northern hemisphere is to turn clockwise, to the right; its converse, widdershins, is the mark of the *sauvastika*, and brings ill-luck because it is not the way of the world.[38] Thus, there is a revolution which moves in direct accord with the sun, and one in which the back is always to the sun. Maximus's troping, as we have seen, is a negative heliotropism which, after half a revolution, would meet up with the setting sun he so desires. However, the way of the father is clockwise, in the other direction. Thus is he whirled first one way, then the other, like the Mole in "West Gloucester," spinning manically on its "star-wheel" nose in the middle of the highway, "like a flower dizzy/ with its own self" (M,III,26).

In the third Maximus volume, the whole textual ensemble takes a turn as poems like "I have been an ability" begin to spiral to the left, on the page itself. The typography appears to veer off westward, but somehow manages to preserve its deference to the paternal trope; to read it, one must turn the page eastward—"My beloved Father/ turning this page to Right/ to write/ this poem/ in your Praise/ in counter/ clockwise/ Circle/ rest Beloved/ Father/ as Your Son. . ." (M,III,121). In the same poem, Maximus assumes that his father, like himself, automatically turned to the right upon leaving his house. One evening, however, he loses "space control" and turns left, a "moral" error which causes him to lose his way for a matter of hours. Similarly, the earlier cannibalism of "Stage Fort Park," in which the father is eaten "piece by piece," had engendered a "steep and left-ward twisting" (M,II,151).

Some of these vertiginous contradictions are inscribed in the heliographs which pirouette around the writing of Olson's signature in "Physically, I am home":

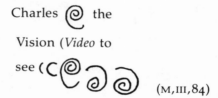

Charles   the

Vision (*Video* to

see (((M,III,84)

Here, in the significance of the name itself, we find both the injunction to turn under the name of the father, and the outlawed will to turn against it. To go right or to go left, Olson's doodled whirligigs are undecided. Elsewhere, when it comes to looking for moral guidance, Maximus consults his own genitals. Short of remarking which way his penis curves, he notes the resemblance of his twisting pubic hairs to the Lybian ostrich feather, which, as Gertrude Levy suggests in *Gate of Horn*, may once have adorned the crown of Egypt, as the symbolic "spiral of entry" which marked off the coronation ceremony as a divine rite de passage.[39]

Twisting westwards, however, makes another of the spiraling poems into the tightly packed "rose of the world" (M,III,104). It rolls itself up by folding inwards to produce its own autonomous center. This inward slewing seems again to be an evasion of the

in counter   in your Praise

clockwise   this poem

to write

Circle   My beloved Father

turning this page to Right

rest   as Your Son

Beloved   Father

goes forth to create Paradise

Upon this Earth

Secular Praise

of You and the

Creator

Forever

And an end to Hell

—end even to Heaven

a life America shall yield

or we will leave her

and ask Gloucester

to sail away

from this

Rising Shore

Forever Amen [...]

heliotropic law, and yet, like the other flowers of idealism, the lotus and the Black Chrysanthemum, it signals a return to the source of the metaphor, since it simply substitutes its own powers of transformation for those of the sun. The Black Chrysanthemum, for example, is called the Golden Flower on account of its alchemical properties, its ability to turn black into gold, night into day; while the lotus, in Indian myth, plays the more auspicious role of generative organ of the universe. These flowers have interiorized the solar ambition, and so they project rather than absorb light. In "Poem 143: the Festival Aspect," it is the inverted lotus growing down from the sky which deputizes for the sun, now bereft of these "deadly rays" which only figure numismatically;

> ....When the world is one again
> with the Universal the Flower
> will grow down, the Sun
> will be stamped
> on the leather
> like a growing
> Coin   (M,III,73)

Like this "growing Coin," Maximus's heliotropic metaphor has been an "exaggeration, properly heaping up." There is no stopping such a metaphor at any moment to say what it means. In this it evoked Heisenberg's Uncertainty Principle (one of Olson's favorite examples of negative capability), which proposes that it is impossible to measure the mass of a moving object. Maximus's heliotrope, however, is caught between these two imperatives, meaning and circulation (mass and momentum), and so it "moves" in two directions at once. In contrast, then, to Olson's demand for an irreversibly unified, kinetic discourse, we have seen, at another level of his writing, how this demand is reversed and divided, creating a "problem" for subjectivity which cannot be resolved.

In his first published article, "Dostoevsky and *The Possessed*," Olson characterizes Stavrogin as one of Dante's Trimmers, unable to turn with the sun, and unwilling to turn against it: neither faithful to nor rebellious against God:

When dictators offer us states in return for our manhood we too wonder smiling, failing to answer, the world turns, and there's Guernica. For the world always turns and the Stavrogins do not move. Why? Because the essence of a Stavrogin is neuter. He *is* his world's sun, but a sun without a fire and heat of its own. He gives life to others but in himself there is finally no life. He cannot generate himself. And in that immobility lies a further horrible truth—all those separate lives which he dominates when they cross each other, destroy each other. Up to a point he creates, but he creates only finally to destroy. His light is black. And it is just because he does nothing that they destroy each other. They cancel out because he, in his neutrality, lends life to the evil as well as to the good. For Stavrogin is without choice, thus he is without direction and thus he and his world are destroyed. Ultimately, *The Possessed* is a horrible puppetry, the tragedy of the inert, the neuter, the ahuman.[40]

The novel incarnates Stavrogin as the *sun*, the sustaining source of each character as they pass through their respective dark nights. Unable to sustain the self-consciousness of his own actions, however, he will be a black sun, or impotent son, and thus the emasculated object of the kind of anxiety which, we will see in the next chapter, is intrinsic to Olson's poetics.

5.   THE CUTT, THE STILE

1.   Always been, since a summer I was a letter carrier, and walked
     it down, walked it down, 15 miles a day, walked Olson down,
     walked him down, looking him over, delivering a letter, here
     and there.

                                                                 Olson

LODGED IN AMONGST the Eliot-Hayward correspondence which
keeps company with the *Four Quartets* manuscripts in Mag-
dalene College, Cambridge, is a curiously displaced postcard sent
from Gloucester, Massachusetts. Addressed to Ezra Pound in St.
Elizabeth's Hospital, its text reads, "E.P. et famille: Here is my Lady
that Possum stole. Best dead Madonna this side Atlantic. . .Yrs
Olson."[1] The postcard depicts the statue of Notre Dame de Bon
Secours which overlooks Gloucester Harbor from the town, unlike
the "Lady" of "The Dry Salvages," whom Eliot suggests ought to be
placed, if anywhere, at the mouth of a harbor. Notwithstanding
Eliot's claim to something of a vested interest in Gloucester, having
spent the summers of his youth there, Charles Olson asserts his
proprietary rights over the maternal in the manner of a jealous son/
brother caught in the matricidal tangles of a family romance. As
Olson's adopted Muse, this Lady, and notably a "dead" one, is thus
appropriated in the ritual spirit of filial anxiety which marks the
patrilineages of modern American poetry. In Olson's case, this is
done through (an appeal for) the mediation, or the intercession, of
the epic father of Pound himself. And for Olson, inheritance is all
or nothing, a case of primogeniture rather than equal division. "To
write as the fathers to be the father," involves him in a lengthy
series of literary relations obsessively crossed by the conflicts of
filiation "with Finch, Melville, Dahlberg, Cagli, & even Pound":

"the mark of my resistance at no longer being a son. For it is a mere son I have been till now" (O&P,xxiii).

Given this obsession with the male "line" of descent, it is no surprise to find that a family romance is writ very large in Olson's work, in the form of a complex literary fiction which, he claims, involves "two live pasts": "the depth to which the parents who live within us (they are not the same) are our definers," and another mythological begetter (myth as history, geography, demography, economics) which "lies as surely in the phenomenological 'raging apart' as these queer parents rage within us." And, Olson maintains that "the work of each of us is to find the true lineaments of ourselves by facing up to the primal features of these founders who lie buried in us" (AP,39–40). Any study of subjectivity in Olson's work is obliged, then, to account for the way in which these "true lineaments" come together in language itself, on what Lacan calls the "littoral" writing space which is heavily retrenched by the fore-bears of the father's way and the mother's body.[2]

On the "littoral" of *The Maximus Poems*, scored over by the coastal features of Gloucester's geocultural history, it is "Father Sea/ who comes to the skirt/ of the City" (M,II,147), and what resists his advance is the maternal "desperate/ ugly/ cruel/ Land this Nation/ which never/ lets/ anyone come to/ shore" (M,II,119). For the foundling himself, it is clear that "a mother is a hard thing to get away from" (M,II,137), and so in a poem which is a funeral ode for the father, "The Story of an Olson and a Bad Thing," the act of birth is perceived as one in which the maternal role is an asphyxial, or constricting, threat upon the precious birthright of the paternal breath (the poetic afflatus):

> There is birth! there is
> all over the place there is
>
>> And if I, in this smother, if I
>> smell out one thing sharp,
>> or another
>> (where his teeth
>> have been in me, there—
>>
>> even you know, Enemie—
>> I speak as modestly as

broken grass, which,
under the flood, tries
to breathe, to breathe!   (AM,19–20)

Olson's inveterate concern with second births—a poetics of origi-
nation which is, at its best, the brave new world of an archeological
antidiscipline, and at worst, the latest song and dance about the
American self-made man—looks to various ways of breaking what
he perceives here as the stranglehold of vaginal delivery. Hence the
fictions of his earlier poems: "Adamo Me . . ." with its self-beget-
ting, and the attempt to "break the fatal male small span" of his
mother's family by claiming direct lineage from his "father's
mother" in "The K" (SW,159). The price to pay for the excising of
the mother is the return of the repressed—"Is it any wonder/ my
mother comes back?"—the rhetorical question of "As The Dead
Prey Upon Us" (AM,248), in which a dead mother returns to her
house once a week; is it an escape from hell, or to bring a hell to his
own escapism? the speaker wonders. Whatever the answer, it is
plain that Olson's writing accommodates paternity at the cost of the
maternal, in enjoying the universal surfeit of fathers which Melville
had characterized as the emancipated condition of the "all-Ameri-
can" people, sons of all, or *allsons*. In a memoir of his father, *The
Post Office*, Olson eulogizes the male ethic of resistance in his father's political stand against employers who had worn him down
for his union activities. Over the course of his father's life, that ethic
crumbles away, and the consequences is a pitiful one in Olson's
mind: his father falls back upon the Swedish-American societies for
aid, associations which he says "are like mothers anyway . . . keeping their children back from the brunt of this country." This "grave-
ly wounded" condition, moreover, becomes synonomous for his
son with the abject sound of the mother tongue, for it is at this late
point in his life that Carl Olson's Swedish begins to come back to
him (PO,28,54).

Olson's declared intent to be reborn, then, can be read in terms of
a *symbolic debt*, and hence the desire to owe everything or nothing to
the father. In Olson's case, the metaphor of rebirth turns upon the
act of *delivery*, substituting a paternal metaphor for a maternal, bio-
logical function. This paternal metaphor of delivery takes over the

function of the now dead womb, and replaces it with the corrective embryonic space of the father's mail-bag:

> The Return to the Mail-Bag, or
> The Postal Union
> of the Son with the Father
>
> A View, in the Mirror, of Myself
> Age 52   (M,III,21)

The poem refers to a photograph reproduced on the cover of *The Post Office*, showing the father in his letter-carrier's uniform, and the baby Olson standing inside his mail-bag. It is from this mail-bag that Olson grows into a man of letters, bent on delivering his message. In an interview in 1969, he claimed that he has "to go every day a further distance to find what I believe in. I'm getting so that my legs—which happily were a letter carrier's . . ." and there the voice tails off, as if we all knew too (Mu,II,170). In the second Maximus volume, the "Proem" is "a precis/ of land I am shod in,/ my father's shoes" (M,II,137), his legs (or legacy) being the hereditary measure by which his influential poetics of space had been paced out. For one who claimed "to come from the last walking period of man" (M,III,220), it is no surprise to hear Robert Creeley referring to Olson's epic poem as a "walker for us all."[3]

Olson's own experience as a letter carrier extended over three summer stretches from 1931 to 1934, and eleven years later, it was by way of a rancorous farewell to a short but mercurial career in Washington as a New Deal Democrat that he turned down the offer of the Post Office Generalship in the new Truman administration. His postal commission, however, is carried out symbolically in a poetics which incorporates the father's law through the understanding that "people want delivery" (M,II,97). In *The Post Office*, Olson had written a description of the transition from real to symbolic paternity, in which the dead father's metaphor is taken to heart. The father's old-fashioned postman morality is upheld as a prescriptive ruling:

He was scrupulous about a letter. He had the idea that it was made up of words (he had the notion that words have value, as signs of meaning and feeling) and because it was a communication between two persons (the idea

Charles Olson, future man of letters, inside his father's mailbag
(Courtesy the Literary Archives of the University of Connecticut Library)

of a person seemed to have meant something to him). Thus he took himself seriously as the last, and only directly personal agent, of several hired by a stamp to see that a letter reached the person to whom it was addressed, or rather (as I am sure he, with his notions, would have put it) for whom it was meant   (PO,47).

This law of delivery, then, which presides over Olson's firm poetic commitment to providing information, demands that a letter always reach its destination, that the destination is its addressee, and that the addressee, "the one for whom it was meant," is also the one for whom it has meaning.[4] In this way is the paternal injunction introjected into a communication model for Olson's poetics.

Given the obsessive filial attachment that supports such a model, what can we say about the ontology of the letter in Olson's writing, a body of work that is as epistolary, in name, as anything in the language?[5] Much has already been said about what William Aiken calls the "vatic" in Olson's soothsaying oracular stance, a voice inherited from, and studied at close quarters in Pound himself.[6] What is more specific to the form of Olson's letter-writing, however, is what we could call the *viatic* as an economy of address, not only in the route taken by the letter as poetry, but also in its highly oral delivery, or, as Olson put it to Cid Corman, "a via of person pushing" (LFO,2). Olson's letters proper have long enjoyed an occult value as unpolished relics, cursory publications of which have been enough to breathe a grander life into the smallest journals. Any study of the larger sets of correspondence, with Dahlberg, Creeley, and Corman, all now in print, will reveal Olson's practice of setting up relations of debt that often resemble forms of *blackmail*, so often does he profit from the claim of being more sinned against than sinning: his commandeering of Corman's journal *Origin*, fully recorded in *Letters for Origin*, is a good example. More often than not, however, the letter is a nursery ground for an essay or poem, while a few have become primary texts in their own right: thus *A Bibliography on America for Ed Dorn* ends, "OK, this has now become a letter," meaning, for Olson, a different kind of text altogether (AP,14).

Indeed, the mode of address in Olson's letter-text is not that of a dialogue at all, it is more like an apostrophe, a reflexive monologue that alternates between the nominative and the dative, enunciator and enunciated, in an attempt to bring them closer together. So too, the mode of delivery is to be both "the muzzle and the charge," and thus to ensure that the message goes by way of Olson's signature, C.O. (c/o), care of his body itself.[7] The letter is therefore *arriviste* in the Derridean sense, because it depends upon a reconstitution of Olson's body for its full effect, an event that must not take place *before* or *after the letter:* "but that my freshness/ not be opened/ (as my mail must not be before I do)" (AM,136). To dispatch the body whole and straight, this is the dream of the *biogrammé*, one of the essentialist desires that lies behind Olson's poetics of postal exhaustiveness. And when he misquotes Pound's praise for Hulme's dictum, he suggestively writes: "It is true, what the master says he picked up from Confusion; all the thots men are capable of can be entered on the back of a postage stamp" (SW,19) (the original reference was to half a sheet of notepaper). Knowledge, then, is to be found on the tip of a wet tongue, just as the body reappears in the breathing space between lines.

Few of the Maximus letters make anything more than a conventional gesture toward the standard dialogic, epistolary medium. The addresses to Vincent Ferrini, for example, which gave birth to the Maximus sequence, openly meditate on the impossibility of dialogue, where language is such an untrustworthy rendezvous:

"I'll meet you anywhere you say. . ."
"I'll try once more to meet you. . ."
"I begin to be damned to figure out where we can meet. . ."
"It's no use
     There is no place we can meet."   (M,I,20–25)

So strong is Olson's monologic will in this that his desire to inhabit the letter goes even further still. He will follow it to the typographers (a touch point for his early editors), and from there into the printing shop itself, as is described here in an extraordinary explanation of his notion of *typos*, the third of his dynamic poetic functions, after *topos* and *tropos:*

It's type, and is typology, and is typification, and is, in a sense, that standing condition of . . . I mean standing, really, in the very literal sense of substantive or object or manifest or solid or material. We get our word type—which interests me, I suppose, as a writer—from it. If any of you have ever seen a piece of movable type, at the bottom is the letter and the block is above. So that in order, really, to imagine a printer doing it . . . he's under your words in order to make the letters of them. Which always delights me literally, as a problem of creation. In fact, literally, I would go so far—if you will excuse my Americanism—to think that you write that way. That you write as though you were *underneath* the letters. And I take that a hell of a lot larger. I would think that the hoofprint of the creator is on the bottom of creation, in exactly that same sense.   (MU,II,34)

The letters here are *underwritten* as if they were insurance against the death or divisibility of the message. The body is a pledge, and its premium is the "blow" it imparts to the letter, a signature (Olson calls it an "archetype," or "initials" [Mu,I,57–58]) that naturalizes the otherwise inert medium of language. For Olson, it was the use of the typewriter that promised to restore the hieratic qualities of this kinetic act to the author-producer, and thus solve the rationalist problem whereby "man is estranged from that with which he is most familiar." He claims, for example, in a letter to Corman, that "the revolution I am responsible for is this one, of the identity of a person and his expression (that these are not separable)" (LFO,106). This is also how Olson attempts to respond to the "problem" of subjectivity which he construed in "Projective Verse" as the "lyrical interference of the individual as ego" (SW,24). Olson's way of doing away with this "interference" is to collapse the enounced subject into the role of enunciation: "How do you, how as a person, not only a poet, does one live one's own image, rather than use it simply for writing—which has been a three hundred year old problem in English and now is broken." The solution, as we shall see, which Olson will try to work into *The Maximus Poems,* is one which is just as old: "an attempt to bring this thing closer and try to talk as though it was *I* rather than some creature like I said I call Maximus, who's been the person that's presided" (Mu,II,27). With the body to back up each word, there would be no interference, lag or gap in the "effect" of subjectivity, a lag of the sort which Ed Dorn, Olson's most assiduous student, dramatizes in *Gunslinger:*

> . . . . The Ego
> is costumed as the road manager
> of the soul, every time

        the soul plays a date in another town
        I goes ahead to set up
        the bleachers, or book the hall
        as they now have it.
        the phenomenon is reported by the phrase
        I got there ahead of myself
        I got there ahead of my I
        is the fact
        which not a few mortals
        misread as intuition.

The character thematized as "I" is allegorically killed off and then revived in the course of Dorn's poem. Olson's anxiety about the fickle identity of "Maximus," and his attempt to stabilize that identity with his own body, cannot be resolved in the same allegorical manner. As the Maximus sequence grows in length, this problem throws Olson back on to increasingly precarious ground; his body becomes the only (if ambivalent) referent of the poem.

2.   the poem drooping shy and unseen that I always carry, and
        that all men carry. . . . our lusty lurking masculine poems
                                                    Whitman

    Olson's favored term for the immanence of the enunciatory body is "resistance," in which the dynamic force of "natural," bodily energy is incorporated, and then presented as a verticality acting as a check on a horizontal movement. This idea of resistance, for example, governs Olson's prosodic concern with quantity, and in particular with the syllable as a phallic measure (the body scanning the line), weighting each syllable as it "penetrates downwards." In Shakespeare's late plays, these verticalities "tend at any time to increase the standing against the running power of verse," while in Dante's *De Vulgario Eloquentia*, Olson finds that "the resistances of feeling, thinking, and acting" all conspire to form the maximum ballast of "breath (aspirate) accent quantity, all three at once" (SW,35,37). Stopping the line like this is an assertion of the poet's dominant will over the assumed plastic instrumentality of language (an analogue of the Welsh poets who "stop the battle" (M,I,97) in order to hypostatize the events in verse).

Clearly, the keenness of this autonomous will—"how, to get it, up" (LFO,129)—is associated with phallic consistency and Olson's own unambiguous regard for a truly phallocentric activity; posthumanist man, in Olson's mind, now had the opportunity to harness "primordial & phallic energies & methodologies which . . . make it possible for man, that participant thing, to take up, straight, nature's, live nature's force" (HU,23). In the Yucatán, he discovered stone stelae, the tops of which bore traces of red paint, and concluded that, like the Greek cult of Hermes which placed phallic *herms* at crossroads, the Mayans had found a productive cultural space for phallic worship. Such an activity is only productive, however, when the glyphic signifier holds down the real: "It is difficult to reify this now, because none of us, now, find it easy to take a phallus as an image (i have a hunch we reverse the ancients, and make metaphors out of bananas and such rather than, as they, make the phallus, in a sense, a metaphor. For my assumption is that they took the phallus—& sex—as simply man's most immediate way of knowing nature's powers—and the handiest image of that power" (LFO,57). In a series of lectures at Black Mountain, Olson outlines the movement of Cro-Magnon man away from the cultural iconography of the cave, wall-painting, the cup-hole, and the Venus statuettes, to the "art of the sign of speech," and its correlation with the dominance of the phallic as both a "real and abstract" image: "notice this doubleness, that man, from the beginning, took the real as at once literal & abstract, that both the cup-hole and the Venus could stand for the red-force as later man's phallus and language could stand likewise" (OL,10:52). Similarly, in his *Reading at Berkeley*, Olson suggests that his embarrassment with the phallicisms of the first Maximus poem was due to the flimsiness of the image as an *image*, which "is a lotta bullshit, unless it's really the same as the fact, literally" (Mu,I,136). Language, then, associated at its origins with a phallic signifier, must be constantly reactivated by the proximity of a real phallus.

Hermes himself appears in a late Maximus poem as a model of the man who "ought never to be/ anything but wielding/ his/ sky-tale/ *his* leather phallus *his*/ dildo" (OL,9:70). As messenger and letter carrier of the gods, an alternating father/son of Priapus, and a friend of fishermen, he is an Olson through and through. His ithyphallic stone, moreover, doubling up as a boundary marker to set the limits of the letter carrier's route, joins with the other stone elements of a phallic worship fully intact in Olson's work.[8] These stones are a corrective to the omphalocentric "navel of the Earth" at Delphi, the "E on the stone" in "The Kingfishers" which Olson designates as the symbolic birthmark of rationalist culture. All of the images Olson employs to replace the "navel" are outrightly phallic, the most conspicuous being the Diorite Stone, a quasi-vegetation figure from Hurrian myth, which obeys Hesiod's growth principle in swelling to be "27,000 miles tall" so that it has to be severed by a meat cleaver (OL,9:44). The identification with Maximus, who stands "on Main Street like the Diorite/ stone" (M,II,51), is explicit. The topography of the later poems is marked by the increasing attention devoted to standing stones, like the "stone soldiers" of the "undressed" monoliths in the diorite rock formations around the Annisquam river. From the phallic mothers of the Madonna figurines in Gloucester's back-gardens, and the "lingam" of City Hall itself, to the "great Menhirs," "dromlechs," and "cromlechs" posted offshore in Settlement Cove, these sizable stone erections set out the topographical limits for Maximus's thinking. The only stone feature of Goucester's landscape which is significantly antiphallic is nonetheless used to support the notion that Nature sanctions the patrilinear game of resistance. This rock formation is called the Whale's Jaw, and Maximus recalls the father standing inside it: "I have a photograph, him/ a smiling Jonah forcing back those teeth/ Or more Jehovah, he looks that strong/ he could have split the rock/ as it is split . . ." (M,I,32). Unlike Melville, who "agonized over paternity," and whose later, sexually ambiguous heroes were therefore "soft, hermaphroditical Christs" (CMI,104), Olson wants to present Maximus as a successful son, one who would take up the father's resistant example of warding off castratory threats like that of the Whale's Jaw.

As I have suggested, Olson's resistant front draws imaginary support from the fantasmatic totality of a fully corporate body: "his body intact and fought for, the absolute of his organism in its simplest terms . . . the house he is, this house that moves, breathes, acts" (SW,13). It is this body, in a Projectivist poetics, that is seen as the reliable producer of breath, and also a new democratic medium for grounding the poetic afflatus in the organ of the lungs. The poet must go "down through the workings of his own throat" to the lung, the undifferentiated source of aspiration (SW,26). In bypassing the "workings," however—the contours and outcroppings of the oral and nasal cavities, the glottal walls, etc.—the projective poet must bypass the full scale of phonic difference, for it is in the "workings" that the vocal apparatus eroticizes what Barthes calls the "grain of the voice," where the heterogeneous materiality of the body is registered phonemically.[9] Olson's manifesto proposes to put *breath* before *sound*, because the lung is a more functionally homogeneous vehicle for the whole and undivided body. The ear, Pound's phonic guide, is a poor cousin, because it passively registers all sounds, and, in contrast to the phallic swelling and contraction of the lung, is only an inert one-way valve.

The projective thrust of breath is a sexualized act, and its preferred base, as Olson points out to Creeley, is a phallic one: "if you hide, or otherwise duck THE ORAL as profoundly phallic—if you try to ignore the piles of bones . . you leave out the true animal bearing of the species and in the end. . . . you pay for it by sex, and sex alone, becoming the only ORAL, and thus the very inversion of the whole PHALLIC base—you get the present ultimate DELIQ-UESCENCE (example Hitler, who, was a copralagnist [sic])."[10] George Butterick has perceptively glossed a line from the first Maximus poem—"faun and oral/ satyr lesbos vase" (M,I,4)—with the letter extract above. The prodigiously phallic presence of the satyr is made to compensate for the literal orality of lesbianism. The mouth must only be a place of projection, a portal through which the bad object is expelled. Ginsberg's oral performance is a striking example of his projective inspiration, with its ultimate claim to a discourse of exorcism, to a psychophysiological deliverance from the repressive taboos of Western speech formation. Although he does not share the Beat taste for spontaneity, Olson's respect for the "mousike" or *enthousiasm* which Plato had so mistrusted in the Homeric poets,[11] is drawn from the same desire for full bodily expression as Ginsberg's "yoga of breath" or McClure's archly Romantic credo that "poetry is a muscular principle, an athletic song or whisper of fleshly thought."[12] Increasingly, Olson's reference to the body becomes an occult one. In one of his "incongestible" essays in the Sixties, he had proposed a new psychology of the humors called *proprioception,* which involved "SENSIBILITY WITHIN THE ORGANISM BY MOVEMENT OF ITS OWN TISSUES" (AP,16). Proprioception, "the property of one's own perceptions," or, as Olson preferred it, "the physical soul," marks the beginning of an obscure terminological adventure which culminates in his late protestations of some sort of orthodox faith in references to God as "fully physical" (M,III,13).

The other side of Olson's commitment to the body is the chauvinism of its political appeal, especially apparent at Black Mountain in the curricular insistence on bodily involvement in every workable area of community practice from field labor to poetry reading. As Martin Duberman notes, under Olson's term as rector, the elective elitism of the community was such that it increasingly assumed "the 'natural' superiority of some men over others (and almost all men over all women), and—in direct opposition to the style which prevails in most of today's communes—the necessity of leading *hot* lives and of asserting (usually through indifference) the *supremacy* of man over nature."[13] Almost as an extension of this Olympian ideal of *free* bodily enterprise, Olson's early drug encounters with Leary and Ginsberg bolstered his belief in a physicalist revival of the old dream of free will: "the advantage of the autonomic drugs . . . is simply they restore the fact that we live in the autonomic system, which, as far as I understand, is *to preserve our organs from our will* . . . it's without interference of the will" (Mu,I,49). The result of this would be to free the assumed *native* desires of the body. The same Lawrentian innocence which led Olson to patronize the lifestyle of the modern Mayans and their "natural law of the flesh," tempts him with the lure of a liberationary discourse— the prototype of a later discourse of the sixties that is based upon the "free body," the article of the hippy faith, and the core of a sexual politics aimed against the despotic law of puritanical imperialism; cure the body and the mind will follow, as Reich had argued of the political "neuroses." My concern, here, however, is not with the particular shortcomings of that cultural politics and its ideologies of freedom. Nor is it with the moral irresponsibility of Olson's phallocentric "Lawrentian innocence." On the contrary, what I have been arguing is that Olson's critical attention to the unity and autonomy of the body is a direct consequence of his theoretical crusade against the *false* "interference" of subjectivity, and in favor of a more "natural" mode of experience. If that crusade forces him to espouse, finally, a *disembodied* poetics, whether spiritually or politically, then it should also reveal the irony of its own contradictory relation to the practice of subjectivity within language itself.

3.　　　　The scale of the painting became that of the painter's body
　　　　　　　　　　　　　　　　　　　　　　Frank O'Hara

Notwithstanding the legendary giantism of Olson's own frame, the orthopedic totality of the bodily image is writ large across *The Maximus Poems,* its fullest projection being that of the world's body itself, a conflation of Earth and Ocean, before "Earth started to come apart at the seams, some 125 million years awhile back." While the map of this undivided continental mass is reproduced on the cover of the second volume, the true "mirror stage" of human history is recorded in "On First Looking Out Through Juan de la Cosa's Eyes." There, Columbus's cartographer, the first to produce a *mappemunde,* is credited with the discovery of the world's "identity." This representational feat Olson holds to have "completely changed the human species, literally" (Mu,I,64), a feat prefigured by Troilus's hindsight from the seventh sphere, and culminating perhaps in Yuri Gagarin's "look at the whole world over his shoulder in one glance." In his Atlas-like role, Maximus features variously in the colossal cosmic projections of the later sequences, identified with the likes of Ptah and Ymir, the respective Memphite and Norse gods of creation, and from whose bodies the world is manufactured. When Maximus is not in this cosmic position—"the end of the world/ is the borders/ of my being" (M,II,127)—his body is stretched tightly across the topography of Gloucester, or its sister city, Dogtown.

These images of self-projection belong to a familiar Renaissance episteme of discovery. In the lavish cartographical conceits of Metaphysical poetry, for example, a poetics of exploration takes as its metaphorical guide for the conquest of newfoundlands the projected features of the female body. To carry out his contract with the known world rather than an unfamiliar one, Maximus enlists his own body. The economy, however, is the same, for it reveals a bodily wholeness as a sum of parts. Donne provides the appropriate metaphor in "The First Anniversarie":

> . . . . .nothing
> Is worth our travaile, grief, or perishing,
> But those rich joyes, which did possesse her heart,
> Of which she's now partaker, and a part.
> But as in cutting up a man that's dead,
> The body will not last out, to have read
> On every part, and therefore men direct
> Their speech to parts, that are of most effect;
> So the world's carcasse would not last, if I
> Were punctuall in this Anatomy.

Drawing upon the formative science of anatomy, which, at this stage, is little more than a taxonomical exercise in the naming of parts, Donne's metaphor is that of a *parsing* of the body, in the sense of the grammatical exercise now pedagogically defunct. For Olson, this kind of parsing is a suitable athletic preparation for the philospher-kings. Despite Maximus's antirationalist claim that "no Greek will be able/ to discriminate my body" (M,II,14–15), this was precisely the inspiration for Olson's book on the body, intended as a primer for the "fables of the organs" project, neither of which was written. It was to be "a record in the perfectest language I can manage of the HEART, LIVER, BRAINS, KIDNEY, the organs, to body them forth, to give a full sense of the instrument of the organism, approached on the simplest of premises" (O&P,82). In the course of undergoing various hospital tests which were to confirm the terminal nature of his cancer, a machine was used to print out a full physiological description of Olson's bodily condition in much the same way as a seismograph might record the changing condition of the earth's body: "My levy/ like saying the inside of me/ printed direct/ My soul really exists—it is me when physically/ I am spectographic and intellectually my words."[14] Olson delighted in the idea of such an analysis. A sequel I much prefer, however, primarily because of its trans-proprioceptive nature, was the doctor's announcement that the source of his patient's pain had been located in "a special nerve called the maximus nerve," a junction where the nerves intersect before entering the brain.[15] Like the classic hysterical symptom, it is as if part of the body was trying to "speak" the Titanism of Olson's own writing neurosis.

Elsewhere, the parsing model is regularly pressed into service:

My own wrists and all my joints, versus speech's connectives

(M,I,43)

      the crucialness being that these places or names
      be as parts of the body, common, & capable
      therefore of having cells which can decant
      total experience.   (AM,274)

Each "cell" is a miniature Gestalt that can reproduce the experience of the whole body regardless of the combinations into which the cells are thrust. The most productive application of this functionalist model is in dance, Olson's favorite projective discipline. In "Syllabary for a Dancer," a series of letters written for the Indian dancer, Nataraj Vashi, he describes the exemplary importance of dance for the modern writer who

has been forced, today, to re-awake his attention to the kinetics of words, to the syllables as the eyes and fingers of his medium, to the nouns & verbs as the torso and limbs, to the connectives as the ankles and wrists of speech, and to his total use in any given go as more than the sum of any of these parts, or of their revelances to each other, as a dance which has achieved its implicit form is more than the body and its movements, is, actually that thing we used to call the beauty of it.[16]

The astral body returns here, despite Olson's close attention to the "syntax" of body and language, and despite his lifelong opposition to a metaphysics of the abstract—"and I don't mean at all any asiatic passivism" (LFO,54).

The political metaphor made possible by this homology, between parts of the body and parts of speech, is closely associated with the logic of the Platonic "body politic," for a regime like that of the

Republic rules not by speech alone, in the *dictatorial* manner, but along with the totalitarian support of its appeal to bodily consistency:

> by the rule of its parts by the law of the proportion
>   of its parts
> over the World   over the City   over man   (M,III,40)

This is how the political will of the *wanax* figures in *The Maximus Poems* is maintained. As the warrior high-king of the Myceneans, and associated by Olson with Celtic *Ari-Ri* heroes like Cuchulain who exercise their rule from the literal evidence of the ruler's body, the *wanax* proves the continuing worth of his claim to sovereign power by an outright show of exhibitionism.[17] Enyalion, the Cretan war-god and composite hero of the third Maximus volume, is thus in the "service of the law of the proportion/ of his own body," for he is only as good as his last public showing; "the beautiful one Enyalion/ who takes off his clothes/ wherever he is found/ on a hill/ in front of his own troops,/ in the face of the men of the other side, at the command/ of any woman who goes by" (M,III,38).

There is a level at which this economy of bodily parts can be said to articulate writing itself, rather than serve merely as a compositional model or method, as it does, for example, in Olson's adoption of the Greek epic formula of *rhapsodia*—"songs stitched together"[18]—as the rubric for *The Maximus Poems*. In a judicious article, Rosemarie Waldrop suggests that the structural organization of Olson's writing works by relations of contiguity rather than similarity. In other words, it moves horizontally, metonymically spreading into adjoining areas of meaning like a map, and unlike the metaphorical plan of allegory, simile, or image, each plagued by their "vertical transcendence." Distinguishing this impulse from the "metaphorical" project of *The Cantos*, Waldrop argues of Olson's "Tyrian Businesses," an apparently metaphorical poem, that there slides beneath this surface another economy, "this time by contiguity, namely the parts of the body."[19] Her reading lists successive references in the poem to the waist, the breast, the buttocks, the scalp, the womb, the voice, the penis, the heart, the nose, the tail, the face, the eye, the teeth, the stomach, the vagina, the rib-cage (I have added one or two of my own). Far from outlining a metonymic economy of bodily parts, however, it seems to me that Waldrop has actually uncovered a metaphorical movement, and one which comes full circle, like that of the heliotrope which I discussed in the last chapter. Each of these parts, of course, is an image of the whole, while the shift from part to part is an invitation to join up all the dots, and fill in the outline of a full body: "As a man is a necklace/ strung of his own teeth" (M,I,37). The most consciously metonymic organization of text in Olson's poem is the section given over to fragments of dictionary definition as his glance crosses the pages of his Webster's: from "heart" to "heather," from "metaphrast" to "metacenter," from the "nose-twist . . . my trophy" to "the toc" or tropic bird, and so on. That such a motivated attempt to transgress the codes of compositional technique should still unconsciously fall under the gravitational pull of the bodily image, is a salutory lesson for Olson's "open" poetics in general. And it will remind us that no poetry is *free*, no matter whether one wants to do a good job or not.

Waldrop closes her argument by linking the spatial organization of Olson's text with his extrinsic *push* across the American land-scape. In doing so, she revives the old project of constructing a *different* American solution to the European problem of time and history.[20] Ever since his graduate thesis on Melville, Olson had clung to this epic ambition, and *Call Me Ishmael* had indeed pro-posed a number of related projects for the American writer to pur-sue: to explore, for example, how a cultural politics of American geography might be written. Despite the lessons of Carl Sauer, however, despite his own eulogizing of the migrant spirit, and de-spite his research plans for further work on the Mayans, on the American Indians, and on a prose epic about the West, Olson *stays put*, and binds himself obsessively to the confined spaces of Gloucester's topography. More of a prison—"Limits/ are what any of us/ are inside of" (M,I,17)—than a working exile, it is Glouces-ter's hold on Olson's bodily history, rather than its convenience as a productive working "space," that increasingly determines his rela-tion to the local.

4.   But the page is missing. As my page is. I have to know
        my own missing page. It's there. I can send for it. . . .
        Only I don't do it. Why not?

                                                        Olson

   Both Donald Davie and Don Byrd have suggested that Gloucester
has no special privilege as a place, and that Olson had no "mystical
compulsion" to present it as such, or to *choose* it for some particularly topical value.[21] To insist on this, however, is to see *The Maximus Poems* as an *anonymous* text, stripped of any part of the desire
to literally map out a bodily subjectivity across Gloucester's topography: what Maximus calls "the topological as a prime and li-
bidinal/ character of man" (M,I,144). In exploring this desire, I shall
argue that it is not manifest through any consuming image of
wholeness (Maximus *covering* the earth) but through a series of
cumulative associations with Gloucester's *detachment:* geographi-
cally, as a littoral, estranged from the mainland; historically, drained
of the founding idealism of its settlement; economico-politically, in
decline ever since the productive balance of its early fishing industry; and symbolically, disinherited from the temporal spaces of
Olson's childhood, spent there as a summer resident. All of the textual anxiety provoked by these losses is bound up and emblematized
in the metaphorical wound which figures prominently throughout
Olson's work—as the Cut: a canal slashed through marshland in
1643 by the first minister of Gloucester in an attempt to facilitate
shipping access to the Annisquam River from Gloucester's harbor.
The Cut is not only the central landmark in Maximus's historical
and topographical adventures. It also serves as a castration trace,
the site of any reading of the symbolic debt in Olson's poem.
   As the image of the Cut suggests, there is a counterpoint to the
ambitious fables of wholeness like the creation myths and the
mappemunde in *The Maximus Poems.* Maximus's vast, imaginary em-
pires are divided by lines of fragilization, like the great rifts formed
in the earth's crust by the breaking up of the continental plate. One
of these rifts, the Cabot Fault, runs through Gloucester itself, and
Maximus, like Antony, does the splits across it: "one leg upon the
Ocean one leg/ upon the Westward drifting continent" (M,III,37).

His task is to supervise the splitting, and to bridge the subsequent gap, and so we will find him "at the place of the parting of the seams of *all* the earth" (M,III,166). Similarly, Olson's own speculative account of Western history emphasizes moments of discontinuity which separate the periodic ideologies of the "human universe": 3378–1200 B.C., the Sumerian thrust of the first metropolitan "will to cohere" interrupted by a successive "will to disperse"; the East/West cultural division of 450 B.C., with Herodotus inaugurating the rational order of *logos;* in 1630, the birth of Cartesian subjectivity, and also, coincident with Gloucester's founding, the protohistory of capitalism: 1910–1950, the modernist parenthesis, and finally 1956, the new millennium of the poets.

If this display of historicism strikes us as somewhat willful, there is little that is gratuitous about the role of the Cut in the "personal" history of Olson's writing. He describes it as "a river which I have only recently discovered is a prime image of all my experience, of woman of birth of my own town of me—of who I am, the subject of my work" (OL,10:20). Olson's own history is straddled across the Cut, his childhood spent in summers in Stage Fort, and his later writing period spent "over the Cut" on Fort Point, in the city proper. The exact time of that crossing over coincides with his first attempts at writing, while living in a boarding house on the canal bank in an area known as Kent Circle: "Wrote my first poems/ and an essay on myth/ at Kent Circle/ at Kunt Circle" (M,II,129). "Kunt Circle" is libidinally overdetermined, not only because of its inverted triangular shape, but also on account of its numerous sexual associations for Olson, including several concurrent love affairs, his declared desire for his landlady, and the clearly fetishistic memory of his Aunt Vandla, who lived nearby at "90 Middle, the gambrel/ which is sliced off" (M,II,181)—the knowledge and disavowal of her "phallic" cut displaced from its lower position onto the door handle, or on to her throat where she wore a gaudy brooch to cover a goitered swelling. (This is the same aunt who had made him the "gift" of the Cut as a child in the form of a cardboard toy village, associated by Olson from then on with "the whole Cut" [M,I,85]).

An early poem, "The Twist," gives us a sense of Olson's sexual investment in the Cut, for it is there that the puzzling memory of his first poem is resolved. In 1940, he had written of the canal:

"Stretched fabric across the hips of the earth/ French cut/ Discovering the global curve beneath"; and thirteen years later, in "The Twist"—"the Annisquam/ fills itself, at its tides, as she did/ the French dress, cut/ on the bias" (M,I,82). According to Butterick, the association is from a dream statement, itself a displacement of an erotic memory of his wife in a French dress, "cut on the bias."[23] Our next discovery in the poem is that the name of the English river which links Worcester (the name of Olson's American birthplace) with Gloucester is the Sever(n), its own Cut, and thus a counterpart of the Annisquam (or Annie's Quim, as of Cape Ann), which, in Olson's words, "binds my own psyche."[24] Seeking a vantage point safe from the hazards of this densely sexualized landscape, it is the bridge over the Cut which serves Maximus as a position from which to disavow all proximity to these castration threats:

> . . . . .They tear down
> the Third Ave. El. Mine stays
> as Boston does, inches up.
> I run my rails
> on a monorail.   (M,I,85)

It is from this bridge that the annual memorial service for Gloucester's lost fishermen is conducted in the form of a floral tribute thrown into the Cut. As "the flowers break off," the "calyx and the corolla," their labia, are scattered onto the teeth of the dog-rocks which guard the entrance to the Cut's tidal waters, while the "anther" and the "filament," the male pollen-bearing stamen "drives on" upstream, and is thus preserved intact. The dog-rocks themselves (Scylla "in the Charybdises of the Cut waters" [M,I,52]), are associated with a canine agent of castration referred to throughout Olson's writing: from the early postal encounters with snapping dogs (one Airedale in particular, who appears in a photograph of the father in The Post Office "in a new uniform, with Cuppy pawing him to the shoulders like some mythic lion" [PO,38]) to the more explicit anxiety of "Stevens Song"—"canine/ head piercing/ right through the letter carrier/ trousers and into the bone" (M,III,33). Tyr, Norse god of war, however, appears as a figure who heroically accepts the loss of his "living hand" (M,III,47) as a pledge to appease the dangerous wolf dog Fenris. His qualities are thus prized *at the cost of his loss,* or on account of his bodily debt. Such a recognition of the value of an enabling lack does not extend to the "father" figures in Olson's work. William Stevens, for example, the "first Maximus," who is stripped of civic privileges that include the ownership of the Cut (from 1642), is seen merely as an object of unwarranted persecution. So too, in the case of Olson's father, whose privileges of seniority are withdrawn by his employers, whose letter carrier's shoulder is "dropped" from the weight of his mail bag, and whose physical hardships cumulatively contribute to his early death. What the son owes to the father's loss is displaced or else denied altogether.

The history of the Cut itself reveals this economy in a more literal way. Legally established in 1641 as a passage subject to toll, a fixed, enabling debt designed to pay off the builders over the course of the next twenty-one years, Olson is appalled to discover that it was still being used over sixty years later to exact payment upon users and thereby swell profits. This fact is confirmed by the will of Stevens's grandson, which describes the Cut as "a certain priviledged place . . . where vessels pass through for money." Olson reads this as a sign of the city's "perjorocracy" (with some of the Poundian trappings of "usury"). In the same way, the fishing industry had pushed its profit margins far beyond the thirty-thousand-dollar debt upon which the settlement was originally founded, thereby moving its "monies/ away from primary production and trade" (M,I,72).

Increasingly, Olson meets the Cut's symbolic debt head-on. In "The Carpenter," the poet records the purchase of Babson's *History of Gloucester,* a second-hand copy which has one page missing, "the crucial page, the page which tells about the Cut." It is simply a matter of asking the Library of Congress to send a photostat—"only I don't do it. Why don't I?" This missing information is holding up the "poem I promised can be written." The delay takes on significant dimensions when it threatens to reveal "how one puts one's signature under the table where nobody . . . sees it." What it questions is the "authorization" of information in *The Maximus Poems,* for it is at this point that the very loose identity of Olson/Maximus begins to drift apart: "My own/ are not Maximus's. I cannot inform you direct. I am merely/ the maker. I only see what's underneath/ the table. You mustn't ask me/ to disclose that way" (OL,6:52–54). The same identity crisis writes itself into "Maximus, in Gloucester, Sunday, XLV," as "the/ plague of my own unsatisfying possible identity as/ denominable Charles Olson," for at the end of the poem the text claims its origin in Stage Fort Avenue, which is across the Cut, instead of in Fort Square, where Olson lives (M,III,80). Similarly, in "Maximus to Gloucester," the view across the Cut, from one address to another, is seen as a mirror-image, "like backwards/ of a scene/ I saw the other way/ for thirty years" (M,I,107). The Cut, then, plays an enabling role as a seal of authorial identity for *The Maximus Poems*. But to do so, its function as a castration trace must be disavowed: Olson, in "Maximus to Gloucester, Letter 11," for example, claims that his father's grave is in Stage Fort Cemetery, in the proximity of the Cut, when it is actually situated back in Worcester's Swedish cemetery.[25]

As a consequence, perhaps, of Olson's haunting claim that he finds it "impossible, like they say around here, to get across Cut Bridge" (Mu,II,110), it is Maximus's quest as "Citizen of the Cut, now standing for election" (OL,6:61), to restore the missing page, and span the "Promised Land" of the Cut. In order to be the infallible son, his electoral platform must be *on* Cut Bridge itself, and this indeed is increasingly the place of enunciation of *The Maximus Poems* as it moves into the last volume. Finally, the only way to maintain control over the subjective core of the poems is for Maximus to literally speak from the bridge over the Cut, thereby keeping the castratory at bay, offshore: "no more dogs/ to tear anything/ apart . . . / no more dog-rocks for the tide/ to rush over not any time again/ for wonder/ the ownership/ solely/ mine" (M,III,53) Sovereign rights over the Cut, once exercised by Stevens, are now there to be repossessed and defended. Hence, in the extraordinary "Oceania" sequence, Maximus sustains an all-night vigil on the bridge, observing his sentinel-like defiance of a police cruiser on patrol in the bay. The mandate to his little principality carries with it familiar powers of regal fiat:

> And the tide
> came to a stop

> while I wrote up to the last line over
> on the bridge
> abutment (actually
> swinging
> gate of
> bascule   (M,III,156)

This is the ultimate show of *resistance* in Olson's writing. The tidal waters are "stopped" as the Cut is forced to close under the actual bodily weight of Maximus. The closing of the Cut cancels the symbolic debt, for body and voice, "Olson" and "Maximus," are brought together in the same enunciating position, and thus the pseudo-autobiographical "interference of the individual as ego" is dispensed with.

Similarly, in "Golden Venetian Light . . ." where Maximus chooses to consecrate the filial will of his sun-worship, the "ripping red river" is suddenly stilled, coagulated, and cleansed by "Zeus' dust," the paternal seed now taken up autonomously by the son (M,III,212). "Astride the curb of the embankment," Maximus chooses the Cut as the site of sun-worship in order to consummate his long observance of phallic shrines (in this case, it is one of Gloucester's stone herms, "the Aldermen's polished granite statement"). As the most hieratic of *The Maximus Poems*, "Golden Venetian Light . . ." seals the veneration with which we have seen the Cut invested in Olson's work. It also lays open to question Davie's comment about Olson's lack of any "mystical compulson" in choosing to write from and about Gloucester. Davie is guided by Williams's example in insisting on the *local*: Williams, for example, writes of Poe that "what he wanted was connected with no particular place: therefore it *must* be where he *was*."[26] In analyzing Olson's symbolic debt, I have, in a sense, been exploring Williams's statement in the light of Freud's *wo es war, soll ich werden*, which describes the psychic force of the "local" subjective makeup at another level—"where it [the id] was, there I [the ego] must be." Freud's meaning rests upon the understanding that the *place* of subjectivity is necessarily determined by unconscious effects: every place, then, is a "particular" place, not by arbitrary choice, but by psychic necessity. Hence it is the Cut that "chooses" or determines the economy of subjectivity in *The Maximus Poems*. Olson is "chosen" by Gloucester, just as Hawthorne is "chosen" by Salem, and Thoreau by Concord. Each, in turn, tries to write his way out of that external determination/ internal necessity that comes with a "sense of place": Hawthorne, who exorcizes his ancestral sins in *The Scarlet Letter*, Thoreau, who obsessively records his self-determination in *Walden*, and Olson, whose Maximus willfully mans the Cut, and asserts imaginary control over the fate of *The Maximus Poems*.

5.   The Genetic
                                is Ma the Morphic
                                is Pa . . .

Maximus's position on the bridge reminds us of Olson's own chosen role as a literary watershed, his "bridge-work" (the title of a section from "Proprioception") serving to act as a "ramp" "fr the Old Discourse to New," and also across the Atlantic, "bridging a peninsula too to/ a continent" (M,III,150), in establishing a new community of English-speaking poets with British writers like Jeremy Prynne and Andrew Crozier. The Old Discourse, in its more local form as distinct from the full span of the Greek *logos*, dates from the moment of Cartesian subjectivism: "exactly/ 300/ years/ writing/ at the stile" (M,II,129). Among the poems that draw on information from Gloucester town records from the seventeeth century, a "stile" is mentioned as leading into the field adjacent to "the Cutt" during this period. For Olson, this becomes a metaphor for the old "stile" of discourse that lifts language over the real, in other words, a discourse of abstractions. Just as surely, it is associated with the *stele*, or herm, that marks out the delivery route (if not also with the phallic *stylus* of inscription). The corrective model for the "male style" of the Old Discourse is to be

                      Femine
                      Writing so that all the world
                      is redeemed, and history
                      and all that politics,

> and "State" and Subjection
> are for once, done away with,
> as the reason
> of writing.   (AM,295)

This is a powerful claim, but then womanhood, Olson insists, "is power enough to blow/ the world apart" (OL,9:64), a nuclear source whose energy might be tapped and then employed in the filial "resistance" game played out in so many of the countercultural wars of the sixties. In his proposed restoration of the feminine, Olson takes up the inheritance of Goethe's "eternal feminine," the oldest muse, or life-force, of the artist, and thus the longest-standing male property of all. Truth is held there in the woman as other, but it is veiled and arcane, an "alternative" field, as "dangerous as any/ misleading lady" (SW,186); or in Chaucer's maxim, frequently cited by Olson—*mulier est hominem confusio*—a meaningfully obscure order of reality, protecting a much richer logos which must finally belong to man himself. This is Olson's last quest, *cherchez la femme*, and it takes him not by way of Freud's "riddle of femininity," but by the less royal road of Jungian archetypology (and more specifically, the Great Mother, partial object of the Feminine Archetype).

In the Goethean *Poetry and Truth*, Olson characterizes poetic production in terms of an autonomous process involving "the blow upon the world" by which archtypes are fashioned in the unconscious and then "projected" on to the poet's conscious writing space like an "imprint," or Paracelsian "initial" (Mu,II,9,34,44). To Olson, this suggests a fully *typed* speech of pure "archetext," where language would be shaped through the cosmological patterns of myth into a constant "condition of the universe" beyond all concrete engagement with subjectivity (Mu,I,56–60). Myth is simply the natural language of the psyche; "by giving it shape," Jung writes, "the artist translates it into the present."[27] Olson's interest in the mythical type of the Great Mother takes the form of various manifestations of the Earth Mother: the Norse Bestla, for example, "Earth mass mother milk cow body" (M,II,163) (and her invert, the Egyptian Nut, who spans the sky "from toe to tip of hands/ over the earth" [M,II,150]), the Greek Gaia, the Mexican Mayanuel, and Hesiod's Earth herself. As a result of these "identifications," the synergy of man and land proposed by Sauer takes on its full mysti-ficatory trappings. Like Donne's Newfoundland, and Williams's America, the land is conceptualized as a woman's body, its surface a tabula rasa for male writers to inscribe at will: "like this one we/ few American poets have/ carved out of Nature and God" (M,III,173–74).[28]

To Olson, restoring the feminine is like reappropriating the once-denied maternal body. In Olson's poetics, however, this is a spir-itual task, involving submission to the "feminine principle," or *anima*, Jung's transformative source of human change and redemp-tion. The natural function of the *anima* is to liberate the uncon-scious, where "feminine power" is lodged, and to activate, as Erich Neumann puts it, "the law of compensation by which the uncon-scious, through dreams and visions, through its reactions and its action-determining mechanisms, equals the one-sided deviations of the centro-verted conscious personality."[29] In other words, the composite harmony which accompanies the "feminine principle" subsumes and effaces all subject-centered experience.

Recalling Olson's last fabled days in hospital, Robert Duncan remembers him holding forth to friends about his liver, or "live-her" condition, the Jungian transformation in its final stages of claiming the body on behalf of the feminine.[30] On that deathbed, Olson writes his last letter, a text called "The Secret of the Black Chrysanthemum"—"I have not/ written or made the dictation to my self" (OL,4:35)—which contains, and passes on, the putative mysteries of transformation inasmuch as they have been revealed to him. This occult correspondence marks Olson's own transforma-tion from Hermes the messenger to *Hermes Trismegistus*, or *Ter-Maximus*, the author of all mysteries and father of the alchemical faith. Sealed in an envelope inscribed "The Secret," it is his literary will and testament, handed over to the "adopted" son of his last days, Charles Boer.[31] In the presence of the body to the letter, this carefully staged bedside ritual enacts the law of delivery for posthumous posterity. Because it is a paternal delivery, and thus a dead letter, it guarantees the handing down of phallic power by *postal* descent, thereby consummating the most deep-seated princi-ples of Olson's poetics.

JOHN ASHBERY

6. DOUBTING JOHN THOMAS

1. It is only that you happen to be wearing this look as you arrived at the end of your perusal of the way left open to you, and it "froze" on you just as your mother warned you it would when you were little.

Ashbery

One day in the year 1929, a painter asked me: "What are you doing there? Are you working?" I replied, "Yes, I'm making collages. . . ." Then he whispered in my ear, "And what kind of glue do you use?"

Max Ernst

COMMENTING ON John Ashbery's third book of poems, *Rivers and Mountains* (1966), Richard Howard suggests that "here was perhaps the first poet in history in whose work anxiety (with all its shaping, climax-reaching concerns) had no place, a poet for whom the poem was poem *all through*."[1] It is itself a grandiose claim, perhaps as "shaping" and as "climax-reaching" as any. Nonetheless, Howard's general point seems to me to be significant in the light of the arguments I have advanced on the topic of Eliot and Olson's theoretical anxieties about the "problem" of subjectivity. What is important about Ashbery's work, however, is not that it has been stripped of anxiety, nor indeed that it offers some even-handed solution to the problems of subjectivity. On the contrary, we will see that the anxiety and/or the problem have merely been *displaced*. These are no longer problems to be dealt with externally—by willfully acting upon language in the theoretical name of some other subjectivity that is more "true" or "natural"—but rather, problems to be described and displayed within language itself, within the "poem *all through*." In pointing to certain aspects of this internalization of the question of subjectivity in the work of Ashbery, I shall be concerned particularly with its spatial and temporal effects, phenomenological or otherwise; temporal and spatial effects which have come to be seen as the respective objects of theoretical anxiety for Eliot and Olson. It is not my intention, however, to present Ashbery's writing generally as a solution to the "failures" of Eliot and Olson, nor, on a larger polemical scale, am I proposing this comparison in terms of some hierarchical ascendency of postmodernist values over those of modernism. In this respect, Ashbery's "displacement" simply brings us closer to our current or present-day theoretical *horizon*, a fact which should be acknowledged at a number of levels of interpretation. This "simply," however, conceals a much more significant epistemological shift, and one which should also be acknowledged in its own right—a shift in which language and subjectivity are no longer perceived as contingent and answerable to willful change, but in which linguistic subjectivity is accepted as given and necessary.

Ashbery's literary star shot to public prominence when his sixth collection, *Self-Portrait in a Convex Mirror* (1972), won three national book prizes. Since then, the title poem (and the painting upon which it reflects) has been enlisted in the public and critical imaginary as somehow defining the "look" of late modernist writing: (to put it in those same imaginary terms) its appetite for diffraction and loss of legitimate perspective, its mannered dialogue with a highly precarious representation of the self, and the parodic, almost allegorical bent of its framed surface, wrought to a sumptuous high finish. In that poem, Parmigianino's celebrated painting is seen as projected from the "surface" of the convex mirror which Richard Howard interprets as the "blazon en abyme," or emblematic device, of all of Ashbery's writing.[2] Since Ashbery has chosen not to espouse or elaborate any kind of substantial poetics outside of his poetry, critics, like Howard here, have been obliged to isolate such devices embedded within the writing, from whence they serve to comment on the author's constructive aims. Before we can allow such devices to speak in an unmediated fashion, before they are allowed to *reflect* upon experience, especially the experience of writing (as high modernism does), we must, however, ask some questions about the conditions of that articulation; in short, we must examine the grounds of its enunciation. For even if Ashbery's work can be read as an internalization of what had hitherto been situated on the "outside" of the poem, it is no less immune to the contradictory, or divided, effects of enunciation with which I have been concerned in earlier chapters. Rather than accept the "statement" of the convex mirror, then, at its face value, as an emblem of irony, I shall try to place it within another circuit of meaning, one which governs the construction of meaning itself. Perhaps in the course of this complex process I shall also be reproducing, and not just analyzing, some of the strategies at work in Ashbery's later writing, where a statement is uncannily revealed both as a representation *and* its example: "We wore these for a while, and they became us" (W,33); "Noting the grain of the wood this time and how it pushes through/ The pad we are writing on and becomes part of what is written" (W,73). But this is the risk of all writing, critical or otherwise, and it is the lesson of Ashbery's poetry as much as it is the lesson of any theory of language or poetics. And again, this is something to accept rather than disavow or celebrate.

In a 1977 interview with the *San Francisco Review of Books*, Ashbery describes his purchase of a book of reproductions of paintings opened up for display in a Provincetown bookstore at the page of the Parmigianino plate: "the funny thing is, when I went to find that bookstore, it had completely disappeared. There was no trace of its ever having been there. It was like De Quincey looking in vain for the store where he first bought opium. Being kind of susceptible to all kinds of mystical, superstitious ideas, I felt that this bookstore had just materialized for a few moments to allow me to buy this book and then vanished."[3] Although De Quincey had entertained a similar opinion about the celestial origins of the purveyor of his prize, "sent down to earth" as he put it, "on a special mission" to himself, his account of the opium merchant's subsequent eclipse reaches ever greater heights of incredulity: "the reader may choose to think to him as possibly, no more than a sublunary druggist: it may be so, but my faith is better: I believe him to have evanesced or evaporated." A footnote to De Quincey's astonishing observation records that *evanescence* was a seventeenth-century way of "going off from the stage of life," a privilege of royalty, however, and not one normally extended to the street druggist's lot. The footnote concludes with a couplet from an ominously named "MR FLATMAN," who is clearly disaffected with the all too public nature of Charles the Second's death: "Kings should disdain to die, and only *disappear;/* They should *abscond*, that is, into the other world.[4] MR

FLAT-MAN's royal road is one characterized by an absconding *into*, not an absconding *from*, and we can thus perceive it as an allegory of the slippage which *contains* the unconscious as its vanishing point. For it is consciousness which absconds into the unconscious, and not vice versa, as the more common metaphors of *irruption* and *surfacing* would suggest. Freud reminds us that "consciousness is in general a highly fugitive state. What is conscious is conscious only for a moment."[5] Lacan goes no further in his claim that this is practically an "ontic" function of the unconscious, imagined as the opening up of a slit which gulps down consciousness at every moment's notice.[6] The need to disappear is a constituting one, founded as it is upon the virtuality of a lack; to be able to constitute a visible object, for example, one must first of all be capable of making it disappear. So too, for both Ashbery and De Quincey, a charmed departure marks a moment of initiation, while their common, superstitious response reveals the *fetishistic* double side of belief, accompanied by all those features of infantile credulity we associate with secret knowledge.[7] Anticipating that this fetishistic response will be crucial to any reading of Ashbery's work in general, how "literally" are we to read it here?

Five years earlier, Ashbery's "new spirit" had been announced in *Three Poems* by the appearance of an "expressive sheen" which ordinary things had begun to assume, "a prismatic space that cannot be seen, merely felt as the result of an angularity which must have existed from earliest times . . . so that one realizes one's self has dwindled and now at last vanished in the diamond light of pure speculation" (TP,41). That "expressive sheen" might remind us of the lambent gleam of the bookstore display and its glittering prize for the poet's eye, its satisfying and necessary disappearance, but just as important, its satisfying and necessary exposure, just for him, and just for a moment, so that he might enjoy the privilege of "pure speculation" forever after. Freud's 1927 paper, "Fetishism," details the significance of the *shine* as a fetishistic precondition of his famous patient's case.[8] The shiny surface, however, is not the fetish itself, but its condition; Guy Rosolato suggests that it derives from a displacement of the shine on the head of the mother's imagined penile erection.[9] This condition assumes a level of translation (in the patient's case, a "literal" one, from English *glance*, perception of the maternal lack, to German *Glanz*, the shine, and its occulted signifier, the *glans* of the penis itself), a translation involving a displacement onto another part of the body, in the patient's case, the nose.

Parmigianino's painting still has its lustrous moments, the "gloss on the fine freckled skin" and the "lips moistened as though about to part"—effects translated from the glossy surface of the mirror, and copied, as Vasari described, onto a wooden hemisphere to be paraded before a "stupefied" Pope and his court. A mirror, then, the only object that cannot be seen *for what it is*, is posed as the object of the painting. But what of the object in the poem, which appears to come and go, to be present and absent as the narrator's meditational will demands?

> The balloon pops, the attention
> Turns dully away. . . . .   (SP,70)

> As I start to forget it
> It presents its stereotype again   (SP,73)

> A breeze like the turning of a page
> Brings back your face. . . . .   (SP,76)

It is as if the vagrancy of the object, its oscillating between presence and absence, were somehow the guarantee of the poem's subjective fixity. So too does the fetish come to represent both the presence and the absence of the maternal phallus, its recognition and its disavowal at one and the same time, thus ensuring the security of its secret knowledge, even in the face of what appears to be an untenable contradiction. Rosolato argues that the loss of the desired sexual object is like a flight of perspective, and that the fetish object can thus be paired with a "perspective object," an object which is foregrounded when the fetish is invested with maximum erotic power, and pushed out of sight to its vanishing point when the lack it fulfills lies empty. It shows itself and then hides, advances and then withdraws. Already the drawn-out Mannerist perspective of the convex mirror suggests this sliding scale, "a recurring wave/ Of arrival" throughout the poem, the hand absurdly elongated, almost "big enough/ To wreck the sphere" as it is "thrust" at the spectator, curves around, and swerves "back to the body of which it seems/ So unlikely a part." The contradictory reading of this gesture is a source of confusion, for it appears to "protect" what it "advertises," offering itself both as a "shield" and a "greeting," an "affirmation that doesn't affirm anything," (SP,70). Towards the end of the scenario, however, after much showing and hiding, the object finally loses its power to attract the look, and retreats into the permanent exile of disavowal. That final flight of perspective is quite categorical:

> There is room for one bullet in the chamber:
> Our looking through the wrong end
> Of the telescope as you fall back at a speed
> Faster than that of light to flatten ultimately
> Among the features of the room. . . . . .   (SP,82)

Like the fetish, the object here is no longer "offered." Its capacity to be foregrounded and then dismissed altogether is a guarantee not only of the fetish subject's mastery, but also of a continued complicity with the "secret" knowledge which involves the disavowal of castration. "Self-Portrait in a Convex Mirror" is the poem in Ashbery's work which most readily offers that position and that knowledge to the reader, and consequently it is most readily panegyrized as an example of its author's humanist reflections; it emulates the subjugating manner of a fetishizing eye which keeps its object in "suspension, unable to advance much further/ Than your look. . ." (SP,69).

There is, however, another, more productive side to understanding the structure of fetishism, beyond the simple pleasure of tracking down its giveaway traits. As I have suggested, it is not the meaning of the fetish which is important so much as its relation to meaning itself, inasmuch as this relation governs the vicissitudes of belief which, in Ashbery's case, are part and parcel of our reading of modern poetry; we are compelled to take up a fetishistic position of assuming two contradictory placements of truth at the same time—that the meaning of this poetry is still intelligible, and also that it has no meaning; no one believes each proposition independently, everyone believes both (somewhat like the belief that is maintained in Santa Claus).[10] The condition of art in this context is like Barthes's fugue, which simultaneously and independently delivers a contradictory message: "This is not art," and "I am art."[11] If this is the generalized rule of postmodern cultural consumption then the only sane response to a system that is all "surface" and only pretends to have depth—is *duplicity*. Indeed, in a late unfinished paper, "The Splitting of the Ego in the Process of Defence," Freud, too, was moving toward a recognition that this fetishistic structure of duplicity could no longer be seen as a limited form of perversion, but rather as a generalized condition implied in the very constitution of subjectivity.[12]

In the "mirror's stiff enclave" of "Self-Portrait," then, there is more than the simple narcissism of "enchantment of the self with the self" (SP,72), or as an earlier poem puts it, the Platonic dream of self-completion in an "attractive partner who is the heaven-sent one, the convex one." (TP,57). There is more than the candid mythologizing of the self offered to those who would read the poem as an apologia—reflections on the poet's mind and art—soberly published in a mock dialogue with a Renaissance painter, to match Browning's Quattrocento vignettes. For the other side of the mirror stage is the blank and alienating verso of belief: "this otherness, this/ 'Not-being-us' is all there is to look at in the mirror" (SP,81):

> . . . . You feel then like one of those
> Hoffman characters who have been deprived
> Of a reflection, except that the whole of me
> Is seen to be supplanted by the strict
> Otherness of the painter in his
> Other room. . . . . . .   (SP,74)

If Ashbery's writing insistently repeats this strategy of showing and then hiding, of turning itself back to front, then it is because it tries to accommodate the credulous part of us which *must* participate in the make-believe of meaning, while it undercuts that stable gesture in the same breath, exposing the clichéd props, the stiffened conventions, and the stage machinery of a reading regime which values instant communication. Hence Ashbery's ironic toleration of

the "eternal 'we'," as he puts it, "which gives the impression that
the author is sharing his every sensation with some invisible Kim
Novak."[13] It is the same collusive feint that Freud attributed to the
Jewish joke: the forgery of a temporary belief which wins enough
time for the signifying effect to do its work. In the joke, in contrast
to the linguistic structure of the pun, it is the signifier that is finally
irrelevant, while the confidence trick lingers on to engage its victim
in a giddy state of self-analysis. Clearly this is an altogether different cognitive step from the Cartesian rejection of skepticism (certainty, for Descartes, is found through the conscious knowledge of
doubt). On the contrary, it is the belief itself which is the medium
rather than the goal, as in the scholastic rule of thumb: *credo ut
intellegam*. Ashbery's reader is subjected to all the tricks in the book,
as the decoys and lures of this structure of belief are exposed. Even
the non-dupes err (or as Lacan puts it, *les noms du père*, revealing the
name-of-the-father behind each artful dodge), for Ashbery neither
offers nor imagines any *alternative* deception-free discourse; all language bears within itself this potential duplicity, or sleight of hand.
No sooner has one come to understand the fraudulent makeup of
an initial set of beliefs or meanings than the scene has changed,
and precisely as a result of that understanding, a new deception
takes its place:

. . . . .Then the advantage of
Sinking in oneself, crashing through the skylight of one's own
Received opinions redirects the maze, setting up significant
Erections of its own at chosen corners. . .   (w,70)

For the reader/"spectator," then, a fixed point of view is shown,
first of all, to be necessary, and then impossible, like an effect that
"is apt to be turned off at any moment, leaving the spectator in the
position of Sylvester the cat, who can walk perfectly well on air
until he realizes what he is doing."[14]

Conversely, the position of enunciation is itself marked by the
same counterfeit theatricality; as Ashbery writes in a review of a
Jasper Johns show, "unlike the Romantic, who imagines he is at the
center of things, Johns takes up his position consciously; he thinks
that he might as well pretend to be there."[15] Again, two contradic-

tory propositions are made to coexist: on the one hand, the assumption of subjectivism (or a fixed subjectivity-effect), and on the other, the proof, which is never empirical, of its misrepresentation. Neither of these propositions, however, are privileged, for Ashbery's lesson is about the necessity of this two-sided construction of subjectivity:

> The transversals that haven't stopped
> Defining our locus, have indeed only begun
> To, you are invited and cannot refuse,
> To share this painted wall
> Of painted wooden tulips, the wooden clouds
> In the sky behind it. . . .   (AWK,51)

If we want to provide anything more than an impressionistic account of this invitation that "cannot" be refused, then we must pay particular attention to these "transversals," for they belong to an explicit subtext that functions as a referent for all of the "visuals" in Ashbery's writing[16]—the tradition of perspective in Western painting. To begin with, however, we must recognize how Ashbery's relation to the art world has been explored, thematized, and, I would argue, misrecognized by critics.

Ashbery's twenty years and more of weekly art reviewing for *Art News, Art International, The Herald Tribune, New York, Newsweek, The New Republic,* and others, placed him in a routine of writing about painting, which irradiated his poetry. His very close association with the art world in New York and Paris has prompted critics to put his work alongside that of Frank O'Hara, James Schuyler, and others of the New York School, under the sign of the "painterly" poem.[17] In *Frank O'Hara: Poet Among Painters,* for example, Marjorie Perloff's working critical assumption is that one can do with words "what the Abstract Expressionists were doing with paint."[17] However theoretically precarious or critically impressionistic this may be, it begs the traditional metaphor of *ut pictura poesis.* A good example of this is Perloff's unproblematic resolution of the paradox at the heart of O'Hara's famous conundrum-poem, "Why I Am Not a Painter," of which she concludes that O'Hara proposes, when all is said and done, that "poetry and painting are part of the same spectrum," and that "art does not tolerate divisions; it must be viewed as process and not product."[19] If, as Perloff suggests, the poem is a "profound jest," or a "stupid answer" to a "stupid question," then that is normally a sign, in O'Hara's writing, that it is a very serious question indeed. For we learn to read O'Hara with a very real sense of comic relief, a kind of kitsch *comedy politic,* if only because, as he put it, "in a capitalist country, fun is everything," or since "art is not your life, it is someone else's," if not lived, then owned, protected, and leased elsewhere.[20] In answering an equally "stupid question"—why R.B. Kitaj is a "literary" painter—Ashbery makes the important point that language, "unlike Sherwin-Williams paint, or anyone else's, 'covers the earth.'" One does not *choose* to use language in the same way as one chooses to use paint; one is born into language.

Not least of the effects of O'Hara's poem, then, is to question, if not directly resist, the sloppy logic of the *ut pictura poesis* equation. However, even if we accept Perloff's thematic on its own terms, and recognize with O'Hara himself that, in deference to the dogma of action painting, the surface had to be kept up, "high and dry, not wet, reflective, and self-conscious,"[22] it is clear that Ashbery's work, by that same criterion, engages another art history altogether. For his is the heresy (at least for the Abstract Expressionists) of illusionistic space: a writing "surface" that will drop, disappear for long stretches, lose its voice, shimmer and reflect with the falsest of lights, and generally betray its complicity with the lures of subjectivism—trap-doors, sliding panels, and false bottoms—by employing a whole inventory of "optical" tricks learned and inherited from the discourse of Renaissance perspective. In Clement Greenberg's canonical account of modernist art, the Cubist dilemma of choosing between the "depicted flatness" of a surface reality and the trompe l'oel of spatial illusion was resolved by favoring the former, the "eye-undeceiving trompe l'oeil," rather than the conventional "eye-deceiving kind" with its insistence on representing the illusion of plasticity and depth.[23] Greenberg's acid test of spectator-subjectivity—that one should not be induced to "poke a hole" in the canvas—would flunk a Doubting Thomas of Ashbery's persuasion, fitfully struck by his double-edged revelation of the window on the wall *and* the wall itself. Indeed, a more appropriate fellow-traveller for Ashbery would be Houdini, who vehemently proclaimed, and demonstrated for that matter, that it takes a profound knowledge of the art of illusion to expose even the cheapest of frauds: in his case, a lifetime's experience of escapology to challenge the tartufferie of a nation's spiritualist mediums.

In order to pursue this "art of illusion" in Ashbery's writing, we must account for the history of subject-construction in Renaissance perspective as a high-fidelity eye, or panoptic *passe-partout*. In the ideal arena of spatial perspective, first worked out in the geometrical Euclidean manner by Alberti, a perfectly symmetrical world is engineered for the eye by the superimposing of two triangles whose bases coincide with the picture plane, and whose apexes are designated, respectively, as point of view and vanishing point. All of the possible points on any of its planes are determined by a spray of orthogonal light beams which split up and classify its infinite space according to the harmonic code of optical reason. The mirror is the last judgment on any painting produced within that code because it can *legitimize* the theses of perspective by returning a look perfectly, thereby proving that point of view and vanishing point are reversible and virtually coincident. A Husserlian domain of pure visibility opens up, stretching from the foot to the horizon of things and back again:

> We aren't meaning that any more.
> The question has been asked
> As though an immense natural bridge had been
> Strung across the landscape to any point you wanted.
> The ellipse is as aimless as that,
> Stretching invisibly into the future so as to reappear
> In our present. Its flexing is its account,
> Return to the point of no return   (HD,23)

For the spectator, ideally positioned at the focal point of the world's "pure" attention, this sliding scale of distance fetishistically shores up the metaphysical subject. As Jean-Louis Baudry has argued, it has been the "ideological function" of art to produce this effect ever since the Renaissance, and in so doing, "provide the tangible representation of metaphysics which the wholeness and homogeneity of that vacuumed space offers up to a transcendental field of vision."[24] "Is it correct for me to use you to demonstrate all this? Perhaps what I am saying is that it is I the subject, recoiling from you at ever-increasing speed just so as to be able to say I exist in that safe vacuum I had managed to define . . ." (TP, 15). Because of the structural equivalence of point of view and vanishing point, the painting can be said to see itself, to look back at itself. It can also be said to articulate itself, since its optical space is recited according to a discourse, or rhetoric, of seeing; the look is both the subject of enunciation and the enounced.[25] In a classical painting, then, the tableau is presented as if the narrator were absent, the point of view is bodiless and transcendental, a voyeuristic apparatus available for the "unauthorized," scopic use of the spectator:

> It insists on this picture of "history"
> In the making, because there is no way out of the punishment
> It proposes: sight blinded by sunlight,
> The seeing taken in with what is seen.   (AWK, 90)

There is, however, a conventional strain of Dutch painting that anticipates Ashbery's desire to expose the "invisibility" of this look, and it is indeed one which employs the convex mirror in place of the vanishing point, thus throwing back the loop upon the spectator in the form of a different or distorted space neither "inside" nor "outside" the "real" space of the painting—Van Eyck's *Arnolfini Wedding Portrait* is the most celebrated example: others include Hans Memling's *Virgin and Child* (Bruges), Quentin Metsys's *Money-lender and Wife* (Louvre), and Petrus Christus's *St. Eligius* (Metropolitan, New York). Deprived of our genitive possession of these paintings, we are literally caught short in terms of their convexed perspective, oscillating between the predicative point of view and the more unlikely position of recognizing that we are being gazed upon.

In an interview, Ashbery mentions the example of Vermeer placing one "of his own paintings on the wall of the background in one of his paintings, like mutually reflecting mirrors, leading to infinity,"[26] but this euphuistic, Borgesian gesture hardly does justice to the devastating simplicity of the convexed effect. More germane would be the painting from which his third volume of poems takes its title, De Chirico's *The Double Dream of Spring*, in which the retreating orthogonals, actually traced out on the picture surface, coincide and merge with those of another picture surface within the picture, thus cutting off access to the vanishing point, and slicing into our expectation of the concavity of the tableau. De Chirico's iconographical passion, like that of Ashbery, was for the "consonance of the Renaissance" (SP,74), "the beginning, before an angel bandaged the field glasses" (TCO,56); the wrenched, idiomatic use of perspective in his painting produces multiple vanishing points, exaggerated foreshortenings, and conflicting planes, all "effects" which are recognizable in Ashbery's writing.

So too with the capricious Mannerist experiments with established pictorial codes, experiments, like those of Parmigianino, that both assert and repudiate their formalism at one and the same time. To say that Ashbery is a Mannerist poet, however, is to fall back again upon the impressionistic discourse of *ut pictura poesis*. What is more important is to recognize how a conventional discourse about perspectival point of view is internalized, *thematically* and *structurally* within the fickle and contradictory space reserved for subjectivity in his poetry:

> He would cook up these goulashes
> Make everything shipshape
> And then disappear, like Hamlet, in a blizzard
> Of speculation that comes to occupy
> The forefront for a time, until
> Nothing but the forefront exists, like a forehead
> Of the times, speechless, drunk, imagined   (AWK,44)

Here the "vanishing point" turns into something else; it is rerouted on to a contiguous plane, the proximity of which draws our attention but also invites us to reexamine the preceding one. The resultant "illusion," like Gombrich's rabbit/duck, persists, and our understanding of its duplicity only increases its ambiguity; there is no more a secure position of "fence-sitting/ Raised to the level of an esthetic ideal" (DDS,18) than there is a quasi-Nietzschean celebration of perspectival relativism.[27]

This kind of ambiguity can be compared and contrasted with the more "mechanical" effects of that marginalized perspectival tradition in which geometrical hallucinations are constructed within perspective cabinets or in the curiosity form of the anamorphosis. Impossibly oblique at first, the anamorphic point of view is restored to its "normal" aspect with the aid of a cylindrical mirror. In "Lithuanian Dance Band," for example, the world is stretched out to its distorted limits:

> For today it looks compressed like these lines packed together
> In one of those pictures you reflect with a polished tube
> To get the full effect and this is possible
> I feel it in the lean reaches of the weather and the wind
> That sweeps articulately down these drab streets
> Bringing everything to a high gloss.   (SP,53)

The appearance of this "high gloss" reminds us of the fetish,[28] and in particular, the fetishized perspective object which comes or goes at will; as Jurgis Baltrusaitis points out, the anamorphosis is a verification of, rather than a challenge to the principles of perspective,[29] for if it suggests a lack, "like the face on a deflated balloon, shifted into wrinkles, permanent and matter-of-fact, though a perversion of itself" (TP,6), this is only a temporary "detumescence," and can be recuperated into an object of visual mastery by applying its "key."

It is this mechanical "peep-show" aspect which Ashbery recognizes as part of his consuming interest in the "heightened voyeurism" demanded by the work of Raymond Roussel.[30] In a review, he writes of the "svelte, secret resonance" of Roussel's visual chicanery, like "a Chinese box that one turns over and over, certain that there is a concealed spring somewhere, that in a moment, the lid will fly open, revealing possibly no more than its emptiness, but proving at any rate that reality is only a false bottom."[31] Many of Roussel's long poems, narrative scenarios of extraordinary visual detail, open up through the imaginarization of a conventional, everyday point of view: in the case of *La Source*, a watering scene inscribed on a bottle label on a cafe table; in *Le Concert*, a vignette in the letterhead of a sheet of writing paper; and in *La Vue*, a seaside tableau viewed inside the base of a pen-holder.[32] Roussel's writing celebrates a *correct* point of view as the key to its mysteries (his posthumous *Comment j'ai ecrit certains de mes livres* reveals the "secrets" of his compositional techniques) and more often than not contains its own self-reflexive instructions about how the text itself is to be viewed, read, and understood (it is no surprise that one of Ashbery's earliest and most anthologized Rousselesque poems is called "The Instruction Manual").[33] *Nouvelles impressions d'Afrique*, for example, is composed by means of a cumulative series of parenthetical subdivisions; when the ninth level of bracketing is reached, the parentheses close one after the other. The effect is palindromic, for the text is read by shunting each narrative segment from the back to the front until a piecemeal narrative emerges. Knowledge of the text, then, is a secret, to be learned and applied mechanically.[34]

Ashbery, however, has suggested that the parentheses in *Nouvelles Impressions* are employed to speed up the disintegration of language in a way comparable to that in which Mallarmé used blanks to produce those " 'prismatic subdivisions of the eye' which he mentions in the preface to *Un coup de dés.*"[35] The visual or virtual implications of Mallarmé's use of the "blanc" are, of course, an important facet of the modernist assumption that words can become or behave like things, that poetic language can accede to a more plastic configuration of the real in its "tactile" moments than can ordinary discourse.[36] Language, in other words, can be naturalized: the calligrammes of Apollinaire, Max Ernst's picture poems, the dream of a plastic transcription of experience to which Pound's ideographism and Olson's glyphism, as we have seen, are irresistibly drawn. Clearly, this is not Ashbery's dream, and one need only cite his own comments, in a review of a *"Paroles Peintes"* exhibition in Paris, about his "deep dislike for poetry given the status of an object, printed in thundering type and illustrated."[37]

If Ashbery's perspectival "effect" is to be distinguished from this modernist emphasis on surface and materiality, it should also be contrasted with the hermetically self-reflexive practice of Roussel's compositional strategies. For Roussel, the mechanics of visual construction are the vindication of his text. Ashbery's work, as I have suggested, thematizes this mechanical construction of subjectivity *in order to demonstrate* its spurious or fetishistic premises. As the phantom of the opera in "Faust" appears to have overlooked, "hungers . . . must be stirred before disappointment can begin" (TCO,47). In this early poem, the hunger of the audience for illusory meaning depends upon the sumptuous stage setting. Representation, however, in the shape of the orchestra musicians and stage hands, is on strike (this is a real crisis in which hunger is not "just another topic"). The following question is posed. If the "phantom" apparatus of representation could be seen for what it was, and seen through a phantom window, "painted by the phantom/ Scene painters, sick of not getting paid, of hungers," then "the hungers could begin for real" in the divided desires of the audience. So too in the play, *The Heroes*, where Theseus fearlessly exposes the confidence trick of the Minoan labyrinth and its horrid resident as a hoax, "a great big doodle-bug made of wood and painted canvas." No need for a ball of yarn, the minotaur is vanquished by the "indifference of a true aesthete" with an eye for a booby trap.[38]

It is Ashbery's strategically ambiguous appeal to the necessity of these trick effects that characterizes his challenge to the weather-beaten subjectivism of classical humanism: "an end to the 'end' theory whereby each man was both an idol and the humblest of idolaters, in other words the antipodes of his own universe, his own redemption or his own damnation, with the rest of the world as painted backdrop to his own monodrama of becoming of which he was the lone impassioned spectator" (TP,64). Unlike Eliot and Olson, who oppose this tradition head-on and who are consequently obliged to pursue their own "end" theories, Ashbery's method is to show how the Faustian humanist lives on, and *also* how he can be led astray by a process of conventional disorientation, like the character of Faust, himself the model of humanism, "drifting" about in the "tunnels" of the opera-house stage, "in search of lost old age" (TCO,47).

As a result of Ashbery's method, "remnants of the old atrocity subsist, but they are converted into ingenious shifts of scenery" and characterized as "a sort of 'English garden' effect" (TP,27), landscaped to catch the knowing eye. In his concern with the planned obsolescence of the beauty spot, the one-dimensionality of the facade ("No one criticizes us for lacking depth" [W,61]), Ashbery is as much a landscape poet as Wallace Stevens, and indeed one who takes this conventional genre seriously enough to transform its rules by demonstrating how closely they regulate our voyeuristic pleasure. Contrast this with other poetic models of perception: the *scope* of Maximus, and the idealism of his historico-geographical coordinates of visibility; or two earlier notions of invisibility, Hopkins's *inscape* and Eliot's *escape*, the former a poetics of grace in which the labor of signs is divinely assumed, the latter an attempt to secularize that same concept of transcendental authorship. Ashbery's poetic experience is that "everything is landscape," and that is a way not only of talking about the conventionally exhibitionistic construction of the world, but also of pointing to the conventional makeup of the social fabric itself, beyond which there are no "alternative" powers of appeal, whether divine or natural.

Ashbery, then, insists on conflating O'Hara's distinction between the classical "landscape-with-poet" and the romantic "poet-in-landscape":[39] both are involved simultaneously in a "horizon in whose cursive recesses we/ May sometimes lie concealed because we are part/ Of the pattern. No one misses you." (W,61). O'Hara's heroic embodiment of the poet-in-landscape is, of course, Jackson Pollock, in whose work he finds the conceptual perfection of his notion of *insight*: "by being 'in' the specific painting, as he himself put it, [Pollock] gave himself over to cultural necessities which surround art as an occasion of extreme cultural concern, encumbrances external to the act of applying a specific truth to the specific cultural event for which it has been waiting in order for it to be fully revealed. This is not automatism or self-impression but insight."[40] As the art swallows up the artist's subjectivity, or drips it across the canvas à la Pollock, the unmediated takes over: "I am Nature." It is the story of the American sublime (produced after the sublime has historically lost its meaning).

(One might just as well choose Ruskin's distinction between the high, creative poet—Dante, if no one else, for Ruskin—and the exponent of the "pathetic fallacy"; the first possesses "a great centre of reflection and knowledge in which he stands serene, and watches the feeling, as it were, from far off," while the second affects a state of mind "in which reason is unhinged . . . by an excited state of the feelings" to such a pitch that "he cannot speak of the sea without talking of 'raging waves,' 'remorseless floods,' 'ravenous billows,' etc."[41] Again, we would have to say that both of these elements are ambiguously present in Ashbery's "landscapes"—the cliché of sentiment *and* the ironic knowledge of its contrived articulation.)

If, as I have suggested, Ashbery's work represents a move away from the *naturalism* of the American sublime, then it also exhibits a less obsessive relation to the cultural nationalism of the American "heritage." It promotes a "negative feeling of being at home," as he wrote of Joan Mitchell's work, herself an *apatrides* (as opposed to an *expatriate*) who lived, like him, in a Parisian "climate of indifference" much more productively than she might have done in "the intensive care-wards of New York."[42] So too of Joan Bishop, who spent roughly the same time abroad as Ashbery, from the mid-fifties to the mid-sixties, living only obliquely through the turbulent New York scene of the time—"reversals and surprises, palace revolutions, deathbed conversions, posthumous knightings, anathemas, miraculous presages, eclipses, earthquakes, and floods."[43] In this context, it does seem somewhat misplaced to try to recontain Ashbery within the obsessive superstructure of a theory of *repatriation* as Harold Bloom has done, a critical scenario in which the poet must always be seen "swerving" away from his precursors, in Ashbery's case, the composite father of Whitman/Stevens, the patrician overlords of Bloom's canon of American transcendentalists.

Similarly, there seems little in Ashbery's work that points toward the American modernist obsession with cultural specificity or Americanicity. In *The Tennis Court Oath*, for example, a spurious opposition is set up between the two poems, "Europe" and "America." Neither makes any attempt at cultural inclusiveness, nor are there any recognizable signs of specificity, except for the occasional, gratuitous, and ironic reminder that the text should somehow be living up to at least some of the expectations addressed by the title. This is Ashbery's transatlantic literary joke, and like O'Hara's poem about oranges, it is a serious jest, in this case, at the expense of the separatist tradition which stems from Lawrence's *Studies in Classic American Literature* and Williams's *In the American Grain*, and wears itself down to the threads in Olson's reduction: Europe = Time, America = Space. This is not to suggest, however, that Ashbery's writing is entirely immune to what he calls "the drama of an American conscience, lavish, beautiful and rigid."[44] Indeed, his high kitsch delineation of American suburban life (and the surrealism of Hollywood is a subgenre of this) is, in many respects, a more significant response to everyday, commodified modernity than are the many celebrations of non-Western or pre-Western mythologies that passed for political platforms among the Beats, the Black Mountaineers, Snyder, Bly, and other late modernists. The novel, for example, which he cowrote with James Schuyler, *A Nest of Ninnies,* is one of the most mercilessly polished of his suburban discourses. Reaching out to touch the farcical underbelly of the Jamesian tragicomedy of manners with its membranous imitations of the higher "aesthetic" life, it exposes the full necessity of a whole range of cultural allusions upon which the *narrative* structure of suburban life obsessively depends. The precarious irony of these narrative effects is something which Kenneth Koch, for example, a much more accomplished comedian than Ashbery, cannot reproduce with the same serious interest.

In contrast, however, to the parricidal vows issuing from every corner of the American counterculture during the sixties, Ashbery, along with O'Hara, kept his distance from polemical programs which called for direct political action in one form or another. In response to the charge of a lack of commitment over the Vietnam question, Ashbery wrote in a 1966 issue of *Bookweek* that "Frank O'Hara's poetry has no program, and therefore it cannot be joined. It does not advocate sex and dope as a panacea for the ills of modern society; it does not speak out against the war in Vietnam or in favor of civil rights; it does not paint Gothic vignettes of the post-atomic age; in a word, it does not attack the establishment. It merely ignores its right to exist and is thus a source of annoyance to partisans of every stripe. . ."[45] If Ashbery and O'Hara flagrantly refuse the poet's prophetic voice, they do not seek to challenge the unearned privileges of that voice, for this would be to fall into the same circuit of aggression. The "nuptial quality," as O'Hara puts it, of Ashbery's writing means that "he is always marrying the whole world,"[46] which is to say that the poet's polygamous inheritance is not poethood itself, nor its privileges, but the whole symbolic, or social, order which comes with a given language. Once the language is accepted, then the only oppositional activity proper to the poet is to expose and thereby impoverish an established class of looking and writing that has been standardized and conventionalized within that language.

As a result of this, the political appeal of Ashbery's work is low on the scale of visibility. There is no significant attachment to socioeconomic markers—"home/ Is a modest one-bedroom apartment,/ City-owned and operated" (SP,23)—nor any passionate revolt against an elitist literary knowledge, that of "using what Wyatt and Surrey left around" (SP,19), and neither is there any "committed" adoption of language as an instrument of terror leveled against a "bad" political object. Ashbery's response, by contrast, is to the universality and prolixity of the language system as a whole. Language, unlike paint, covers the earth, subjects are switched on like "talking engines" (AWK,88), and "sentences suddenly spurt up like gas" (DDS,57). The insatiable systematicity of this discourse recalls Olson's threat of an endless or unstoppable oralizing, but it operates beyond the willfulness of any one single mouth. So too should we distinguish it from what David Antin calls "uninterruptible discourse," or poetry's unsociable and monologic habit of closing itself off from the world; Antin's alternative "interruptible" discourse, and his postexistentialist question—what am i doing here?—gesture toward a new liberal rationalism which could accommodate, Socratically, any oppositional point of view.

Finally, we are obliged to look for a metaphor or model for the discursive inclusiveness of Ashbery's "talking engines." It would not, however, be one drawn from the traditional modernist concern with the metaphors of mechanical production, or overproduction. We would turn instead to the conceptual terms of the "software" or information revolution, where the spectacle of a culture effortlessly producing data about its own signifying processes offers a more appropriate representation of the kind of pseudosurface that is reproduced in Ashbery's poems. Subjectivity and its effects, then, are constantly circulated, as if on a screen: "our habits ask us for information" (DDS,83). The early "Fragment," for example, reads like a piece of computer "papyrus," stripped, however, of any Sapphic resonance (unlike, for example, A.R. Ammons's *Tape for the Turn of the Year*, written on a printout tape over a set period of time):

Continuing inquiry and reappraisal of always new
Facts pushing past into bright cold
As from general spindles a waterfall of data
Is absorbed above by command . . . .　　(DDS,82)

The circulation of data is, of course, controlled from elsewhere. When subjectivity becomes little more than an "active memorial," loss begins to fill up the poem, as if the speaker, as part of the sham, "were choked by sighs and tears, and had forgotten/ The reason why he was telling the story" (DDS,83). Despite the irony, the dissembling, and the make-believe, there is a body, as we will now see, being implicated in all of this.

2.　　　　The body is what this is all about and it disperses
　　　　　In sheeted fragments, all somewhere around
　　　　　But difficult to read correctly since there is
　　　　　No common vantage point, no point of view
　　　　　Like the "I" in a novel . . .

　　　　　　　　　　　　　　　　　　　(SP,56)

Any account of perspective and point of view, as we have seen, is necessarily limited to certain systematic assumptions about Euclidean space, its uniform code, and/or distortions of that code. Indeed, within the classical discourse of "art history," there have been no rules for discussing the successive problems faced by the historical "avant-garde" other than those which govern the desire to resolve one overriding problem—the perfect representation of space: how to build a higher vault, how to induct the monumental outline or avoid the statuesque in painting, how to break down the unnatural symmetry of a landscape, record deep space, perceptible motion, multiple perspective, optical space as opposed to trompe l'oeil, how to forgo the frame and, finally, the gallery. Greenberg, for example, chronicles the modernist movement according to the same narrative formula in depicting the irresistible advance of an art *Geist* which resolves a series of formal problems by privileging the qualities of flatness, "surfaceness," and "artificity." In his account, the crucial early choice for modernism, faced with "mutually exclusive alternatives," was to prefer representation over illusion (the optical Braque over the pictorial Picasso). The choice, even when it had been made, however, was plagued by the problem of "being thrust back into at least a memory of deep or plastic space."[48]

The significance of this comment goes beyond Greenberg's anxiety about the spatial component, or the relation to point of view with which I have been concerned in Ashbery's work up until now. On the contrary, it is Greenberg's allusion to "memory" which I will now pursue, and in particular, the suggestion that memory is a *flaw*, a breach of the undivided spatial presence within which the modernist artwork is assembled, both theoretically and epistemologically.

Generally speaking, it is the temporal component of subjectivity which tends to be repressed in theoretical accounts of representation. This temporal would complement the spatial if only it could be articulated ideally:

> *This* thing, the mute, undivided present,
> Has the justification of logic, which
> In this instance isn't a bad thing
> Or wouldn't be, if the way of telling
> Didn't somehow intrude, twisting the end result
> Into a caricature of itself   (SP,80)

Enunciation, however the "way of telling" always will "somehow intrude" and divide or displace the spatial present. However much it intends to apply itself to the problems of "focusing" the meaning of a dialogue about images and imaginary meditations, "Self-Portrait in a Convex Mirror," for example, increasingly falls prey to a rather arbitrary series of memories, the Eliotic "cold pockets/ Of remembrance, whispers out of time" (SP,83). The failure of consciousness is mimed, thematized, and ironically lamented.

Where do we begin to look for textual signs of a temporally induced displacement, the "deprivation or logic/ Of strange position" (ST,74) to which Ashbery alludes in a recent interview: "I want to move to some other space when I write which perhaps was where I had been put without being fully conscious of it"?[49] An obvious reference would be the notorious short life of his personal pronouns (what David Shapiro calls the "shiftiness" of the shifters),[50] and the resulting tendency of his writing to move through a whole spectrum of identity in a matter of lines. Ashbery has offered his own description:

the personal pronouns in my work very often seem to be like variables in an equation. "You" can be myself or it can be another person, someone whom I'm addressing, and so can "he" or "she" for that matter and "we"—it doesn't really matter very much, that we are all aspects of a consciousness giving rise to the poem . . . and I find it very easy to move from one person in the sense of a pronoun to another and this again helps to produce a kind of polyphony in my poetry which I again feel is a means towards a greater naturalism.[51]

Even if it is used here to sanction the dislocation of identity, this appeal to a "greater naturalism" should be familiar enough by now: the fallacy of "mimesis of the way experience and knowledge come to me, and I think to everybody."[52]

Whether or not we accept the positivism of this claim, it seems to me that the mere act of manhandling these pronouns seems to contribute very little in itself to the powerful negativism which affects the personality of Ashbery's poetic practice. To support this view, one could cite the example of *Three Poems*, a text which appears to adhere more faithfully to an I/Thou address (the Thou, as Ashbery has revealed, was inspired by his analyst) than any other of Ashbery's long poems. What affects us in *Three Poems* is neither the fear that the pronouns are declining erratically behind or beyond our conceptual understanding, nor, despite the conventional intimacy of the address, the assumption of a singularly flat and austere anonymity. What we do find in this writing is a complete loss of "voice," a phonic vacuum which has swallowed up all of the "personality" endemic to a sense of identity; the identifying marks have been scrubbed out, leaving the ruthlessly spare and neutral surface with a bare minimum of bodily support. Only occasionally, in the cracked texture of the prosaic cloth does a "voice" distinguish itself, "reciting the only alphabet one knows" (TP,11), and reminding us of how ironically this bloodless style has been constructed. The obvious referent is Eliot's late purgatorial discourse, devoted to the stylistic abandonment of all bodily traces. Clearly, *Three Poems* does not share the same obsessive commitment to negativity, or at least it does not present that stylistic will in an unmediated manner, as a serious attempt to reform the ways of linguistic subjectivity. On the contrary, its response is to *internalize* that will as a conventional level of discourse, colliding with the expectations set up by its appearance as a naturalistic discourse.

Not least of the results of this reflexivity is to complicate the notion of "originality" which we traditionally assume as a way of responding to poetic voice. Roger Shattuck, for one, has objected to this loss of voice, complaining that there is more "visual thinking than music" in Ashbery's writing, thus setting it apart as a deviation from what he sees as the more progressive tradition of modern poetry (the Symboliste celebration of music). Ashbery, he claims, "forces his poetry to wear the seven veils—and then refuses to let it dance."[53] Shattuck's response is important, not so much because of what he perceives, but rather because of what he fails, or refuses, to perceive in Ashbery's own "refusal." To put it in the most reductive terms, his criticism appeals to those values of authenticity and sincerity which the modernist poet *qua* poet is presumed to be able to reveal naturally. The contrived value of Ashbery's project, however, does not lie in the mere refusal of that notion of originality. For as Shattuck's observation suggests, albeit indirectly, it engages the conventional expectations of "voice" and all the trappings of voice *at the same time* as it "refuses" them. The result is an effect we have already described, the exposure of a poetic cliché, which in this particular context would be the spectacle of a body that knows its way around the vowels, and can strike up a professional routine on request, as if it were born to the trade (perhaps "the difference between someone who is in love and someone who is merely 'good in bed'" [TP,11]). When one loses the faculties of a language that has been learned, it is the aphasic or the amnesiac, rather than the purgatorial, that is induced, and this again collides with the conventional irreversibility of the way in which naturalistic writing incorporates memory, or memories. The hint of a remembered "earlier" body is evoked but only as an absence or "repoussoir" in which "the negative outlines of our never doing define their being" (TP,11), like the diapositive of a fossilized vessel, its "rotting spars sketched in phosphorus" (AWK,117). I shall now try to describe the temporal effect of this remembered body in a more elaborate way.

I have suggested that classical point of view suppresses the problem of enunciation and temporality. Lacan invokes the Freudian critique in proposing that point of view is split up over the course of its "logical time," because it is divided between a double registration of material experience, both in the conscious and the unconscious: "the appearance/disappearance takes place between two points, the initial and the terminal of this logical time—between the instant of seeing, when something of the intuition itself is always elided, not to say lost, and that elusive moment when the apprehension of the unconscious is not, in fact, concluded, when it is always a question of 'absorption' fraught with false trails."[54] Consciousness fetishistically straddles the distance between these two different times: "the whole thing is calibrated according to time's way of walking sideways out of the event, at the same time proceeding in a straight line towards an actual vanishing point" (TP,23). And memory divides the body's attention in the same way, pulling apart the classical optical geometry:

> The prettiness urges
> Far into the body, deep
> Into the coffin of reactions, splitting light
> Into two unequal portions. One
> For me, the other for my things
> Like my memories and the changes I'd
> Want to introduce each time. . . .   (AWK,60)

What is there to say linguistically about the conjunctive relation between visual and auditory signs? In a famous paper, Roman Jakobson argues that the distinction between the "spatial" (visual) and the "temporal" (linguistic) arts is quite categorical: "a complex visual sign involves a series of simultaneous constituents while a complex auditory sign consists, as a rule, of serial successive constituents."[55] The opposition should not, however, be understood as mutually exclusive, since the simultaneous synthesis of a visual perception is always preceded by a series of successive search processes, and vice versa for the language model. Jakobson concludes another paper by claiming that the comprehension of the sequential aspect of a series of signs is seized "at one and the same time" as the perception of its concurrence, and he compares this altrified moment to the "modern psychological problem of *immediate memory* . . . or *short-term memory*."[56] When these two operations occur at the same time, long-term memory is suspended; the temporality of the sequence is disavowed, or at least incorporated into the "spatial" dimension. We have already encountered this contradictory form in the structure of fetishism, where, clinically speaking, it offers a solution to the conflict perceived by the child between an instinctual demand and its prohibition, the latter the result of a newly perceived reality like the fact of sexual difference. Freud notes that fetishism is "a very ingenious solution of this difficulty," but goes on to point out that "success is achieved at the price of a rift in the ego which never heals but which increases as time goes on."[57] The spatial present of the fetishistic belief, then, is increasingly threatened by the divisive effects of holding in place the memory of the original fetishized moment.

The description of the "fetich" which Ashbery offers in *Three Poems* does indeed emphasize the disavowal, or at least the transformation, of temporality: "Fetishism comes into being only when there is a past that may seem more or less attractive when compared with the present: the resulting inequality causes a rush towards the immediate object of contemplation, hardens it into a husk around its own being, which promptly ceases" (TP,70). Ashbery's "definition" of the "fetich" (it is, of course, an "anthropological" one) could be read as a critique of the modernist supplication of the past, especially the modernist solution to the problem of trying to write about history while living within it—the solution of employing the past to produce a unified present. History is never confronted head-on in Ashbery. His problem is that of *writing time,* as opposed to history; "something about time/ That only a clock can tell you; how it feels not what it means" (HD,29). Time, in this respect, becomes the durational content rather than the subject matter of Ashbery's writing. This is a lived phenomenological difference, and it runs up against what Barthes, in his strange last book, calls "our race for impotence: to be no longer able to conceive duration, affectively or symbolically."[58]

A favorite Ashbery scenario, for example, is the "haunted landscape" which seems to have only just been evacuated by persons or by an event, leaving a "kind of outline, distant, yes, but warm,/ Full of the traceable meaning that never/ Gets adopted. Well isn't that truth?" (AWK,98). If "time and land are identical," then it is because our incomplete point of view no longer tallies with a sense of what is felt to be unsaid or latent, what the landscape depends upon, in its absence, to invest itself with meaning. It is like Freud's discovery, on casting his eyes around the "familiar" terrain of the Acropolis for the first time, that "it really does exist," an equivocal response in the light of his confidential desire that it be too good to be true, and that he might be able to preserve the suspension of disbelief experienced as a child, learning about Ancient Greece at school. The "truth" of this revelation would not apply to a purely empirical context, like that of coming across the Loch Ness Monster stranded on the shore, that is, something we have never believed in—but rather in the surprise of realizing that something like the existence of the Acropolis was actually an object of doubt in the first place.[59]

The terra incognita of Ashbery's landscapes is haunted by a similar sense of incredulity, by the anxiety that they might become meaningful, that everything which had been missed, delayed, wrongfully announced, or merely displaced, will come suddenly to a point and reveal a significant arrangement of meaning. This is the anxiety of *waiting* which "invests everything like a climate" (SP,14), the anticipation, not of something to come, but of something that may have already happened. It is a part of the desire for an eternally lost object, "until we too/ Are parted like curtains across the empty stage of its memory" (AWK,104). And it is then that a kind of double life is discovered in the memories of another parallel body that is being lived out alongside our "own." Fetishism yokes these two together; both are believed but one is disavowed. The anxiety it provokes, however, is what Ashbery's writing articulates.

Clearly this is not the anxiety which we discussed at the beginning of this chapter. Ashbery's anxiety is a *chronic* one, and chronic in that it is an anxiety about time, or the divided feel of duration:

> The roar of time plunging unchecked through the sluices
> Of the days, dragging every sexual moment of it
> Past and lenses: the end of something.
> Only then did you glance up from your book,

> Unable to comprehend what had been taking place, or
> What you had been reading.   (HD,2)

What is the possible origin of this time? The "scene of a crime," of the attempt to efface the existence of a crime? In Ashbery's case at least, the answer is not bound up with the punishment of nomination:

> Mountain ash mindlessly dropping berries: to whom is all this?
> I tell you, we are being called back

> For having forgotten these names, for falling like nameless things
> On unfamiliar slopes. To be seen again, churlishly into life,
> Returning, as to the scene of a crime.   (DDS,44)

In contrast to the serious theater of naming which we discovered in Eliot and Olson's work, "Ash" and "berries" fall like "nameless things" throughout Ashbery's writing; paternity is no longer emblematized, except in a mock-heroic way. In "Wet Casements," a name is mentioned at a cocktail party, and overheard by someone who carries it around in his wallet while "bills slid in/ And out of it" (HD,28), an economy of the name which is fully "circulated." Similarly, there is a long history of mishaps in the delivery of letters in Ashbery's work. They either arrive absurdly late, "forty-odd years after" they were posted (DDS,75), or at an inappropriate time ("as we gallop into the flame" [TCO,58]), or, most catastrophic of all, when "you have ripped it open not knowing what it is,/ The two envelope halves lying on a plate" (SP,45). There are no trusted letter-carriers here.

If Ashbery has too much time on his hands, and mistakes letters for interior communications, then O'Hara proposes, in his "Personist" manifesto, that he has no time at all to write letters: "if I wanted to, I could use the telephone instead of writing the poem."[60] The distinction is a useful one, if only because it speaks to the different chronic sickness about time which is displayed in O'Hara's I-do-this-I-do-that poems:

> and I am sweating a lot by now and thinking of
> leaning on the john door in the 5 SPOT
> while she whispered a song along the keyboard
> to Mal Waldron and everyone and I stopped breathing.

Here, time has run out. And if there is nothing more to be said, then it is because the unsaid is not important in O'Hara's work, so much is his writing a case of "going on your nerve" that subjective time settles around a very personal bodily rhythm. O'Hara, in a sense, goes too fast to be able to think about reproducing a "natural" stream of consciousness, while the anxiety bred on that "nerve" is a by-product of the short-term memory, or memo-pad narrative— What have I forgotten today? Whatever it is, it's nothing important, but trying to remember it will keep the poetic body on the go, as here, in the eponymous "Anxiety":

> there are no alternatives, just
> the one something.
> > I have a drink
> it doesn't help—far from it!
> > > I
> feel worse. I can't remember how
> I felt, so perhaps I feel better.

So too with a textual device that has become a trademark of the New York School (witness Ted Berrigan's religious observance of it)—the gratuitous citation of time and place: "it is 12:20 in New York, a Friday." This is O'Hara's ironic reversal of the conventionally privileged epiphanies of creative insight. It does suggest, however, that time, in the last instance, is a responsible phenomenon, and not a source of those contradictions which are attributed, instead, to the fickle rhythms of a "decadent" body. In effect, O'Hara is afraid of running out, not only of time, but also of wit, alcohol, novelty, and joie de vivre. Ashbery's compulsion to speak—"that I sing alway" (HD,88)—and the insatiable condition of that speech— like "a spoiled child asking its mother for something for the nth time" (TP,85)—has a share in that anxious consumption. The origin of his other anxiety, however, is in the impulse *not* to say everything, to record that there is in fact something that cannot be said, an inadmissible idea, word, fact or moment which perhaps was never articulated, but whose absence is now reinvented ad infintum:

> . . . . Each of us circles
> Around some simple but vital missing piece of information,
> And, at the end, as now, finding no substitute,

Writes his own mark grotesquely with a stick in snow,
The signature of many connected seconds of indecision.
What I am writing to say is, the timing, not
The contents, is what matters . . . .   (HD,85)

This lacking condition is openly and repeatedly thematized in Ashbery's writing: "the word that everything hinged on is buried back there; by mutual consent neither of you examined it when it was pronounced and rushed to its final resting place. It is doing the organizing, the guidelines radiate from its control; therefore it is good not to know what it is since its results can be known so intimately" (TP,95). The fully revelatory manner of confessional poetry takes this knowledge at its face value, working it over until some central proposition surfaces. In suggesting again that this conventional, confessional manner is taken up thematically in Ashbery's work, one has to add that his compositional method is, at the same time, directly governed by the failure, or the negative capability, of such a revelation; the "hole that hatches me into reason" (ShT,38) is an absent knowledge that breeds "a randomness, a darkness of one's own" (HD,61). Every event, then, as it appears on paper, is also an epilogue, the effect of a written, porous memory, like the Icaresque scene in "As You Came from the Holy Land," where something momentous is happening in the sky, "but the sun is setting and prevents you from seeing it" (SP,7). This effect is so recurrent in Ashbery's writing that it establishes itself as a set of conventional rules. For Bloom, this belatedness is seen as an entertaining, picaresque allegory of the poet writing his own "history of someone who came too late" (SP,7). In Bloom's reading, Ashbery presents just one more manifestation of the archetypal filial struggle, "another failed version of the questing self."[61] To see this anxiety stripped of its personal referent, to see it generalized and displaced on to a secondary level of conventionalization, is to approach the problem of the failure of language *tout court* to fully articulate a "questing self." The elusive trail of Ashbery's "it," for example, as an almost universal, roving substitute for any contextual referent, takes on most of the burden of poetic *personality* which would otherwise be recuperated into the kind of allegory of poethood which Bloom has written about. One is reminded of the

"it" in Henry James, the occulted or unspoken fact (of carnal knowledge, generally) which supports the vast and gorgeous superstructure of the later novels.

Eliot said of James that his mind was too fine to be violated by an
idea. The *idea* in Ashbery is almost always a cliché which complies
with an imaginary demand for meaning:

> The voice of reason is heard for a hard, clear moment,
> Then falls still, if for no other reason than
> That the sheriff's deputies have suddenly coincided
> With a collective notion of romance, and the minute
>   has absconded.   (SHT, 42)

An idea, or image, of romance confronts the *moment* of its own
representation, and displaces the durational effects of that moment:
"the minute has absconded." By contrast, the continuing debate
about "it" generates more time and space than can be functionally
contained:

> We do not have it, and they
> Who have it are plunged in confusion:
> It is so easy not to have it, the gold coin, *we* know
> The contour of having it, a pocket
> Around space that is an endless library   (AWK, 97).

The source of this "endless library" is the written memory of a
displaced moment, object, or fact. A kind of warmth plays around
their vacated forms: "the outline of an eddy that traced itself/ Before
moving on" (AWK, 116). And there is something of the infantile
demand for *leftovers* which presides over the anxiety generated by
these absences: "the child's devotion to this normal, shapeless en-
tity" (RM, 35). Like the cutouts of Matisse, stranded in a chromatic
spectrum of new events, these lively relics are still umbilically
linked to their originating context, and their eroticized edges or
outlines still radiate some of the heat of their original meaning.

Ashbery's commitment to this "leaving-out business" (RM, 39) is
often cited as the source of a defined poetics; what appears to be a
compositional principle in the early work is taken up as a thematic

or discursive topic in the later poetry. The obvious point of reference is Mallarmé—"*je n'ai crée mon oeuvre que par élimination*[62]—
whose reified absences figure both concretely (the *blancs*) and figuratively (the Symboliste "spaces") as a formal code of invention.
Ashbery's own Mallarmean attack on the language surface is all but
exhausted by *The Tennis Court Oath*, which "pushes far into amnesiac" in an attempt to reach the unsociable, syntactical limits of
language. The less spectacular but more politic work that follows
cannot be addressed, however, without assuming "a slightly guilty
air of naturalness" (TP,38): the discursive account of language itself
as a "leaving-out business," and the implied contradictions of subjectivity, "always past, yet always in question, on the surface/ Of
the goggles of memory" (DDS,89). In the later work, then, absence
is no longer essentialized as an ideal medium, but taken up at the
level of its conventional effects, effects that are no less authentic,
but which are shown to mediate, or block access to the "authenticity" of their origins.

Macavity, the stylish master of absence, is never too far away to
be invoked (in one "it" poem, curious cats "followed it/ Down to
the glen where it was last seen" (ShT,44):

. . . . the catgut
Of abstract sleek ideas that come only once in
The night to be born and are gone forever after
Leaving their trace after the stitches have
Been removed but who is to say they are
Traces of what really went on and not today's palimpsest? For what
Is remarkable about our chronic reverie (a watch
That is always too slow or too fast)
Is the lively sense of accomplishment that haloes it
From afar . . . .   (AWK,66)

Notwithstanding Macavity, it is clear that the discussion of time in
Ashbery's later work increasingly comes to refer, directly or not, to
the "case" of Eliot. In "Litany," Ashbery's longest poem (the long
poem as duration and not the "long poem" tradition of the modern
American epic), *Four Quartets* acts almost as an explicit subtext;
passages pick up an allusion, first of all in a parodic manner, but

then slip into a kind of parallel step, underlined by the "parallel" texts of the poem itself:

The dust blows in.	The pattern of the city,
The disturbance is	The formula that once made sense to
Non-verbal communication:	A few of us until it became
Meaningless syllables that	The end.
Have a music of their own,	
The music of sex, or any	The magic has left the
Nameless event, something	Drawings finally.
That can only be taken as	They blow around the rest—tumbleweed
Itself. This rules ideas	In a small western ghost town
Of what else may be there.	That sometimes hits and sometimes misses.

(AWK,4)

Similarly, earlier in *Three Poems*, the aped confessional banality of the prose allows Ashbery access to areas of religious discourse where the reader knows he has no serious business to conduct: words are "broken open and pressed to the mouth" (TP,6) in the presence of "the secret feelings of an administrator beyond the bounds of satisfying intimacy" (TP,18). John Lehmann writes about the attempt "to construct out of the everyday world, a heaven without the furniture of theology,"[63] and we are reminded of Eliot's remarks about the "insufficiently furnished apartments" of Milton's Hell, filled only with "heavy conversation" (SE,321). But these discourse-filled "apartments" are as staged and illusory as any of Ashbery's visual effects; faith is only "a new way of being seen" (TP,39).

In pointing to Ashbery's "tolerance for negativity," particularly his quotidian acceptance of repeatedly shapeless expressions of (in)significance, David Shapiro describes a dominant "antinomian" temper in the poetry as whole.[64] This seems to hold good as a way of talking about the rather ambivalent attitude toward the privileges of epiphany, either in terms of an order of grace, or as a more domestic flight from meaning—although this is not the real thing and has no special meaning, you, the individual, are somehow implicated in it, if only because of the memory of some possibly unknown event which is part of your history: "perhaps the explanation lies precisely here: what we were witnessing was merely the reverse side of an event of cosmic beatitude for all except us, who were blind to it because it took place inside us" (TP,114). Again we encounter a *déjà vu* which is also a *jamais vu*, unable to sit still on the surface of memory. Again it makes serious fun of Eliot's anxiety about the Word:

> . . . . It all boils down to
> Nothing, one supposes. There is a central crater
> Which is the word, and around it
> All things that have a name, a commotion
> Of thrushes pretending to have hatched
> Out of the great egg that still hasn't been laid.
>
> (AWK,55)

As a safeguard against this anxiety, we could add the poetics of *agnosticism* to Shapiro's "antinomianism," an agnosticism derived, literally, from a "thought-not-possible," and which manifests itself as a skepticism, not about the real (or the transcendental), but about the conventional survival of its representations or symbolic expressions. Belief, then, for the agnostic and mystic alike, is merely a disquisition about the capacity of language to present a case for the real, or represent its point of view. In other words, it is an opinion about the (im)mediacy of language itself.

Earlier, I suggested that a different kind of *chronic* anxiety was generated by Ashbery's poetry. Eliot's "insignificant" moments were ones which had somehow escaped signification—unseen, unheard, perhaps even unlived. Memory had begun to be the medium of another kind of redemptionary time, through which filtered the God-given past. Ashbery's work realizes this as a fully expanded writing practice or compositional method; this time, however, is *invented*, rather than *discovered* as it is in Eliot, where the phenomenological apperception of experience depends upon a disclosure of more authentic, transcendental forms.

The rhythm of reading the longer poems, however, works to maintain the "lived" consistency of this "other" time, but a time which has little of the imaginary consistency of the "fables that time invents/ To explain its passing" (DDS,46) by perfectly reproducing a supreme fiction from memory. If only because of its formal structure, "Litany" (*Lis-ta-nie* in French—Read your denial) is perhaps the best example of the way in which these durational effects are divided and distributed. Its two "simultaneous and independent" monologue texts, echoing again the classic fetishistic circuit, each acknowledge and disavow the other at one and the same time; occasionally, they present some cross-reference—a synchronous sound, a common word, a contiguous meaning—that almost gratuitously establishes their mutual resonance. A related time is built up between the two columns of the poem, a time that is entirely artificial but which draws upon our divided attention in a manner that is real enough:

> It's only after realizing this for a long time
> That you can make a chain of events like days
> That more and more rapidly come to punch their own number
> Out of the calendar, draining it. By that time
> Space will be a jar with no lid, and you can live
> Any way you like out on these vague terraces,
> Verandas, walkaways—the forms of space combined with time
> We are allowed, and we live them passionately,
> Fortunately, though we can never be described
> And would make lousy characters in a novel.   (AWK,85)

Ashbery's point here seems an appropriate one with which to conclude this argument for a non-naturalistic time, for it reminds us of the classical novel's various experiments with subjective time. From *Tristram Shandy* to *Ulysses*, from *style indirect libre* and the Jamesian point of view to the Beat narrative rap, the dominant impulse is to represent or reproduce a more natural form of subjectivity, whether in the form of an "interior consciousness" or in the simulation of the *proper* sequence of a reader or character's time. We do not find any such sympathy with a natural consciousness in Ashbery's writing. Perhaps only allegories of the unconscious are prepared to refuse to identify with a waking life. This, of course, need not entail a refusal of life, but rather, as we shall see in the next section, an acceptance of language.

3.

Art has to be constantly re-begun, or as the
Red Queen noted, one has to run very fast
in order to remain in the same place.

Ashbery

From *The Tennis Court Oath* onwards, and in contrast to that volume, Ashbery commits himself to a declarative, if not an explanatory, level of discourse. I have described some of the ways in which that discourse courts meaning in order to expose the fraudulence of its representations: "It is the law to think now. To think becomes the law" (TP,4). It is a discourse that pretends to know what it is doing, to such an extent that words are both employed as messengers and reified as events acting in the world: "It is they who carry news of it/ To other places. Therefore/ Are they not the event itself?" (AWK,5).

Increasingly in the later work, the meaning of a line implodes or collapses into itself, describing, in the same moment, how that collapse came about. Many of the concluding lines or half-lines of poems in *Shadow Train*, for example, ironically transcribe their own conventional necessity as the *terminus ad quem* of a light, logical meditation construed across the space of sixteen classically strophed lines: "the idea/ Warning, waiting there like a forest, not emptied, beckons" (ShT,1): "the poem is you" (ShT,3); "the night we now knew" (ShT,4); "One last question" (ShT,6); "We only have to begin on time" (ShT,8); "the hoofprint in the dust" (ShT,16); "One for the books" (ShT,21); "We are all soiled with this desire, at the last moment, the last" (ShT,22); "A blight. Spared, though" (ShT,31); "surprised, somewhat, but sure" (ShT,38); "and the minute has absconded" (ShT,42); "This is all there is" (ShT,46); "Or so I've been told" (ShT,50). In a review, John Bayley suggests that these poems mime "the act of evanescence, swooping on the sixteenth line to a vanishing point . . . . like the grin of a Chesire cat," invoking "evanescence" and "vanishing point" in a much more figurative way than I have done earlier.[65] However, if these poems "die naturally," as Bayley claims, then they also implicate the conventional necessity of that death by playing up the fate of those last lines, somewhat like the tag-fetishism of the alcoholic's "one for the road." Is there anything "natural" about an ironic denouement such as the following?

. . . . . . You remain a sane, yet sophisticated, person:
Rooted in twilight, dreaming, a piece of traffic.   (SHT,40)

Here, in "We Hesitate," the conclusion we are offered presents a *decreasing* order of thematic certainty articulated within a formal structure of cumulative affirmation. From the infallibity of "sane," to the thin contingency of "a piece of traffic," any collusion with conventional logic is both artificial and contradictory.

It would be easy to go on and interpret such willfully self-concious effects in the more general light of those *postmodernist* practices that have been viewed, in recent years, as offering a highly ironic commentary about problems of mediation and representation. Indeed, there is no doubt that many of my polemical descriptions of Ashbery's work have been drawn (implicitly rather than explicitly) from a larger cultural reading of the withdrawal from modernism. Postmodernism itself can be read in terms of its concern with its own lateness, or posteriority, as a culture of secondarity. Subject to the same "failures" or enunciation which inspired the first wave of modernism, postmodernism returns to these same problems, not however to solve them, but to examine the codes and conventions which govern the representability of these problems as "problems" of subjectivity, history, etc. More often than not, then, postmodernist practices are understood through their reference to a complex range of conventional assumptions about styles and forms from the past; the given fact of these conventions is a starting-point for any exploration of meaning. Even the modernist belief in cultural continuity is internalized as a conventional fact, to be engaged and then displaced, rather than unsystematically vandalized by the indiscriminate use of the device of formal discontinuity. In *Poetic Artifice*, for example, Veronica Forrest-Thompson argues for an antirealist writing which is not captivated by its flat rejection of conventional meaning, syntax, or logic, but which is alert to traditional levels of conventional expectancy, and insists on its "artificial" construction as a challenge to other liguistic orderings of the world. This kind of writing demands "that unmeaningful levels be taken into account [so] that meaning be used as technical device which makes it impossible as well as wrong for critics to strand poems in the external world."[66] Much of what I have said about Ashbery appeals to a similar "realism" about the ways of challenging realism, especially with respect to the fetishization of conventions, like that of point of view.

This, however, is a book about modernism, or at least what it perceives to be modernist. Rather than generalize some of the tendencies suggested by Ashbery's work, by presenting them in the context of a different or redemptive postmodernist point of view, I want to finish by restating some of the polemical distinctions that I have made concerning the "failure" of modernism, and to do so in the light of those elements of Ashbery's writing that bear a close relation to late, or advanced modernism.

For the most part, the critical hosannahs which honor Ashbery's poetry today do so at the cost of one perceived "failure": the general boycott of his second volume, *The Tennis Court Oath*, regarded by some as little less than a shocking mistake and by others as no more than a youthful aberration. "We all have graves to travel from," it observes, and despite its singular resemblance to *The Waste Land* in composition, construction, and effective appeal to discontinuity, Ashbery's decision to "travel from" *The Tennis Court Oath* into more traditionally acceptable, formal provinces has been greeted with as much relief as Eliot's journey out of the wasteland was met with disappointment, and anger. Notwithstanding Ashbery's own recent, playful reminder—"the critics always get everything wrong"[67] —the parallel is either too fleeting or else much too complex to pursue here. The importance of *The Waste Land*, however, as a historical and conventional referent, is one which we will bear in mind and discuss later.

The very nature of the critical resistance provoked by *The Tennis Court Oath* invites some kind of psychoanalytical interest. Bloom, for example, refers to it as "a fearful disaster" or a "collapse into such a bog" of "calculated incoherence."[68] Williamson connects it to "the vertiginous quality of adolescent consciousness."[69] And Shapiro sees it as an infantile disorder which is worked through and placed in check by a more mature "ego development" in the next volume.[70] Shapiro's specific complaint is that it presents "merely a glamorous dream imagery," a comment which is significant if only because it heralds much of the subsequent reception of Ashbery, favorable or otherwise, that has been colored by a reaction

to the "dream" status of his writing:[71] "Something like living occurs, a movement/ Out of the dream into its codification" (SP,73). If
we are to take this "dream" element in Ashbery 's work seriously,
and thus subject it to a more systematic Freudian examination, then
I would argue that a distinction must be made between the way in
which the dream is experienced—from the psychological stand-
point of the dreamer—and the "codification" of the dream itself
inasmuch as it reveals the way in which the unconscious operates
through the "rhetoric" of psychic communication. As I have suggested, we can hope to find in this distinction a model for what I
have variously described under the double-edged category of *failure:*
the attempt to use language to construct a predetermined (or theoretical) subjective position—in this case, the "natural" psychology
of a dreamer's consciousness—and hence the relapse into reproducing another form of subjectivism; and secondly, an acceptance of the failure of subjectivity in language, manifested by the
psychic displacement of consciousness—and, in this case, it would
be the operations of what Freud calls the dreamwork. Somewhere,
perhaps, in the critical space between these two tendencies lies a
more interpretive reading of Yeats's claim (in a more utopian context) that "in dreams begin responsibilities."

To begin with, we should acknowledge the extent to which a
stock of references to dream conventions is present throughout
Ashbery's poetry, from the Keatsian "Have I awakened? Or is this
sleep again?" (TP,4) to the neoclassical associational daydreaming
in "Self-Portrait in a Convex Mirror" which distracts the narrator.
Many of the poems in *The Double Dream of Spring* end in morning
scenarios, or reveilles, "readying its defences again/ As day comes
up" (DDS,42), as if preparing the reader for a gentle awakening.[72]
Contributing to this kind of reading is the frequently staged opposition between the "sieved dark" of night, "trifoliate, strange to
the touch" (HD,50), and the "thawing nerve" of waking into the
"open, moist, impregnable order of the day" (TP,9). Night retains
its Gothic mystique as the oneiric guardian of arcane truths, while
"the rest is up to the scribes and the eunuchs" (AWK,91), the
dream-interpreters whose killjoy job it is to "rationalize" the
dreamwork.

Even if this extensive array of mythological conventions harks back to the impressionistic notion of an assumed dreamer-narrator, we expect to find such a gesture undercut. Indeed, what Ashbery calls Dreamland frequently appears as a gaudy Disneyworld, worked up into a literary fantasy:

> Yet whereto, with damaged wing
> Assay th'empyrean? Scalloped horizon
> Of Cloud-Cuckoo-Land? O land
> Of recently boiling water, witches,
> Misgivings, ships
> Pulling away from piers
> Already slipping deep into the norm
> Of blue worsted seas?   (AWK,31)

The relations of this visual logic are, of course, to be read as spurious, and like all mock exteriors, their formal interest is summoned up, as it were, out of the blue, to match the counterfeit depth of our expectancy. It is our passing through that is a "facade," before we discover that the clouds "are pulled along on invisible ropes" (HD,50), or that someone has thrown a switch to release the "immobile Niagaras that hover in the background" (AWK,114). Prospero's "cloud-capp'd towers" turn up of course in Hollywood— "a turret here, an art-deco escarpment there" (HD,34), and so in a place which is no less rich than it is strange, an overdetermined curiosity makes us look twice, and ask: What lies behind the facade? It is a question that Freud had meditated upon at length in his discussion of the dreamwork, noting how certain constructed fantasies, or "facades," seem to be always already there, as precast elements of the very structure that accommodates the dream thoughts.[73] Even when these facades are exposed as "fictions," their effectiveness persists. As Ashbery often observed, in interviews and art reviews, there is a necessity about the "look" of certain landscapes or things, as if they had to exist in that way to tally with the demands of some personal psychic configuration which now recontains itself fantasmatically in the impression which that image makes: or perhaps also in the "fleeting moments" in writing when one gets the idea "of a structure that doesn't exist in English."[74] The result is a language full of meaning which is not, however, a discourse; it is like

waking up
In the middle of a dream with one's mouth full
Of unknown words takes in all of these;
It is both the surface and the accidents
Scarring that surface, yet it too only contains
As a book on Sweden only contains the pages of that book.

(SP, 55)

The "surface" here, like the facade, appears to have depth and dimensional meaning, but is also no more than the literal "stuff" of its contents, or its lettering.

Ashbery's "dream images," then, have the requisite high visibility which the dream content demands, for the primary criterion for inclusion in a dream is the figurability of a series of dream thoughts—whether something is capable of being represented or not, in its censored pictorial form or otherwise.[75] Freud's *Entstellung*, the distorting or censoring effect of the dreamwork, is literally a *dis-figuring*, which is to say that it cuts up and rearranges the primary dream material, transforming what was perfectly recognizable in its original form into the conventionally absurd, secondary level of dream logic. If we extend the *Entstellung* metaphor to the realm of literary activity, we see that it would only correspond to those instances of cutting up a text that has already been understood, and *not* to the cutting up of found material in order to produce new patterns of meaning. Ashbery's constructivist experiments in *The Tennis Court Oath* belong to the latter category, while it is the cut-up work of John Cage or William Burroughs, for example, which approaches the demands of the censorship model. A Cage lecture, in its uncut draft form, is often a strikingly polemical discourse, subsequently broken down and "dis-figured."[76] By contrast, the "free speech" we are offered in Ashbery's Dreamland (AWK, 104) is constructed from disparate and gratuitous sources; the Surrealist *acte gratuit* is not here an index of expressivity. In "Europe," the most "cut-up" of all of Ashbery's texts (incorporating fragments, among others, of a pulp adventure story, *Beryl of the Biplanes* by William Le Queux), the sources themselves are inherently uninteresting.

In this respect, then, any attempt to seriously correlate the dreamwork with the impressionistic assumption of a "dreamer" at the core of Ashbery's work must be discarded. The question of "free speech," however, stubbornly haunts attempts to link experimental writing with some conception of the unconscious processes—another myth of natural writing. In "A Note on the Prehistory of the Technique of Analysis," Freud cites the source of his famous method of free association as an essay by one Ludwig Borne, entitled "The Art of Becoming an Original Writer in Three Days," in which Borne advocates writing down "for three days on end . . . without fabrication or hypocrisy, everything that comes into your head."[77] The Freudian interest in free association does not lie, however, in the opportunity such a practice offers for the liberating effects of spontaneous self-expression, but on the contrary, in the way in which it throws light upon the operations of repression in a linguistic context. "Freedom," in this respect, is only worthwhile inasmuch as it reveals the *necessity* not only of censorship but also of those psychic determinations which work at the level of and the level below censorship. For Freud, there is no free speech as such, only a different arrangement of variously determined discourses. The Freudian point of view, then, runs counter to the expressionist myth about creative spontaneity, which holds that extemporaneous discourse is a vicarious, if not direct, link with the more authentic truths of the unconscious. Among American writers, it is the ideology of Beat discourse which most fully adopts that myth, asserting its democratic availability to every turned-on individual, as opposed to poets born to the rhetorical manner:

—If possible write "without consciousness" in semi-trance (as Yeats's later "trance writing") allowing subconscious to admit in own uninhibited interesting necessary and so "modern" language what conscious art would censor, and write excitedly, swiftly with writing-or-typing-cramps, in accordance (as from center to periphery) with laws of orgasm, Reich's "beclouding of consciousness." *Come* from within, out—to relaxed and said.[78]

Unlike Kerouac here, Olson, as we have seen, was no great believer in spontaneity, but subscribes nonetheless to the naturalism of an "open" poetry. At a different level of organizing the same myth, the expressionism of Roethke and Berryman mediates the spectacle of confessional authenticity, where the poet's problems are presented as an example of an "interesting" psychology, or a sophisticated consciousness.

For Ashbery, however, a more important frame of reference is Surrealism, the most serious cultural attempt to follow through the automatism of the associationist technique. In an art review in 1968, he suggested that "we all 'grew up Surreal' without even being aware of it,"[79] and that ever since "the declaration of independence" [of the "Republic of Dreams"] was signed in the twenties, "the space of dreams—deep, shallow, open, bent, a point which has no physical dimensions or a universal breadth—is the space in which we now live."[80] Ashbery's gesture is a conventional tribute to the utopian aims of the Surrealist project: the dissolution of the barrier between sleeping and waking, a lifestyle and a literature lived in much the same way as one dreams. Breton's manifesto-bound fascination with Freud drew the Surrealists toward a kind of writing which modeled itself on the contradictory logic of the unconscious. In this respect, Breton's is another sophisticated plea for naturalism, another attempt to transcribe the universal thought processes (his interest in psychoanalysis is seasoned with a taste for spiritualism which led him increasingly into a rapprochement with Jung) of the human condition through the medium of a superconscious or super-real individuality: "SURREALISM, n. Psychic automatism in its pure state, by which one proposes to express verbally, by means of the written word, or in any other manner, the actual functioning of thought. Dictated by thought, in the absence of any control exercised by reason, exempt from any aesthetic or moral concern."[81] Ultimately, the attempt to produce this "pure state," Breton's call for a more true *moi*, or an expanded condition of consciousness, speaks to the kind of expressionistic psychologism we have been discussing. In the later manifestos, this appeal becomes more and more specific. The first Surrealist magazine to be published in America, for example, bears the title *VW*: "the first V with its axis on the EGO and the reality principle, the second W on the SELF and the pleasure principle — the resolution of the contradiction tending only to the continual systematic enlargement of the field of consciousness."[82]

Again, one can make a limited claim for the kind of psychologistic attention that Ashbery devotes to this idea of the *universality* of consciousness in his writing: his interest, for example, in a "polyphony" of consciousness, or the "greater naturalism" which might be provided by any chosen means of impressionism, even at the level of "the kind of impression you get while riding in a car, changing the radio station, and at the same time aware of the passing landscape. In other words, a confused but insistent impression of the culture going on around us."[83] No matter how problematic as an effect of language, I have suggested that this same descriptive psychology is more difficult to reproduce in the case of the dream condition, where the subject, deprived of any control over the events, is almost the spectator of someone else's dream. Because this is a lived effect, it cannot be simulated by simply trying to represent the absurd relations of dream logic. It has been widely argued nonetheless that much of Ashbery's poetry is intended to echo this condition in all of its shifting, somnambulent grounds.

A dream poetics of this sort, moreover, merely revives the familiar criterion of realism—to accurately reproduce a typical event, or in this case, a typical discourse. (A simple example of this contrived mentalism is "Worsening Situation," written from the point of view of a psychiatric inmate, and ending on a note which resonates with the reader's suspicions, rather like the last lines in Browning's "My Last Duchess": "Lately/ I've been looking at old-fashioned plaids, fingering/ Starched white collars, wondering whether there's a way/ To get them really white again. My wife/ Thinks I'm in Oslo—Oslo, France, that is" [SP,3–4]). In a letter to O'Hara, Auden offers the standard realist response to such a poetics: "I think you (and John for that matter) must watch what is always the great danger with any 'surrealistic' style, namely of confusing authentic non-logical relations which arouse wonder, with accidental ones which arouse mere surprise, and in the end fatigue."[84] Auden's critique could be read in the context of the Lockean tradition of associationism, in which the "reality" of linked ideas was posited in the objects themselves according to the natural postulates of Reason. Indeed, he sounds not unlike Dr. Johnson, prepared to accept the "wondrous" conceits of the Metaphysical poets on condition that there must somewhere be a rational limit to the stretching of Nature's laws of association. On this conceptual level, the "limit" is always a "rational" one. Surrealist poetry in English, for example, like the work of Philip Lamantia, David Gascoyne, Michael Horowitz, or the Deep Image movement (Bly, Simpson, Wright, Kelly) has devoted itself to an expressionist zeal for conceptual inventiveness, rather than pursuing the French concern with phonic associationism (*"allez, la musique!"*). The result is distinguished only by its "scenic" unintelligibility as a daring series of thoughts or images, vying to outdo each other in the transgression of rational or logical relations. Rather than willfully avoid logical relations in this manner, Ashbery, even at his most transparent, is preserving the rigorous logical structure of language relations, at the same time as he is gratuitously engaging different levels of the same discourse:

> They dream only of America
> To be lost among the thirteen million pillars of grass:
> "This honey is delicious
> *Though it burns the throat"*   (TCO, 13)

> And by no other moment, we have come down
> At last to where the plumbing is.
> We had hoped for a dialogue.
> But they're rusty.   (AWK, 99)

These parts of speech are ambivalently held together under the formal pressure of being placed in logical conjunction. Elsewhere, it is a purely phonic set of relations that binds together a line or a phrase: "The lake a lilac cube" (TCO, 13); "A torn page with a passionate oasis" (TCO, 59); "a sail stunned in a vast haze" (AWK, 45); "this wide berth of lights like weeds" (AWK, 73); "You see the sand-lots still foaming with the blood of light" (ShT, 12); "The segments of the trip swing open like an orange" (W, 9). Such moments of acoustic dexterity conform absolutely to Breton's prescriptions for *l'enchaînement musicale,* or rather, the proviso that things, in poetry, should be heard first and seen later (Breton's *auditif*: clear listener as opposed to the visionary *clairvoyant*).[85]

Ashbery is barely committed, however, to this *alchimie du verbe*; assonance and alliteration are infrequently and gratuitously strewn around his work. As I have suggested, there are other ways in which his writing confronts the "dreamwork" in terms of a process of inscription or dictation. And there are a number of metaphors available to invoke such a process: the art of "Pyrography," for example, of burning designs or letters onto a material surface with a hot, metal instrument (HD,9), or in "The Skaters," in the description of "flame-writing" with a "solution" of nitrate and potash, the writing being visible only "in the gaps" between the clouds of smoke as "solution-writing" (RM,50)—as in a dream interpretation, we are not sure how *literal* this "solution" is. These metaphors of writing belong to the ambivalent, double register of meaning that is so insistent in Ashbery's work. All too often, a reference to the discourse of writing becomes a reference to the textual surface itself in a metaphorical operation of the type which Freud suggested was at the heart of the dreamwork. In effect, it is in Ashbery's thematic and structural use of such operations that we can speak more successfully about a "dream" poetics, a poetry that is like a dream, not because it tries to reproduce certain impressionist effects, but because it is subject to the same kind of codes, or rhetoric, of meaning which govern the dreamwork.

Before elaborating this idea with respect to *The Tennis Court Oath*, we might briefly mention two other possible responses which have been alluded to earlier. The first is concerned with a rather graphic desire to break the law and get away with it: "Police formed a boundary to the works/ Where we played/ A torn page with a passionate oasis" (TCO,59). Scattered throughout the volume are complaints against an overlegislated language: "I was almost killed/ now by reading/ on trial" (TCO,16): "Have you encouraged judge/ inked commentary" (TCO,68): "The editor realized/ its gradual abandonment" (TCO,65). It is no surprise that Ashbery's title recalls one of the most famous "unfinished" representations in history, David's proposed painting of the French revolutionary oath. In this respect, the liberationary feel of these disjunct poetic forms is quite premonitory of the full spate of experimental modernism which carried American poetry through the turbulent sixties. The facile interpretive dilemma—any fixed reading closes the "open" poem—presented by this order of formalism is actually a conventional discomfort that is thought out for us, and described as it is given, in Ashbery's later work:

> . . . . We are afloat
> On our dreams as on a barge made of ice

Shot through with questions and fissures of starlight
That keep us awake, thinking about the dreams
As they are happening. . . . . . .   (AWK,82)

Nothing so courteous, however, is permitted in *The Tennis Court Oath*, where the more appropriate metaphor would be that in which the dream thoughts are broken up by the dreamwork and jammed together, as Freud put it, like "pack- ice."[86]

A poem like "Europe," moreover, evokes a range of conventional historical meanings that goes beyond its formal discontinuities. In this respect, it bears comparison with *The Waste Land*, not only because it confronts formalism with historicism, but also because it incorporates what Eliot's poem has already done. In contrast to the anxiety of Eliot's cultural moment, "Europe" sounds cheerful, relieved that the agony has moved on:

> To employ her
> construction ball
> Morning fed on the
> light blue wood
> of the mouth   (TCO,64)

The baroque facade of the European myth has long since been slated for demolition, but the wrecking ball, in accord with the environmental doublespeak of the day, is said to be engaged in "construction." The wrecking and the construction are carried out on the same linguistic register—the mouth-music of "light blue wood"—beyond any serious external appeal to the stockpile of cultural references which supplements *The Waste Land*. For four decades, Yvor Winters's critique of the "fallacy of imitative form" has stuck tenaciously in one way or another to our reading of *The Waste Land*: the broken form as a simple reflection of social and cultural confusion. No longer viable as a means of representation by the time of Ashbery's "Europe," this formal device becomes internalized as an object of knowledge at the level of a literary convention, and thus becomes a referent at that same level. In much the same way Freud had noted that the absurd or madcap logic of the dream was often a conventional way of representing an element of absurdity or irrationality in the dream thoughts themselves.[87]

(Other examples would be the long naming-lists of the first twenty-two pages of *The Vermont Notebook*, and the way in which they domesticate the conventional Dadaist taxonomy; or the ironic incorporation of the modernist *ubi sunt*? within the beautiful inventory of the world's rivers, catalogued in "Into the Dusk-Charged Air".) At this conventional level of meaning, the questions raised by Eliot's poem—Who is speaking? Who is Phlebas the Phoenician? and what is his structural role?—are entirely rhetorical. In Ashbery's poem, the stakes are different—Where are we linguistically when this poem is being read? If there is a significant distinction between these two types of question, then it arises from the difference between the allusion, Eliot's expressive principle, and the lexical bricolage which constitutes the formal organization of "Europe"; one is primarily a literary device, the other is a linguistic design.

Without straying much further into the realm of linguistics, we can suggest that *The Tennis Court Oath* displays a "rhetoric" of meaning, rather than a grammar of meaning which would be encoded within a set of fixed relations between subject, language, and cultural referents. Rhetoric, in this sense, would be understood as a display of the associative paths taken by the signifier: in other words, not a simple taxonomy of various figurative operations (anadiplosis, chiasmus, hendiadys), but a way of describing the component substitutions and displacements which make up these operations.[88] The "rediscovery" of Freud's attentiveness to the two "sovereign" operations of the dreamwork, condensation and displacement, was largely inspired by the thesis that the unconscious obeys processes of a linguistic nature, that is, processes which are also active in language. Dream logic, even at its most gratuitous and absurd, is determined by strict codes of linguistic necessity; *there is no free association.*

It is in the context of these operations that we can speak of the "dream logic" of *The Tennis Court Oath*: its lexical juxtapositions and metonymies, its syntactical decomposition, etc. Any systematic account of such operations is beyond the scope of this author, and this book. I have chosen, nonetheless, to list a few examples culled from Ashbery's text. No attempt is made to catalogue the operations at work in each fragment, although most are of a metaphorical nature, governed by phonic association (the classic intercourse of metaphor and metonymy). The elements involved are underlined, and some of my own interpretations of the occulted text are appended in brackets on the right:

(TCO,11) What had you been thinking about
    the face <u>studiously bloodied</u>   [study/ink blots
                                              blotched
    <u>heaven blotted region</u>   (blood) clotted]

(TCO,11) the blood <u>shifted</u> you know   [walls shrink
    these <u>walls</u>
    <u>wind</u> off the earth had made   wind shifts]
    him <u>shrink</u>

(TCO,19) in <u>progress</u>   [progress is halted
    the <u>halt</u> sea   the salt sea]

(TCO,19) a <u>feather not snow blew</u>   [a bird (not slow) flew]
    against the window

(TCO,23) The <u>peanut ship wells</u>   [peanut oil/wells
    Into the <u>desert</u>   ship of the desert]

(TCO,33) The <u>arctic honey blabbed</u>   [sun went over
    <u>over the report</u>   the horizon]
    causing darkness

(TCO,39) The factory to be screwed
    <u>onto palace</u>   [into place]

(TCO,56) Guns were fired to <u>discourage</u>   [discharge]
    dogs into the interior

(TCO,66) . . . . .but the stone
    must be rebuilt. Time <u>stepped</u>   [stopped]

(TCO,67) The librarian <u>shabbily books on</u>   [looks]

(TCO,72) the club had bought <u>aperture</u>   [up her share]

(TCO,72) He ran the <u>ferret</u>   [gauntlet]

(TCO,79) Soon after noon carrying <u>a narrow</u>   [an arrow]

Proper linguistic analysis of these examples must go begging. In the context of this study, however, they demonstrate (better than any theoretical discussion could) the thesis that language is spoken in more than one place, and that subjectivity is a product of, and not the operator of that division. The logic of the modernist project is to pursue that thesis beyond the comfortable terra firma of literary associationism, and that is why works like *The Tennis Court Oath* or *Finnegans Wake,* have been read as "literary failures," and not as a challenge to the idea of Literature, or as texts which no longer qualify. The best response to this is to insist on the continuity between these "experiments" in language, the discourse of traditionally conjunctive literary form, and the discourse of "ordinary" spoken language: "Like the blood orange we have a single/ Vocabulary all heart and all skin. . ." (DDS,82). "Ordinary" language is no less subject to the congeries of figurative operations that mobilizes "poetic" language, and it can accede to poeticity by the simplest of substitutions, whether through well known routes (rhyme, alliteration) or by more novel paths (fresh "rhetorical moments," as manifest in the examples above).

In each substitution or displacement, one element of language comes to stand in for another. The ousted or omitted element haunts the new formation, however, from its position of absence, dividing up the range of meaning, as in a metaphor, and preventing it from ever being fully present. Poetry continues to be the privileged or quarantine space for our cultural experience of this fact: a cordoned-off no-go area where "certain sins of omission go unpunished" (DDS,55) Because of that, it is set aside as a special province of knowledge or perception about how our social subjectivity fails, or else infringes all paternal denying that

> only the other—
>   exchanged another meaning
> here lately   (TCO,83)

THE FAILURE OF MODERNISM:
A CONCLUSION

T HE FAILURE OF MODERNISM, as this book has argued, turns upon the assumption that subjectivity is a problem, and that it can be solved by reforming language itself. At least two questions might reasonably be asked of this proposition. How specific are these issues of language and subjectivity to the modernist period alone? And how strictly defined is my use of this term "modernism"?

Clearly, the perception of subjectivity as a problem to be solved is no longer particularly fresh by the turn of the century. One need look no further that Emerson's famous image from "Nature" for a classic formulation of this idea:

Standing on the bare ground—my head bathed by the blithe air, and up-lifted into infinite space—all mean egotism vanishes. I become a trans-parent eyeball. I am nothing. I see all. The currents of the Universal Being circulate through me; I am part or particle of God.

Certainly language is used here to *support* Emerson's thesis. In fact, the feat of transcendental elevation is suggested, if not wholly en-acted, by a short phonic medley: the alliteration and assonance of "bare," "bathed," "blithe," "air," and "space," sustained by the acoustic play of "uplifted" and "infinite," "mean" and "ego," all of which dissolves, and levels off on the higher transcendental plane with the new finality of "vanishes." Moreover, Emerson's transcen-dental "solution," in the specific form of a model of perception like the transparent eyeball, is one that would look forward to the phe-nomenology of Eliot's poetics of "invisibility" which I discussed in the first chapter. And as for language, Whitman's premodernist vision of *Leaves of Grass* as a "language experiment" offering "new words, new potentialities of speech" to the newest poet of the "American" sublime, responds well to the chauvinistic impulse that we have seen at work in Olson's demand for linguistic reform. As Eliot might have said, however, it is only the *idea* of such things that is fresh and novel to Emerson and Whitman. In other words, they present an idea of the sublime that could be realized within the conventional (and for them, "natural") limits of language, without breaking any serious laws. It is not until the modernist perception, that language is not only pliant but also artificially organized, that Emerson's idea can be acted out in a concrete way by the kind of writing that sought to fashion or wrench language into more "natural" shapes and quotients. Under modernism, the perception of subjectivity as an unnecessary obstacle could at last be combined with the redeeming perception that language can be acted upon at will. In effect, the modernist will rewrites Marx's slogan: the philosophers have only interpreted subjectivity, the point is to change it.

To jump, then, from the premodern to the postmodern, it is all the more significant that certain writers who are active today view this volitional drive to resolve a philosophical problem in literature as one that can no longer be trusted. One of the language poets, Charles Bernstein, for example, offers this opinion:

Much of the spirit of modernism has been involved in the reassertion of the value of what has come to be fantasized as subjectivity. Faced with an imperial reality, "subjectivity" is first defined as "mere idiosyncrasy," that residue of perception that is to be discounted, the fumbling clouds of vision that are to be dissolved by learning. But in just this is the ultimate *subjectivity* of a people: stripping us of our source of power in our humanness by denying the validity of our power over the constitution of our world through language. The myth of subjectivity and its denigration as mere idiosyncrasy—impediments to be overcome—diffuses the inherent power in the commonness of our alienation: that rather than being something that separates us, alienation is the source of our commonness. . . . The poetic response to the imposition of an imperial reality has been to define subjectivity by a kind of Nietzschean turn around, not as "mere" but as "exalted." The image of the poet as loner & romantic continues to condition this response. An unconscious strategy of contrariety develops—that the official manners & forms are corrupt & distorted & only the private & individual is real.[1]

Bernstein, of course, has his own political and theoretical axe to grind, but his response, in this passage, to both the initial wave of modernism and the Romantic resurgence (the "new American poetry" of the fifties and the sixties) seems to me to be accurate. The alternatives which Bernstein's position implies, however, are an indication of a truly concrete withdrawal from the failures of modernism; the implication that subjectivity should be accepted as *given* and thus *necessary* to language, rather than imagined either as superimposed, or as a preexisting source of expressivity which can be summarily dispensed with. James Breslin points out that poets have been announcing the "end of modernism" ever since the early forties, and more often than not, with "the air of a wish for its passing rather than of a lament for what has already gone."[2] The sophist's rejoinder to this might be that modernism is that which revives at the very moment when its demise is being announced. But surely this would only serve to perpetuate the helpless self-aestheticizing of modernist culture by way of its own art forms.[3] The only way of breaking out of such a vicious circle is, finally, to weigh the current social worth of these forms and find them wanting. And modernist culture, despite the strong postwar reaction to the political aesthetics of Pound and Eliot, did not break until the seventies when its traditional oppositional role loses its edge, and when it runs up against a smoothly assimilating technocratic surface against which it has no purchase. Modernism ends when there are no places left to run to—the autonomy of art, the Romantic "psyche," poetic license, the bardic, magic, psychosis, suicide, and even silence.[4]

I have already partially answered my second question about the working use of the term "modernism"; it is employed here primarily to describe an experimental attitude among modern poets toward language and subjectivity, an attitude that embraces both a philosophical appeal to assumed "universal" attributes (of subjectivity: the true, natural, or ego-less) and a practical attempt to implement that appeal in poetic discourse. There are, however, larger and, perhaps, more familiar frames of reference which my discussion takes into account. "Modernism," for example, connotes a particular kind of reaction to history; *history is all or nothing*. Texts either intervene in history, generally to refurbish it with a shape that best conforms to the perceived needs of the present (Eliot, Pound), or else they abstract themselves entirely from the realm of shared historical precepts and strike out on their own idiosyncratic guidelines (Olson's claim that history is a rationalist fallacy, Ginsberg's visionary escape routes). History, from one modernist's eye to the next, is seen to have "failed" in some fundamental way. Paul de Man has commented on the paradox of "defining the modernity of a literary period as the manner in which it discovers the impossibility of being modern."5 Indeed, his exemplary spirit is the Nietzschean dilemma of willfully forgetting all of that which precedes the present, a desire for the tabula rasa of modernity, however, that contradicts, or rather fails to concur with, the process in which history both integrates, and is itself renewed by, modernity. As a result, the "authentic" spirits of modernity and history are "condemned to [be] linked together in a self-destroying union that threatens the survival of both."6 De Man's view of this dialectic between history and modernity is a "comparative" or universal definition, and in this it resembles, if not reaffirms, Nietzsche's own comparative analyses. In effect, it is unable to offer a description of how and why that "self-destroying union" should appear to be more critically pronounced *at any specific point in time*. How, then, would we account for the perception, acknowledged both then and now, that modernism was the very epitome of such a cultural crisis? For Marxists, for example, the "failure" of history was that the "concrete totality" announced by dialectical materialism had failed to emerge in the first few decades of the century; consequently, when it was not being mechanistically interpreted as a homologous reflection of the crisis of liberal capitalism, modernism was seen as one of the forms of intellectual response to that socio-political failure.7 My own approach to the question has been aimed at providing a more local description of the "impossibility" of history, a description that can, on the one hand, be placed in temporal terms (unlike De Man's), and which seeks, on the other, to account for the general sense of cultural failure by examining the modernist critique of traditional assumptions about individual consciousness (unlike the orthodox Marxist reliance on a fixed, determinist model of the relation between history and culture).

History is always articulated from somewhere. The modernist

taboo on subjectivity therefore had two distinct and extreme consequences. The first response was to presume that history can articulate itself, given the requisite formal means, and therefore the poem tries to be long enough and inclusive enough for that to happen (*The Cantos, The Waste Land, Paterson, In Parenthesis, A Drunk Man Looks at the Thistle, The Bridge*; Zukofsky's *A* is exceptional only inasmuch as it acknowledges the subjective source of its artifactual construction). The second and later response was an inversion of the first because it claims that history only exists when one needs it; Olson, for example, insists that the only true history is a history of one's own making, outside of any shared conventions—a history is what one does, rather than what one learns, or is determined by.[8]

Another important frame of reference for the development of my argument is the context of American poetry, and therefore a literary tradition whose insistence on its own, separate, cultural identity could only serve to heighten the modernist obsession with forging new identities. As I have suggested, modernist poetry is a twofold formation, the initial Anglo-American wave and the later American resurgence of the fifties and the sixties among the Black Mountain poets, the Beats, the New York school, and others. In this respect, I largely agree with Charles Altieri's isolation of these two related "moments" in modern poetry although I have difficulty in going along with his view that both moments can be linked, in their respective appeals, to different aspects of "the Romantic experience": an initial Coleridgean commitment to "the creative form-giving imagination" and a later espousal of an "immanentist" or Wordsworthian disclosure of presence in nature and organic process.[9] Whether or not it is any more telling to say that they both "repeat" the Romantic experience, we can say that each moment proposes a certain kind of solution to the problematic of language and subjectivity in its own time and place. This, then, is the basis of their respective consanguinity in my argument, and it is a relation that holds up even in the face of the parricidal avowals of these postwar poets who were determined to avoid the final solutions of high modernism. The initial Anglo-American solution is to crystalize the transcendentalizing strain of European philosophy into a poetics of impersonality, while the later American movement feeds into the myth of a native transcendentalism long associated with theories of organic process and natural theology; each, in effect, seeks a solution that is deemed more true to the phenomenology of experience. Similarly, if the former is compounded out of a radical breakdown of national identities (the myth of the exile: English-speaking modernism is never English, but rather Anglo-American, Anglo-Irish, Anglo-Welsh, Anglo-Scottish and Anglo-Canadian), then the latter just as surely proclaims its complicity with some of the more representative literary myths of American national identity.[10]

In his study of *The Puritan Origins of the American Self*, Sacvan Bercovitch, for example, has shown how a "private" conception of subjectivity became identified with a "national dream" of self-creation:

The connection I speak of is not simply that between the Reformed and the Romantic concept of the self in process. Colonial hermeneutics bridges the considerable gap between christic auto-machia and the Promethean self-creation in terms of exegesis; and it obviates the traditional dialectic between secular and sacred selfhood by fusing both in the framework of auto-American-biography. For both Edwards and Emerson, the image of the New World invests the regenerate perceiver with an aura of ascendant millennial splendor; and for both of them, the perceiver must prove his regeneration by transforming himself in the image of the New World.[11]

Bercovitch traces this continuity to its "origins" in a "teleology of nature" that not only contains a redemptive vision of national history but also looks forward to a truly American discourse that will complete the conditions for individual/national "regeneration." Such a language of nature cannot, in a sense, be fully pursued until the modernist will for language reform offers the bait of converting it from an idealistic dream into a practical exercise: Pound's ideographism, Olson's glyphism, etc. In the same way, the self-transcendence of "regeneration" is only complete when a radical attention to the *medium* announces a complete displacement of subjectivity: Jackson Pollock's "I am Nature." Pollock's identification is an extreme expression of the naturalistic impulse which Emerson had declared to be the coming millennial spirit; the intrusive bias of subjectivism is so radically rescinded that the medium speaks or articulates Nature directly. The first step in this process is always what Olson calls "the getting rid of the lyrical interference of the individual as ego, of the 'subject' and his soul, that peculiar presumption by which western man has interposed himself between what he is as a creature of nature (with certain instructions to carry out) and those other creations of nature which we may, with no derogation, call objects" (SW,24). Eliot's cult of impersonality, the Confessional poets' autobiographical attempts (Berryman, Lowell, Roethke) to forge "the true shape of the psyche," the Deep Image school's surrealistic attention (Bly, Simpson, Stafford, Wright, Kelly) to archetypal expressions of collective subjectivity, Gary Snyder's much copied eschewal of the personal pronoun in his celebration of primitivism, Ed Dorn's "assassination" and resurrection of a character called "I" in *Gunslinger,* and generally, the appeal of almost two decades of a naked or "open" poetics to the spontaneous and unmediated—all of these positions seek to replace a "false" with a "true" or natural subjectivity, and in doing so, they each pursue their own theoretical crusades in a language medium that is assumed to be tyrannically organized.[12]

In arguing that each of these positions somehow observes a common theoretical purpose (and together they span almost sixty years of modern poetry), I do not intend to play down the multiformity of their various approaches, not only to the problem of subjectivity but also to a whole range of issues whether technical or cultural: indeed, three of these approaches have been examined at some length here, in part, for that very reason. Nor do I wish to neglect the very complex and important ways in which poets learn the "lessons" of their precursors, or promulgate a poetics in response to some other existing aesthetic, as in the phenomenon of the "poetry wars." To seek to account for these differences in "generational" terms, however, as an ongoing series of filial choices—as Harold Bloom and, more recently, James Breslin (in a Freudian and a non-Freudian way respectively) have done—seems to me finally to only complement and reaffirm those fictions constructed by poets *for the very purpose of further displacing the problem of accounting for their own subjectivity.*[13] To project this problem onto a fantasized relation with a poetic father is firstly to disavow its immediate and concrete context in language, and secondly to suggest that the struggle to break this paternal relation will therefore lead to a more independent and autonomous poetic discourse, one that will then have neutralized or purged its false idiosyncratic attachments to externally given worlds like that of a poetic influence. In effect, this would be a roundabout way of disclaiming paternity/history, and asserting the self-determination of discourse itself. Again, this is not to deny that these pseudo-autobiographical fictions have a real effect. My own approach, however, has been to examine the problems which these fictions are designed to deflect attention away from, which is to say, those other fictions that are internal to the construction of subjectivity in language. My concentration of psychoanalytical interest on the latter, rather than upon the more melodramatic categories of poetic "personality" ("Pound" or "Whitman," for example, as a more or less unique, expressive force among other poets), betokens a prevalent interest in the literariness of literature rather than in the larger personifications of literary history or literary politics.

Before discussing the psychoanalytical invocation of the "symptoms" in my subtitle, we should first explain how and why the writers examined here might be seen as "symptoms of American poetry." On the one hand, the phrase is designed to distance this study from the critical practice of celebrating writers who are representative, either of a particular school or aesthetic, or else of a particular point of view that is deemed to feed directly into the Americanist literary myths; such a practice germinates early enough in American literature itself, in Cotton Mather's *exempla* of Puritan saints, and is further idealized in Franklin's self-example, and Emerson's cult of "representative men." On the other hand, each of my "symptoms"—Eliot, Olson, and Ashbery—resists being read as a simple *reflection* of different stages of a developing literary history. Symptoms are neither causes nor effects, but share some of the trappings of each. First and foremost, these symptoms are read for their own particularity and then interpreted, when possible, in the larger structural light of history, but it is difficult to distinguish, at any one moment, between these two levels of interpretation. In effect, the respective work of Eliot and Olson is every bit as instrumental in *shaping* the two modernist moments as it is exemplary in serving as a typical product of the dominant literary ideology of their day. Ashbery's case is less straightforward, and this is a major reason for its inclusion alongside Eliot and Olson. Although he starts writing in the late fifties, widespread acceptance and recognition of his work comes late and is still "active" today. If his early work is clearly modernist in inspiration, then it also looks forward to something else, while his later work, which proclaims its immunity to the modernist anxieties about history and subjectivity, is largely devoted nonetheless to an endless discursive presence that is generated by this lack of anxiety. Ashbery's case, then, is no solution to the failure of modernism, but rather a displacment of a continuing problematic. Indeed, it stands on the cusp of many of the dualistic oppositions that are more clear-cut in the projects of Elio and Olson, and is therefore presented partly as a reminder of a "symptom's" wayward resistance to linear readings.

Of all modern American poets, these three present the most lucid evidence for a discussion about the confusion between theory and practice, or more specifically, between subjectivism and subjectivity. This is all the more marked by the dual affiliations of each writer: Eliot is both a poet and a philosopher (his critical theory, as I argue, is unthinkable without the early philosophy), Olson is both a poet and a historian (a theoretical historian, though his interests increasingly came to be pre-Greek), and Ashbery, despite being read generally as a "pure" poet without a poetics, is not only a poet but also an art critic, a fact which has a very significant bearing upon the "visual" presentation of subjectivity in his poetry. As a result there exists, apart from the poetry, a body of theoretical work (for Eliot and Olson, at least, the intended exception being Ashbery) that bears witness to what each writer "knows" rather than what is assumed to have passed, as if by osmosis, into his discursive veins. This is not to say, however, that we must have either a *mechanical* or an *organic* understanding of the way in which an external discourse of knowledge is somehow inscribed within a poetic discourse or style. Indeed, one of the supplementary aims of my argument has been to try to account for this process of inscription in psychoanalytical terms, or at least by referring to a psychoanalytical model of inscription that takes account of both the psychic and the social. For what links many of the foregoing discussions together is a common interest in the body, a body that is not simply the author's and thus subject to his own peculiar psychic history, but also a body that is already socialized by its encounter with language, and thus subject to more universal laws of articulation. Psychoanalysis itself is in many ways a prototype of the modernist experience as it is described here. Freud's work can be read as a critique of the subjectivism inherent not only in the dominant psychologizing of the time, but also in the more general cultural framework of humanist assumptions about the unity of individuality. There are, however, at least three psychoanalytical responses to this critique. The first is historically continuous with the American Freudian tradition of ego psychology, against which Eliot saw fit to inveigh as early as 1930:

I believe that at the present time the problem of the unification of the world and the problem of the unification of the individual are in the end one and the same problem; and that the solution of one is the solution of the other. Analytical psychology (even if accepted far more enthusiastically than I can accept it) can do little except produce monsters; for it is attempting to produce unified individuals in a world without unity.[14]

Eliot's complaint is clear enough; what should not escape us is the ease with which he identifies "problems" and "solutions" (notwithstanding the added irony that his own critical revolution is predicated upon a similar call for unity). The point to be made, however, is that this particular strain of psychoanalytical thinking, like so much of modernism, seeks to produce a more true or natural sense of ego or identity than was hitherto "available." The second kind of response (a mirror image of the first) corresponds to the heady celebration of fragmentation and desire that has been associated with poststructuralism, but which is more generally a product of the modernist radicalism of the sixties and its willed flight from established forms of necessity: Olson's antirationalist cause is one of its most powerfully articulated gestures. The third response, and arguably the most Freudian, could be characterized as Lacanian, and it is the one that has had the most influence on my argument because its primary concern is with the construction of subjectivity in language. That fact in itself brings the study of literature much nearer to those with an interest in psychoanalysis, while it ensures that the practice of close textual analysis need not be approached as a world unto itself, or a world's body, as Ransom put it, but rather as an analysis of bodily claims—in effect, a body's world. More generally, however, it is the Lacanian emphasis on the *necessity* of subjectivity, no matter how strictly defined in linguistic terms, that stands as a critique of the modernist will; and of the three authors discussed, it is Ashbery's work that comes closest to recognizing the necessity to which we are bound in using language.

Despite what this psychoanalytical interest implies, I do not intend to suggest that modernism, generally, did not have a "theory of the subject" in the sense in which canonical poststructuralism stridently claims such a theory for itself. Modernism *did* have a theory of the subject, and it took full advantage of its "aesthetic autonomy" to pursue that theory at all levels of social as well as literary experience. The lesson to be drawn from that experiment has long since been recognized for its undesirable political consequences, indeed so much so that modernism, for some, will always be looked upon as the cultural will that sought to translate abstract theory into political fact through the self-asserted autonomy of its medium, and, perhaps, simply *because it had to find some* external proof for this "autonomy." The powerful irony of this position was a point of departure for the commentaries of many of the "culture critics," especially those, like Adorno, who were themselves apologists for modernism:

[Modernism's] flight into a new order, however flimsy, is a reflection of the fact that absolute freedom in art—which is a particular—contradicts the abiding unfreedom of the social whole. That is why the place and function of art in society have become uncertain. To put it another way, the autonomy art gained after having freed itself from its earlier cult function and its derivatives depended on the idea of humanity. As society grew less humane, art became less autonomous. Those constitutive elements of art that were suffused with the ideal of humanity have lost their force.[15]

The theoretical knowledge generated by poststructuralism has been read by many as a reaction to, and a corrective for, this flawed "ideal of humanity." And in providing a discursive meeting-ground which can accommodate such a fecund mix of philosophy, literary criticism, linguistics, and cultural politics, it may be that contemporary critical theory does indeed offer a practical alternative to the very real modernist dilemma of having either to fall back upon ever fresher formal permutations, or else look the world straight in the political eye, a dilemma which is as much a product as a cause of its internal contradictions. In effect, if this book is a product (though by no means a "pure" product) of poststructuralism, then it is not because it seeks to present a corrective "theory of the subject," nor advocate a more (or less) "humane" writing practice, which would then stand as a redemptive example to the failed modernist cause. That would be to commit even greater crimes, not least of which would be its complicity with a naive idea of historical progress— that history solves problems as it goes along: indeed the very idea of history that modernism initially set out to challenge. If anything, my intention here has been to question further this strain of positivism, a positivism which still dominates the kind of critical history of a literary period which this book might otherwise have been—a history in which each writer solves, or fails to solve the problems of his precursor(s).

NOTES

1. Tying Knots in the East Wind

1. A letter printed in *The Pall Mall Gazette* two days after the funeral in Westminster Abbey depicted the swan song of an entire literary culture in suggesting that Tennyson's funeral "was not the burial of a man, but of a dead literature, and a dead society. The *ci-devants*—the Leckies, the Argylls, the Froudes—who bore the pall, came to bury themselves, not him. He died, I take it, about forty years ago . . ." The letter is quoted by Paul F. Baum in *Tennyson: Sixty Years After* (London: Archon Books, 1963), p. 7.

2. In the published version of his Clark Lectures, David Piper names the two most important Victorian innovations in the context of the poet's image: firstly, the invention of photography, and, after two hundred years—the reinvention of the beard. See chapter 4 of *The Image of the Poet* (Oxford: Clarendon Press, 1982). The full post-Gothic regalia of cloak, hat, and beard is, of course, best compounded in Julia Cameron's "Dirty Monk" photograph of Tennyson. The engraving of Whitman which faces the title page on the first edition of *Leaves of Grass* (1855) presents the other end of the idealistic extreme (and one that I will argue, in my discussion of Olson in chapter 5, is endemic to the tradition of American naturalism): an informal portrait of a working man, bearded, with his shirt open at the neck, one arm akimbo, the other thrust into the pocket of his pants. Whitman's portrait, of course, provides a constant corporeal presence with which to support the oral form of his poetry.

3. Walter Benjamin, "The Work of Art in the Age of Mechanical Reproduction," *Illuminations,* trans. Harry Zohn, ed. Hannah Arendt (New York: Shocken Books, 1969), p. 227.

4. Eliot's laureatelike success is the bittersweet subject of Richard Aldington's little-known but interesting satire, *Stepping Heavenward* (London: Chatto & Windus, 1931): "The life of the late Jeremy Pratt Sybba, afterwards Father Cibber, O.S.B., recently beatified by the Roman Curia."

5. See Jean-Luc Nancy's fascinating analysis of Descartes's own paradigm of "invisibility," in "Larvatus Pro Deo," *Glyph* (1977), 2:15. Descartes's motto is itself adopted from Ovid.

6. "London Letter," *The Dial* (May 1922), 72:510–11.

7. A number of other studies which address the politics of modernism are

close in spirit and methodology to my own theoretical aims, and I have variously benefited from the arguments advanced in these books: Colin MacCabe, *James Joyce and the Revolution of the Word* (London: MacMillan, 1979); Cairns Craig, *Yeats, Eliot, Pound, and the Politics of Poetry* (London/ Pittsburgh: Croom Helm/University of Pittsburgh Press, 1982); Alan Durant, *Ezra Pound: Identity in Crisis* (Brighton, Sussex/Totowa, New Jersey; Harvester Press/Barnes & Noble, 1981); and Paul Smith, *Pound Revised* (London: Croom Helm, 1983). Recent books which address the changing sociocultural conditions of the authorship and readership of modern poetry include David Trotter's *The Making of the Reader: Language and Subjectivity in Modern American, English, and Irish Poetry* (London: MacMillan, 1984), and Robert von Hallberg's *American Poetry and Culture 1945–1980* (Cambridge: Harvard University Press, 1985).

8. Paul Valéry, *The Serpent*, trans. Mark Wardle, with an introduction by T.S. Eliot (London: Cobden-Sanderson, 1924), p.13. Eliot's example of such a "monster" is Monsieur Teste, for which see my discussion of the *tsetse* fly in chapter 2.

9. Anne Bolgan, *What the Thunder Really Said* (Montreal: McGill-Queens University Press 1973), p.181. Preoccupied with her own research in the Houghton Library, Bolgan trips over some steps in the stacks, and comes to rest upon "a largish academic-looking volume which later turned out to be the Bradley thesis." The book which broke her fall had just arrived that day from "the archives of the Department of Philosophy where it had lain undisturbed and virtually unknown for almost forty years."

10. Richard Wollheim, "Eliot and F.H. Bradley," *On Art and Mind* (London: Allen Lane, 1973), pp. 220–49.

11. Lewis Freed, *T.S. Eliot: The Critic as Philospher* (West Lafayette: Purdue University Press, 1979).

12. Walter Benn Michaels, "Philosophy in Kinkanja: Eliot's Pragmatism," *Glyph* (1981), 9:170–201.

13. F.H. Bradley, *The Principles of Logic* (London: Oxford University Press, 1922; 2d ed.), vol. 1, p. 2.

14. F.H. Bradley, *Appearance and Reality* (Oxford: Clarendon Press, 1930; 2d ed.), p. xii.

15. *Ibid.*, pp. 406–7.

16. F.H. Bradley, *Essays on Truth and Reality* (Oxford: Oxford University Press, 1914), p. 161.

17. F.H. Bradley, *Appearance and Reality*, p. 156.

18. *Ibid.*, p. 199.

19. George Lukács, *History and Class Consciousness*, trans. Rodney Livingstone (Cambridge: MIT Press, 1971), p. 115. Lukács later argues that with the discovery of art it becomes possible either to provide yet another domain for the fragmented subject or to leave behind the safe territory of the concrete evocation of totality and (using art at most by way of illustration) tackle the problem of "creation" from the side of the subject. The problem then is no

longer—as it was for Spinoza—to create an objective system of reality on the model of geometry. It is rather *this* creation which is at once philosophy's premise and its task. This creation is undoubtedly given. . . . But the task is to deduce the unity—which is not given—of this disintegrating creation and to prove that it is the product of a creating subject. In the final analysis then: to create the subject of the "creator." (p. 140)

20. Eliot's response to the "betrayal" of Munich 1938 was *The Idea of a Christian Society* (London: Faber & Faber, 1939), a militant philippic against the "hypertrophy of the motive of Profit." However, the persistent theme of cultural holism in his social criticism is afforded its most classically conservative expression in *Notes Towards the Definition of Culture* (London: Faber & Faber, 1948), in which he recognizes the growing liberal voice for governing "elites," but argues that classes, especially the governing classes, have an important social and cultural function to perform:

class itself possesses a function, that of maintaining that part of the total culture of a society which pertains to that class. We have to try to keep in mind, that in a healthy society this maintenance of a particular level of culture is to the benefit, not merely of the class which maintains it, but of the society as a whole. Awareness of this fact will prevent us from supposing that the culture of a "higher" class is something superfluous to society as a whole, or to the majority, and from supposing that it is something which ought to be shared equally by all other classes. (p. 33)

21. *The Sacred Wood* (London: Methuen, 1920), p. 68.

22. Wollheim, p. 247.

23. "London Letter," *The Dial* (August 1921), 71:216–17. "The strongest, like Mr. Joyce, make their feeling into an articulate, external world: what might be more crudely called a more feminine type when it is also a very sophisticated type, makes its art by feeling, and by contemplating the feeling, rather than the object . . . . the charm of Mrs. Woolf's shorter pieces consists in the immense disparity between the object and the train of feeling which it has set in motion."

24. Michaels, pp. 184–85.

25. See Moustapha Safouan's discussion of the philosophical significance of the term *Vorstellung* for Freud in "Representation and Pleasure," Colin MacCabe, ed., *The Talking Cure: Essays in Psychoanalysis and Language* (London: MacMillan, 1981), pp. 75–90.

26. Charles Hartshorne and Paul Weiss, eds., *The Collected Papers of Charles Sanders Peirce* (Cambridge: Harvard University Press, 1931), vol. 5, p. 189.

27. Emile Benveniste, *Problems in General Linguistics*, trans. Mary E. Meek (Coral Gables: University of Miami Press, 1971), p. 218.

28. Edmund Husserl, *Ideas: General Introduction to Pure Phenomenology*, trans. W.R. Boyce Gibson (New York: MacMillan, 1931), pp. 91–113.

29. Benveniste, pp. 224–25.

30. Sanford Schwartz cites evidence to show that Eliot had, in fact, been reading Husserl in 1914. *The Matrix of Modernism: Pound, Eliot, and Early*

Twentieth-Century Thought (Princeton: Princeton University Press, 1985). p. 167.

31. Letter to Stephen Spender, quoted in *T.S. Eliot: The Man and his Work,* ed. Allen Tate (London: Chatto & Windus, 1966), p. 56.

32. The attack on Cartesian "personality" was an *idée fixe* of Eliot's involvement in Babbit and More's New Humanist movement (for which, see my discussion in chapter 3). A typical observation of Eliot's which tallies with the larger claims of the movement is the following, from "Poetry and Propaganda," *The Bookman* (February 1930), 70:599: "We aim in the end at a theory of life, or a view of life, and so far as we are conscious, to terminate our enjoyment of the arts in a philosophy, and our philosophy in a religion—in such a way that the personal to oneself is fused and completed in the impersonal and general, not extinguished, but enriched, expanded, developed, and more itself by becoming more something not itself."

33. John Fekete has written a wide-ranging politico-phenomenological critique of these developments in *The Critical Twilight: Explorations in the Ideology of Anglo-American Literary Theory from Eliot to McLuhan* (London: Routledge & Kegan Paul, 1977).

34. *The Sacred Wood,* p. xv: T.E. Hulme, *Speculations: Essays on Humanism and the Philosphy of Art,* ed. Herbert Read (New York: Harcourt, Brace, 1936), p. 133: Matthew Arnold, "On Translating Homer," R.H. Super, ed., *The Complete Prose Works of Matthew Arnold* (Ann Arbor: University of Michigan, 1960), vol. 1, p. 140.

35. Walter Pater, Preface to *The Renaissance: Studies in Art and Poetry,* the 1893 text, ed. Donald L. Hill (Berkeley: University of California Press, 1980), p. xix.

36. Paul Valéry, *The Art of Poetry,* with an introduction by T.S. Eliot (Princeton: Princeton University Press, 1972), p. xxiii.

37. *The Sacred Wood,* pp. 170–71.

38. One of the clearest statements of the modernist centrality of the eye and its sexual (phallic) corollary can be found in Wyndham Lewis, *Time and Western Man,* (London: Chatto & Windus, 1927), pp. 7–8. Lewis, who has been taking issue with Sade on the questions of "the spasms of sex," has this to say about the "overmastering impulse": "Whatever I, for my part can say, may be traced back to an organ; but in my case it is the *eye.* It is in the service of the things of vision that my ideas are mobilised."

39. All quotations from this sermon that follow in the text are from Lancelot Andrews, *XCIV Sermons* (Oxford: Oxford University Press, 1891), vol. 1, pp. 196–214.

40. Jacques Derrida, *Of Grammatology,* trans. Gayatri Chakravorty Spivak (Baltimore: Johns Hopkins University Press, 1976), p. 14.

41. George R. Potter and Evelyn Simpson, eds., *The Sermons of John Donne* (Berkeley: University of California Press, 1953–1961), vol. 10, p. 237.

42. *For Lancelot Andrewes: Essays on Style and Order* (London: Faber & Faber, 1928), preface.

43. An interesting essay on Derrida's own "negative theology," and which bears upon this debate, is Susan Handelman's "Jacques Derrida and the Heretic Hermeneutic," in Mark Krupnick, ed., *Displacement: Derrida and After* (Bloomington: Indiana University Press, 1983), pp. 98–102.

44. See "Lectures on Genesis Ch. 1–5," in Jaroslav Pelikan, ed., *Luther's Works* (St. Louis: Concordia Publishing House, 1958), vol. 1, p. 233: "But it was very difficult for me to break away from my habitual zeal for allegory; and yet I was aware that allegories were empty specualtions and the froth, as it were, of the Holy Scriptures. It is the historical sense alone which supplies the true and sound doctrine."

45. As the heresies, stylistic and otherwise, proliferated, so the eighteenth century ushered in a new hard-headedness in matters of style and expression, and one, as Perry Miller notes, that was bound up in a claim for the *rationality* of a colonial politics: "a few Christians perceived that the seductive language of modern heresy would not adequately be refuted by old-fashioned dogmatism. In general, it may be said, they were those most sensitive to literary criticism—Cotton Mather was the chiefest—most miserable at having to appear before the wide, wide world as backward colonials. Conscious of inadequacy, they were the most forward in cultivating the new mode of expression, hoping, by concentration upon language, to transform reason into a slogan for colonial orthodoxy without having to submit their beliefs any longer to the relentless scrutiny of formal rhetoric or of 'vulgar logic.'" *The New England Mind: From Colony to Province* (Cambridge: Harvard University Press, 1953), p. 426.

46. Paul A. Welsby, *Lancelot Andrewes* (London: SPCK Press, 1958), pp. 9–28.

47. Sermon at Lent, 1594, *XCIV Sermons*, vol. 2, p. 14.

48. Stanley Fish, *Self-Consuming Artifacts: The Experience of Seventeenth-Century Literature* (Berkeley: University of California Press, 1972), p. 57.

49. *The Sermons of John Donne*, vol. 10, p. 123; vol. 5, p. 160.

50. *For Lancelot Andrewes*, p. 53.

2. "Signifying Matrimonie"

1. Jean-François Lyotard, for example, has provided the valuable concept of the "libidinal apparatus" of history, whereby the social and ideological formations of the moment are *stamped* upon the individual psychic makeup by way of a collective fantasy structure. The most ambitious use of Lyotard's concept in English is to be found in Fredric Jameson's *Fables of Aggression: Wyndham Lewis, The Modernist as Fascist* (Berkeley: University of California Press, 1979). Jameson stresses the "semi-autonomy" or the "objectivity" of the libidinal apparatus inasmuch as it "endows a private fantasy-structure with a quasi-material inertness" (p. 10). His argument demands that this private fantasy-structure be emptied in order for it to recontain the larger and "objective pre-conditions of the narrative structures which inform" it:

not the "familial or archaic" Oedipal ones, but those to be found in the "objective configurations of the political history of pre-1914 Europe" (p. 11). This emphasis differs from my own consideration here of the subjective function of enunciation. In transcending that subjective function, Jameson's interest lies in a more abstract or "collective" subjectivity in the Hegelian shape of fully articulated political *ideas*. Hence the "subjects of history" in his discussion are nothing less than the full-scale ideological collectivities (the "transnational forces of Communism and Fascism") which emerged after World War I to replace the "older diplomatic system."

2. Letter to Eliot (March 14, 1922) in the Pound collection, Lilly Library, Indiana University, Bloomington.

3. *The Idea of a Christian Society* (New York: Harcourt, Brace, 1940), p. 65.

4. Lyndall Gordon, *Eliot's Early Years* (London: Oxford University Press, 1977), p. 79.

5. Tom Matthews, *Great Tom: Notes Towards the Definition of T.S. Eliot* (New York: Harper & Row, 1974), p. 47.

6. Lacan's understanding of *debt* is not based solely upon an economic relation of reciprocity. This explains why the process of "paying off" the symbolic debt is a rather literal interpretation of a much wider and more complex act of exchange which can be better placed within a history of anthropological thought. Marcel Mauss's theory of the *gift* as a "total social fact" in complex economic, cultural, and social activities like the *potlatch*, was important in directing anthropologists away from the simple economic model of truck and barter, with its classical appeal to the acquisitive contract theory of reciprocity. Mauss's thought was taken up in two ways that are crucial to Lacan. Firstly, by Levi-Strauss's application of the gift relation to the structure of kinship systems and the "incest" principle, from which he demonstrates that the "gift" economy is part and parcel of a larger social structure of communication, an idea central to the notion of the *symbolic*, which Lacan adopts intact; and secondly, in Georges Bataille's concept of *dépense*, or expenditure, a one-sided relation of exchange which marks the shift from a "restricted economy" of calculated returns, to the less utilitarian "general economy" of loss and symbolic expense, an idea which is close to the Lacanian notion of desire.

7. Quoted by Lyndall Gordon from a letter (March 7 1914), in Gordon, p. 27.

8. F.H. Bradley, *The Principles of Logic* (London: Oxford University Press, 1922; 2d ed.), vol. 1., pp. 59–63.

9. See Derrida's discussion of a powerful name-play in Jean Genet's writing in *Glas* (Paris: Galilee, 1974). While putting together *The Waste Land* draft in Lausanne in 1921, Eliot was being treated by Roger Vittoz, an early psychotherapist working on the psychiatric fringes. He had treated an earlier patient, Lady Ottoline Morrell, in a way which alludes to my demonstration of name-playing: "he gave her puzzles to do, such as eliminating

numbers from a set of numbers" in an attempt to persuade her that such mental activities could reestablish her "ego-control" and draw her out of her mental torpor. Leon Edel, *The Stuff of Sleep and Dreams* (New York; Harper & Row, 1982), p. 185. An account of the eccentric life philosophy of Vittoz himself can be found in his book, *The Treatment of Neurasthenia (By Teaching of Brain Control),* trans. H.B. Brook (London: Longman's, Green, 1911). The classic pioneer work on anagrams, of course, is Saussure's, for which see Jean Starobinski's *Words Upon Words: The Anagrams of Ferdinand de Saussure,* trans. Olivia Emmet (New Haven: Yale University Press, 1979).

10. Stephen Spender, "Remembering Eliot," in Allen Tate, ed., *T.S. Eliot: The Man and His Work* (London: Chatto & Windus, 1967), p. 52.

11. Eliot signed at least one of his Moot papers (a philosophical coterie at Oxford) with the name, "Metaikos," or *resident alien.* Matthews, p. 126.

12. The "Ode" was published in the first American edition of *Ara Vos Prec,* but was subsequently withdrawn from *Poems* (1920).

13. In his dissertation, Eliot uses this phrase in a discussion of the "denoting phrase": "What we denote when we *denote the denoting phrase* is not the phrase as such, for that is an activity rather than an object, but rather the tendency towards objectification in the direction toward us: that is, the 'word,' the written sign, or the *vox et praeterea nihil*" (KE,130).

Generally thought to be of Senecan origin, the phrase can be found quoted in Plutarch's "Sayings of the Spartans," *Moralia,* trans. F.C. Babbitt (Cambridge: Harvard University Press, 1927), vol. 3, p. 398: "A man plucked a nightingale and finding almost no meat, said 'It's all voice ye are, and nought else.'" The footnote, however, gives the phrase in Latin as if it were already well known, offering no further reference.

14. Sigmund Freud, "From the History of an Infantile Neurosis," *The Standard Edition of the Complete Psychological Works,* trans. James Strachey (London: Hogarth Press, 1953), vol. 17, p. 94 and passim.

15. Serge Leclaire, "Le corps de la lettre," *Psychanalyser* (Paris: Seuil, 1968), pp. 79–96.

16. I.A. Richards, "Mr. Eliot's Poems," *The New Statesman* (February 20, 1926), 26:524.

17. Quoted by Noel Stock in *The Life of Ezra Pound* (Harmondsworth: Penguin, 1974), p. 258.

18. "Dante et Donne: deux attitudes mystiques," *Chroniques* (1927), 3:169.

19. D.D. Paige, ed., *The Letters of Ezra Pound: 1907–1941* (London: Faber, 1951), pp. 234–35.

20. See Alan Durant, *Ezra Pound: Identity in Crisis* (Brighton/Totowa: Harvester Press/Barnes & Noble, 1981), pp. 145–46.

21. *The Letters of Ezra Pound* (December 24, 1921), p. 169.

22. Quoted by Donald Gallup in *T.S. Eliot and Ezra Pound* (New Haven: Yale University Press, 1970), p. 24.

23. Stephen Spender, *T.S. Eliot* (New York: Viking, 1976), pp. 100–3.

24. F.R. Leavis, *Lectures in America* (London: Chatto & Windus, 1969), p. 55.

25. Peter Ackroyd, *Notes for a New Culture* (London: Vision Press, 1976), p. 53.

26. Grover Smith, *T.S. Eliot's Poetry and Plays: A Study in Sources and Meaning* (Chicago: Chicago University Press, 1956).

3. Ego Dominus Tuus

1. Allen Tate, "Irony and Humility," *Hound and Horn* (March 1931), 4:291.

2. George Orwell, "Points of View: T.S. Eliot," *Poetry London* (Winter 1942), 11:58.

3. Edmund Wilson, "T.S. Eliot and the Church of England," *The Shores of Light* (New York: Farrar & Strauss, 1952), p. 439.

4. Stephen Spender, *The Thirties and After: Poetry, Politics and People, 1933–70* (New York: Random House, 1978), p. 18.

5. *The Critique of Humanism; A Symposium,* ed. C. Hartley Grattan (New York: Farrar and Rinehardt, 1930), p. 166.

6. Ibid., pp. 76, 68.

7. *The Criterion* (April 1924), 2(7):235.

8. *The Criterion* (October 1926), 4(4):752–53.

9. See Jacques Maritain, *True Humanism* (London: The Centenary Press, 1938) and *Scholasticism and Politics* (London: The Centenary Press, 1940)

10. *The Criterion* (July 1933), 12 (49):644.

11. Julien Benda, *Belphégor,* trans. S.J.I. Lawson, introduction by Irving Babbitt (London: Faber & Faber, 1929). In his introduction, Babbitt cites Edouard LeRoy, Bergson's disciple and successor at the Collège de France: "Distinctions have disappeared, words no longer have any value. One hears welling forth mysteriously the sources of consciousness like an unseen trickling of a living water through the darkness of a moss-grown grotto. I am dissolved in the joy of becoming. . . . I no longer know whether I see perfumes or breathe sounds or taste colours."

12. Gorham Munson, "Our Critical Spokesman," in Norman Foerster, ed., *Humanism and America* (New York: Farrar & Rinehardt, 1930), p. 253.

13. Sigmund Freud, "Instincts and their Vicissitudes," *Standard Edition,* vol. 14, p. 128.

14. The Complete Poems and Plays of T.S. Eliot (London: Faber & Faber, 1969), pp. 605–6.

15. Ibid., pp. 129–34.

16. Unpublished ms. in the Berg Collection, New York Public Library.

17. Lyndall Gordon, *Eliot's Early Years* (London: Oxford University Press, 1977), p. 61.

18. Ernest Jones, "Madonna's Conception through the Ear," *Essays in Applied Psychoanalysis* (London: Hogarth Press, 1951), vol. 2. See also Gaston Bachelard's analysis of the calorific constituency of the Word in *The Psychoanalysis of Fire* (London: Routledge & Kegan Paul, 1964).

19. Georges Bataille, *Death and Sensuality: A Study of Eroticism and Taboo* (London: John Calder, 1962), p. 135ff.

20. Bertrand Russell, *The Autobiography of Bertrand Russell* (London: Allen & Unwin, 1968), vol. 2, p. 6.

21. Bataille, p. 226.

22. *After Strange Gods* (London: Faber & Faber, 1934): "First-rate blasphemy is one of the rarest things in literature, for it requires both literary genius and profound faith, joined in a mind in a peculiar and unusual state of spiritual sickness," p. 52.

23. See Kenneth Burke's virtuoso discussion of the *vert*-family in Augustine's *Confessions* in *The Rhetoric of Religion* (Boston: Beacon Press, 1961), pp. 62–65.

24. Evelyn Underhill, *Mysticism* (London: Methuen, 1919; 8th ed.). p. 93.

25. Saint Augustine, *Confessions* and *Enchiridion,* Library of Christian Classics (London: S.C.M. Press, 1955), Book X, 16, p. 216.

26. Ibid., Book XI, 12, pp. 254–55.

27. Ibid., Book I, 2, p. 32. See also Jean-Louis Schefer's study of the importance of memory in Augustine's attempt to write the history of his revelations. *L'Invention du corps chrétien* (Paris: Galilee, 1975).

28. Jacques Lacan, *The Four Fundamental Concepts of Psychoanalysis,* trans. A. Sheridan (Harmondsworth: Penguin, 1977), p. 55. The association between memory, the real, and the symptom in Lacan's thought are discussed further in my "Theory and Knowledge in Psychoanalysis," *The Dalhousie Review* (Summer 1984), 64(2):223–46.

29. Donald Davie, "T.S. Eliot: The End of an Era," Bernard Bergonzi, ed., *Four Quartets: A Casebook* (London: MacMillan, 1969), p.164.

30. Allen Tate, "The Reading of Modern Poetry," *Purpose* (Winter 1938), 10:31–41.

31. *George Herbert* (London: Longman, Green, 1962), p. 20.

32. Sigmund Freud, "The Unconscious," *Standard Edition,* vol. 14, pp.196–203. Freud uses Viktor Tausk's example of the female schizophrenic who claimed that her lover's "eyes were not right, they were twisted." She herself explained that she believed that he was untrustworthy. "He looked different every time; he was a hypocrite, an eye-twister," the latter metaphor being what she had actually taken for a literal fact.

33. Gregory Bateson, "Steps Towards a Theory of Schizophrenia," *Steps Towards an Ecology of the Mind* (New York: Ballantine, 1975), p. 194.

34. Anthony Johnson, *Sign and Structure in the Poetry of T.S. Eliot* (Pisa: Editrice Tecnico Scientifico, 1976), p. 96 and p. 169.

35. Ibid., p. 75.

36. Julia Kristeva, *Powers of Horror: An Essay on Abjection,* trans. Leon Roudiez (New York: Columbia University Press, 1983).

37. Ibid., p. 90ff.

38. Georges Bataille, *Oeuvres Completes* (Paris: Gallimard, 1976), vol. 2, p. 14: "I pictured the eye on top of my head as a terrible volcano in eruption, and endowed with all of the ambiguously comical traits associated with the

bottom and its excretions. Now the eye is obviously the symbol of the dazzling sun, and what I imagined of course was that my crown was on fire, since the eye was fixed in a position to observe the sun at the zenith of its brightness."

39. René Girard's theory of "mimetic desire" and its consequences for the *surrogate victim* is particularly pertinent to the analysis of "ritual" drama like *Murder in the Cathedral*. For the definitive example of a nonsacrificial reading, see his account of the Gospels in *Des choses cachées depuis la fondation du monde* (Paris: Galilee, 1978).

4. Out of True

1. Don Byrd, *Charles Olson's Maximus* (Urbana: University of Illinois Press, 1980), p. xiii.

2. Quoted by Robert von Hallberg in *Charles Olson: The Scholar's Art* (Cambridge: Harvard University Press, 1978), p. 151.

3. Sigmund Freud, "Loss of Reality in Neurosis and Psychosis," *Standard Edition,* vol. 19, p. 183.

4. Sigmund Freud, "Neurosis and Psychosis," *Standard Edition,* vol. 19, p. 151.

5. "It is an accident in this register, and in what takes place in it, namely, the foreclosure of the Name-of-the-Father in the place of the Other, and in the failure of the paternal metaphor, that I designate the defect that gives psychosis its essential condition and the structure that separates it from neurosis." Jacques Lacan, "On the Possible Treatment Psychosis," *Ecrits: A Selection,* trans. A. Sheridan (New York: Norton, 1977), p. 215.

6. Plutarch, "The E at Delphi," *Moralia,* trans. F.C. Babbit (Cambridge: Harvard University Press, 1962), vol. 5, pp. 198–253.

7. Gilles Deleuze and Felix Guattari, *Anti-Oedipus: Capitalism and Schizophrenia,* trans. Robert Hurley, Mark Seem, and Helen R. Lane (New York: Viking, 1977). The schizo "produces himself as a free man, irresponsible, solitary and joyous, finally able to say and do something simply in his own name, without asking permission: a desire lacking nothing, a flux that overcomes barriers and codes, a name that no longer designates any ego whatsoever" (p. 131).

8. Bertold Brecht, "The Popular and the Realistic," ed. and trans. John Willett, *Brecht on Theatre: The Development of an Aesthetic* (London: Methuen, 1964), p. 110.

9. See Brecht's "On the Formalistic Character of the Theory of Realism," in Ronald Taylor, ed., *Aesthetics and Politics* (London: New Left Books, 1977), pp. 70–76.

10. For a Brechtian reading of the "classic realist text," see Colin MacCabe's "Realism and the Cinema: Notes on Some Brechtian Theses," *Screen,* (Summer 1974), 15(2).

11. John Irwin has written a literary history of the golden age of the

American myth of the "language of nature" in *American Hieroglyphics: The Symbol of the Egyptian Hieroglyphics in the American Renaissance* (New Haven: Yale University Press, 1980).

12. Benjamin Lee Whorf, "An American Indian Model of the Universe," *Language, Thought, and Reality*, ed. John B. Carroll (Cambridge: MIT Press, 1956), p.58.

13. Jacques Derrida, *Edmund Husserl's Origin of Geometry: An Introduction*, trans. John P. Leavey, Jr. (New York: Nicholas Hayes, 1978), p.175.

14. See Michel Foucault, "The Order of Discourse," in Robert Young, ed., *Untying the Text: A Post-Structuralist Reader* (Boston & London: Routledge & Kegan Paul, 1981), pp. 48–78.

15. Roland Barthes, *Image/Music/Text*, trans. Stephen Heath (New York: Hill & Wang, 1977), p. 192.

16. Allen Ginsberg, Appendix to Poem, in Paul Carroll, *The Poem in its Skin* (Chicago & New York: Follett, 1968), p. 101.

17. Quoted in Hallberg, p. 72.

18. Cid Corman, "On Poetry as Action," *Maps*, 4:67.

19. Geoffrey Thurley, *The American Moment: American Poetry in the Mid-Century* (London: Edward Arnold, 1977), p. 128.

20. Alfred North Whitehead, *Process and Reality: An Essay in Cosmology* (London: MacMillan, 1929), p. 254.

21. Ibid., p. 78.

22. See Benveniste, *Problems in General Linguistics*, trans. Mary E. Meek (Coral Gables: University of Miami Press, 1971), p. 227.

23. Eric Havelock, *A Preface to Plato* (Oxford: Basil Blackwell, 1963), p. 209. A relevant counterexample to Havelock's argument would be the Old Testament, which incorporates all of these paratactic relations but presents phenomenal events in a lacunary fashion, thereby rendering the diegetic illusion of identification impossible. This raises the larger question of Olson's assumption that Western languages are exclusively "Greek" in structure. Bernard Dubourg, for example, has argued that the major part of the New Testament may well have been written in Hebrew, and that the syntactic traces, rich in semitisms, survive rather well in translation ("L'Hebreu du nouveau testament," *Tel Quel* [Spring 1982], 91:55–63). To what degree, then, are these same paratactical patterns held in solution within our own discourse, filtered through the osmotic presence of the Bible, the central text of all Western culture? Erich Auerbach suggests that the Latin translators, at the time of Augustine, had to fight the temptation to efface all vestiges of that paratactical discourse, which would have led to "the far-reaching rationalization and syntactical organization of the Judaeo-Christian tradition." His conclusion was that they did not, and that they took up, in addition, the pseudo-Hebraic trope of the *figura*, a trope which "annihilated" the classical mind "down to the very structure of its language." *Mimesis: The Representation of Reality in Western Literature*, trans. Willard R. Trask (Princeton: Princeton University Press, 1953), p. 74.

24. Michel Serres, "The Algebra of Literature," in Josue V. Harari, ed., *Textual Strategies: Perspectives in Post-Structuralist Criticism* (Ithaca: Cornell University Press, 1979), p. 275.

25. William Spanos has argued for Olson's philosophical affinity with Heidegger's *Weiderholen*, in "Charles Olson and Negative Capability: A Phenomenological Interpretation," *Contemporary Literature* (1980), 21:39–80. Other phenomenological interpretations of Olson can be found in Joseph Riddel's "Decentering the Image," *Textual Strategies*, pp. 322–58, and Paul Bové's *Destructive Poetics: Heidegger and Modern American Poetry* (New York: Columbia University Press, 1980), pp. 217–81.

26. "An Objective," *Prepositions: The Collected Critical Essays of Louis Zukofsky* (Berkeley: University of California Press, 1981), p. 12.

27. Fredric Jameson suggests that the "originality of the concept of realism, however, lies in its claim to cognitive as well as aesthetic status." Again, the reference is to the Lukács-Brecht debate. Lukács's insistence on "the all-round knowledge" of an "overall, objective social context" as a criterion of realism, in no way contradicts Brecht's belief that realism "is an issue not only for literature: it is a major political, philosophical, and practical issue, and must be handled as such." Where they differ, however, is over the ethical question of how best to represent that "general human interest" in a radical way. *Aesthetics and Politics*, pp. 198, 33, 76.

28. See François Wahl's "Le désir d'espace," *Tel Quel* (Fall 1980), 84:39–45.

29. Jacques Derrida, *Edmund Husserl's Origin of Geometry*, pp. 176–77.

30. André Bazin, the critical champion of the movement, writes: "Neorealism knows only immanence. It is from appearance only, the simple appearance of beings and of the world that it knows how to deduce the ideas that it unearths. It is a phenomenology" and, as such, "looks upon reality as a whole, not incomprehensibly certainly, but inseparably, one." *What Is Cinema?*, trans. Hugh Gray (Berkeley: University of California Press, 1971), vol. 2, pp. 64–65.

31. The "detail" of Maximus differs, then, from Barthes's *"effet du réel"*, the super-real of Flaubertian narrative which, in its heightened and gratuitous notation of random objects, puts up a resistance to meaning by emphasizing the superfluous in realist representation. "L'effet du réel," *Communications* (1968), 11:84–89.

32. "It is time analysis be recognized as an opener not to cure but to cause, a freeing of the human being both back into the antiquity of himself and out into fable (dreams as the myth of the individual, sick or not), *l'humanité, c'est l'infirmité*—and the sum of dreams the archetype source of the myth and faith of the race—not some national advertised future health." "Notes to the Proposition: Man is Prospective," *Boundary 2* (1973–74), 2(2):4.

33. George Butterick, *A Guide to The Maximus Poems of Charles Olson* (Berkeley: University of California Press, 1978), p. 524.

34. Ibid., pp. 687–88.

35. Sigmund Freud, "Psycho-Analytic Notes on an Autobiographical Account of a Case of Paranoia," *Standard Edition*, vol. 12, p. 80.

36. Walter Benjamin too had "turned" toward the same kind of dawn: "As flowers turn toward the sun, by dint of a secret heliotropism the past strives to turn toward that sun which is rising in the sky of history. A historical materialist must be aware of this most inconspicuous of all transformations." *Illuminations*, ed. Hannah Arendt (New York: Shocken Books, 1968), p. 255.

37. Jacques Derrida, "White Mythology," *New Literary History* (Fall 1975), 6(1):51.

38. Jane Harrison, *Themis: A Study of the Social Origins of Greek Religion* (Cambridge: Cambridge University Press, 1927), pp. 525–26.

39. Gertrude Levy, *The Gate of Horn: A Study of the Religious Conceptions of the Stone Age, and Their Influence upon European Thought* (London: Faber & Faber, 1948), pp. 114, 176–77.

40. "Dostoevsky and *The Possessed*," *Twice-A-Year* (1940), 5/6:234–35.

5. The Cutt, The Stile

1. Quoted by Helen Gardner in *The Composition of the Four Quartets* (London: Faber & Faber, 1978), p. 34. The letter is postmarked June 14, 1947.

2. Jacques Lacan, "Lituraterre," *Littérature* (October 1971), 3:3–10.

3. Robert Creeley, *Contexts of Poetry: Interviews 1961–1971*, ed. Donald Allen (Bolinas: Four Seasons Foundation, 1973) p. 33.

4. Delivery, then, offers a flawless model for exchange, the friction-free world of the pneumatic dispatch service into which Derrida throws a polemical wrench in the shape of the proposition that "a letter can always not arrive at its destination." In *La Carte Postale*, he outlines a "metaphysics of postality" by which all channels of exchange—literary, economic, philosophic—are regulated, and offers, as a counterprinciple, a number of plays of *différance* as "*dichemination*," in which the path-finding mission of the message or letter is held up, or prevented altogether. *La Carte Postale* (Paris: Flammarion, 1980), p. 61, 154.

5. Robert von Hallberg suggestively points out that Olson's epistolary lineage is "not in the urbane, Horatian tradition but in the apostolic succession stemming from St. Paul," *Charles Olson: The Scholar's Art* (Cambridge: Harvard University Press, 1978), p. 59.

6. William Aiken, "Charles Olson and the Vatic," *Boundary 2* (1973/74), 2 (1/2):27–34.

7. Letter to Vincent Ferrini, November 7, 1950, *Origin* (Spring 1951), 1:5.

8. Ortega y Gasset suggests that the function of the *herms* was originally associated with the Greek *horos*, the Aristotelian term for the limiting aspects of the *logos*, and was thus extended in usage to represent the border of a landowner's property. *The Idea of Principle in Leibnitz and the Evolution of Deductive Theory* (New York: Norton, 1971), p. 11.

9. Roland Barthes, "The Grain of the Voice," *Image/Music/Text*, trans. Stephen Heath (New York: Hill & Wang, 1977), p. 182.

10. Butterick, p. 15. The letter is postmarked February 19, 1952.

11. See Erik Havelock, *A Preface to Plato* (Oxford: Basil Blackwell, 1963), pp. 154–155.

12. Michael McClure, *Jaguar Skies* (New York: New Directions, 1975), p. ii.

13. Martin Duberman, *Black Mountain: An Exploration in Community* (New York: Dutton, 1972), pp. 408–9.

14. Charles Boer, *Charles Olson in Connecticut* (Chicago: Swallow Press, 1975), p. 129.

15. Ibid., p. 145.

16. "Syllabary for a Dancer," *Maps*, 4:10.

17. Butterick, p. 546.

18. Ibid, p. 102.

19. Rosemarie Waldrop, "Charles Olson: Process and Relationship," *Twentieth Century Literature* (December 1977), 23(4):467–86.

20. Waldrop suggests that the poststructuralist focus on the idea of *rupture* as the representative mark of cultural crisis is rendered meaningless when transplanted from the constricted geo-cultural space of Europe to the relative vastness of the American experience of space. Fredric Jameson proposes a similar explanation for the theoretical primacy of "fragmentation" in recent European political thought; the American Left has never enjoyed the cohesion which is necessary in order for fragmentation to be a productive oppositional force. *The Political Unconscious: Narrative as a Socially Symbolic Act* (Ithaca: Cornell University Press, 1981), p. 54n.

21. Donald Davie, "The Black Mountain Poets," in Martin Dodsworth, ed., *The Survival Of Poetry: A Contemporary Survey* (London: Faber, 1970), p. 224.

22. Butterick, pp. 416, 422.

23. Ibid., p. 126.

24. Ibid., p. 127.

25. Ibid., p. 77.

26. William Carlos Williams, *In the American Grain* (New York: New Directions, 1925), p. 220.

27. Carl Jung, "On the Relation of Analytical Psychology to Poetry, *The Spirit in Man, Art, and Literature* (Princeton: Princeton University Press, 1966), p. 82.

28. For a fuller discussion of this metaphor, see Annette Kolodny's *The Lay of the Land: Metaphor as Experience and History in American Life and Letters* (Chapel Hill: University of North Carolina Press, 1975).

29. Eric Neumann, *The Great Mother* (Princeton: Princeton University Press, 1963), p. 330.

30. Quoted by Egbert Faas in *Towards a New American Poetics* (Santa Barbara: Black Sparrow Press, 1978), pp. 56–58.

31. Boer, p. 150.

6. Doubting John Thomas

1. Richard Howard, *Alone With America: Essays on the Art of Poetry in the United States Since 1950* (New York: Atheneum, 1980; enlarged ed.), p. 41.

2. Ibid., pp. 26–27.

3. "Interview with Sue Gangel," *The San Francisco Review of Books* (November 1977), 3:11.

4. Thomas de Quincey, *Confessions of an Opium-Eater* (Boston: Houghton Mifflin, 1876), pp. 65–66.

5. Sigmund Freud, "An Outline of Psychoanalysis," *Standard Edition*, vol. 22, p. 159.

6. Jacques Lacan, *The Four Fundamental Concepts of Psychoanalysis*, trans. Alan Sheridan, ed. Jacques-Alain Miller (New York: Norton, 1978), pp. 32–33.

7. On the topic of secrets (and their relation to fetishism), see the classic account of Octave Mannoni's *Clefs pour l'imaginaire* (Paris: Seuil, 1969). Taking as its cue the familiar line of the analysand, "I know . . . but nonetheless. . . ," he draws out the implications of that disvowal in anthropology and classical Western theater with respect to the conditions of infantile credulity under which we are held by the spectacle of such illusions.

8. Sigmund Freud, "Fetishism," *Standard Edition*, vol. 21, pp. 152–57. "The patient, brought up in an English nursery, had later come to Germany, where he forgot his mother tongue almost completely. The fetish, which originated from his earliest childhood, had to be understood in English, not German. The 'shine on the nose' [in German '*Glanz auf der Nase*'] was in reality, a 'glance' at the nose."

9. Guy Rosolato, "Le Fétichisme dont se dérobe l'objet," *La Relation d'inconnu* (Paris: Gallimard, 1978), p. 25.

10. See Jean Baudrillard's *Le Systeme des objets* (Paris: Gallimard, 1968) for "the logic of Santa Claus," pp. 232–34.

11. Roland Barthes, "Cette vielle chose, l'art. . . ." in *L'Obvie et l'obtus: Essais critiques, III* (Paris: Seuil, 1982), p. 181. Barthes argues that "art" can be best defined as that which returns most forcefully at the very moment it is being destroyed.

12. Sigmund Freud, "The Splitting of the Ego in the Process of Defence," *Standard Edition*, vol. 23, p. 275.

13. "The Impossible" (a review of Stein's *Stanzas in Meditation*), *Poetry* (July 1957), 90(40):250.

14. "Paris Notes," *Art International* (May 1, 1961), 5(4):63.

15. "Brooms and Prisms," *Art News* (March 1966), 65(1):84.

16. Gangel, p. 11.

17. Among others: Jonathan Holden, "Syntax and the Poetry of John Ashbery," *American Poetry Review* (July/August 1979), 18(4):37; Fred Moramarco, "John Ashbery and Frank O'Hara; The Painterly Poets," *Journal of Modern Literature* (September 1976), pp. 436–62; Leslie Wolf, "The Brushstroke's Integrity: The Poetry of John Ashbery and the Art of Paint-

ing," in David Lehman, ed., *Beyond Amazement: New Essays on John Ashbery* (Ithaca: Cornell University Press, 1980), pp. 224–55; Alan Williamson (the phrase, "the first abstract painter in our poetry," creeps in despite Williamson's otherwise incisive discussion of Ashbery's work), *Introspection and Contemporary Poetry* (Cambridge: Harvard University Press, 1984), p. 18. One admirable exception to the list is Richard Stamelman's attempt to deal seriously with the level of critical reflection involved in Ashbery's meditations about painterly reality in "Self-Portrait in a Convex Mirror," in "Critical Reflections: Poetry and Art Criticism in Ashbery's 'Self-Portrait in a Convex Mirror,'" *New Literary History* (Spring 1984), 15(3):607–30.

18. Marjorie Perloff, *Frank O'Hara: Poet among Painters* (New York: George Braziller, 1977), p. 70.

19. Ibid., p. 12.

20. Frank O'Hara, *Art Chronicles: 1954–1966*, ed. Donald Allen (New York: George Braziller, 1975), p. 82.

21. "R.B. Kitaj at the Marlborough," *Art in America* (May/June 1974), 62(3):103.

22. Notes to "Second Avenue," *The Collected Poems of Frank O'Hara*, ed. Donald Allen (New York: Knopf, 1971), pp. 495–97.

23. Clement Greenberg, *Art and Culture* (Cambridge, Mass.: Beacon Press, 1961), pp. 73–75. "Pictorial art had reduced itself entirely to what was visually verifiable, and Western painting had finally to give up its five hundred years effort to rival sculpture in the evocation of the tactile. . . . We no longer peer through the object surface into what is not itself." The most successful defense of this point of view since Greenberg can be found in the work of Michael Fried. See, for example, his classic early attack on the "theatricality" of Minimalist Art in "Art and Objecthood," in Gregory Battcock, ed., *Minimal Art: A Critical Anthology* (New York: E.P. Dutton, 1968).

24. Jean-Louis Baudry, "Ideological Effects of the Basic Cinematographic Apparatus," in Theresa Hak Kyung Cha, ed., *Apparatus* (New York: Tanam Press, 1980), p. 27.

25. See Jean-Louis Schefer's *Scénographie d'un tableau* (Paris: Seuil, 1969), p. 87.

26. "A Conversation with John Ashbery," by Mark Hilringhouse, *Soho News* (December 1981), p. 7.

27. For a brief introduction to some of the problems posed by optical illusions, for philosophers and aestheticians alike, see Mark Roskill and David Carrier, *Truth and Falsehood in Visual Images* (Amherst: University of Massachussetts Press, 1983). In an important book, M.H. Pirenne has argued that perspectival designs which can only be seen from the center of projection (like Pozzo's ceiling in San Ignazio, Rome) are so perfect that they are easily distorted, often simply by stepping to the side, whereas "lesser" illusions seem to be able to work from a decentered point of view. His deduction is that the spectator must always be aware of the real charac-

teristics of the picture surface *at the same time* as he or she registers the illusion of the represented scene, and that this knowledge helps to compensate for the distorted percept of the scene when viewed from the "wrong" position. *Optics, Painting, and Photography* (Cambridge: Cambridge University Press, 1970).

28. In Lacan's famous discussion of the anamorphosis in Holbein's *The Ambassadors*, the optical effect is interpreted on the level of a castratory threat; the painting is "looking" at the spectator and not vice versa. Holbein's anamorphosis, however, is not one which is intended to be viewed with an optical aid, it can only be seen from an oblique angle, *just* as the spectator is leaving its field of view. *The Four Fundamental Concepts of Psychoanalysis*, pp. 85–89.

29. Jurgis Baltrusaitis, *Anamorphoses* (Paris: Oliver Perrin, 1980), p. 7.

30. Hilringhouse, p. 5.

31. "In Darkest Language," *New York Times Book Review* (October 29, 1967), 72(41):62.

32. Ashbery's comments are in "Craft Interview with John Ashbery," by Janet Bloom and Robert Losada, *New York Quarterly* (Winter 1972), 9:20.

33. A more recent example can be found in Maurice Roche's "optical" writing, which is frequently constructed within, or else contains, visually oblique inscriptions like the anamorphosis. The illusions are often no more than a tissue of precise instructions about how it works, where its "key" mechanism is located, and where one must stand in order to "get the picture." See Claudia Reeder, "Maurice Roche: Seeing is (not) Believing," *Contemporary Literature* (1978), 19(3):351–77.

34. For a fuller discussion of *Nouvelles Impressions*, see Roger Cardinal, "Enigma," *Twentieth Century Studies* (December 1974), 12:53–56. The fetishization of the "mechanical" construction of the art work is a modernist touchstone, best embodied perhaps in an apparatus like Duchamp's *Large Glass*, where the invitation to the spectator to strip the bride bare includes the striptease option of stopping before it is too late, before sexual difference is revealed. Duchamp's piece is a *bachelor machine*, an apparatus in which man is transcendentalized within a mechanical process, where his disciplined eroticism renounces procreation in a reversal of the myth of virgin birth. For the application of this modern myth in the work of Poe, Jarry, Lautréamont, Lang, H.G. Wells, Ernst, Kafka, Tinguely, Warhol, and others, see Harald Szeemann, ed., *Le Maccine Celibi/The Bachelor Machines* (New York: Rizzoli, 1975).

35. "Re-establishing Roussel," *Portfolio and Art News Annual* (1962), 6:106.

36. In *Discours, Figure* (Paris: Klincksieck, 1971), Jean-François Lyotard attempts to revitalize the *ut pictura poesis* equation by reviving the opposition between a commonly referential register and an essentialist "poetic" attempts to revitalize the *ut pictura poesis* equation by reviving the opposi-

tion between a commonly referential register and an essentialist "poetic"
expressivity which language cannot fully incorporate. This latter is a *figural*
space, a plasticity which "remains to be seen" as sensible, both "on the
edge of discourse" (p. 13), and internal to it: Mallarmé's writing, for example, transcends its prosaic function, and reaches out for the power of "being
seen" or "figured" (p. 62).

37. "Paris Notes," *Art International* (January 1963), 17(1):79.

38. *Three Plays* (Calais, Vermont: Z Press, 1978), p. 7.

39. Frank O'Hara, "Rare Modern," *Standing Still and Walking in New York*,
ed. Donald Allen (Bolinas: Grey Fox Press, 1975), p. 80.

40. Frank O'Hara, *Jackson Pollock* (New York: George Braziller, 1959),
p. 12.

41. *Modern Painters*, III, chapter 12, *The Complete Works of John Ruskin*
(London: George Allen, 1904), vol. 5, pp. 210–11.

42. "An Expressionist in Paris," *Art News* (April 1965), 64(2):44, 63.

43. "Post-Painterly Quattrocento," *Art News* (December 1966), 65(8):40.

44. Frank O'Hara, *Jackson Pollock*, p. 21.

45. "Frank O'Hara's Question," *Bookweek* (September 25, 1966). See also
the issue of September 4, and Ashbery's letter to the editor in *The Nation*,
(May 8, 1967), 204(19):578.

46. *The Collected Poems of Frank O'Hara*, p. 266.

47. David Antin, "what am i doing here?" in *Talking at the Boundaries*
(New York: New Directions, 1976), p. 23.

48. Greenberg, p. 73.

49. Sue Gangel, p. 13.

50. David Shapiro, *John Ashbery* (New York: Columbia University Press,
1979), p. 144.

51. "Craft Interview," pp. 21–25.

52. "An Interview in Warsaw" with Piotr Sommer, in Michael Palmer,
ed., *Code of Signals: Recent Writings in Poetics* (Berkeley: North Atlantic
Books, 1983), p. 305.

53. Roger Shattuck, review of *Houseboat Days* in *New York Review of Books*
(March 23, 1978), 25(5):38–40.

54. Jacques Lacan, *The Four Fundamental Concepts of Psychoanalysis*, p. 32.

55. Roman Jakobson, "On Visual and Auditory Signs," *Phonetica* (1964),
11:218.

56. Roman Jakobson, "About the Relation between Visual and Auditory
Signs," in D. Walthen-Dunn, ed., *Models for the Perception of Speech and Visual
Form* (Cambridge: MIT Press, 1967), p. 6.

57. Sigmund Freud, *Standard Edition*, vol. 23, pp. 275–76.

58. Roland Barthes, *Camera Lucida*, trans. Richard Howard (New York:
Hill and Wang, 1981), p. 93.

59. Sigmund Freud, "A Disturbance of Memory on the Acropolis,"
Standard Edition, vol. 22, p. 241.

60. Frank O'Hara, "Personism: A Manifesto," in Donald Allen and Warren Tallman, eds., *The Poetics of the New American Poetry* (New York: Grove Press, 1973), p. 354.

61. Bloom, *Figures of Capable Imagination* (New York: Seabury Press, 1976) p. 191.

62. Henri Mondor, ed., *Eugene Lefebvre: sa vie, see lettres à Mallarmé* (Paris: Gallimard, 1951), p. 341.

63. David Lehman, "The Shield of a Greeting," *Beyond Amazement*, p. 118.

64. Shapiro, pp. 32–33, 104.

65. John Bayley, "The Poetry of John Ashbery," *London Review of Books* (September 2–15, 1982), p. 3.

66. Veronica Forrest-Thompson, *Poetic Artifice: A Theory of Twentieth-Century Poetry* (New York: St. Martins Press, 1978), p. 132.

67. "An Interview in Warsaw," p. 295.

68. Bloom, pp. 172–74.

69. Williamson, p. 123.

70. Shapiro, p. 165.

71. Two examples of critical treatment of the dream theme are Cynthia Evans, "A Movement out of the Dream," *American Poetry Review* (July/August 1979), 18(4):33–35, and Marjorie Perloff, "Mysteries of Construction," *The Poetics of Indeterminacy* (Princeton: Princeton University Press, 1981), pp. 248–87.

72. Christian Metz has suggested that the classical narrative film offers the same gentle exit out of the dreamlike condition it has reproduced for the spectator in the movie theater darkness. "The Fiction Film and Its Spectator," in *The Imaginary Signifier*, trans. B. Brewster, C. Britton, A. Guzzetti, and A. Williams (Bloomington: Indiana University Press, 1982), pp. 99–147.

73. Freud observes that this kind of fantasy is like "the facade of an Italian church in having no relation with the structure lying behind it. But [the fantasy] differed from these facades in being disordered and full of gaps, and in the fact that the portions of the interior construction had forced their way through it at many points." *Standard Edition,* vol. 4, p. 211. See Dalia Judovitz's valuable discussion of the "facade" in "Freud: Translation and/or Interpretation," *SubStance* (1979), 22:29–38.

74. "Craft Interview," p. 28.

75. Sigmund Freud, *Standard Edition*, vol. 5, p. 340.

76. It was Tristan Tzara who provided the blueprint for this kind of cultural activity:

To make a dadaist poem
Take a newspaper.
Take a pair of scissors.
Choose an article as long as you are planning to make your poem.
Cut out the article.

Then cut each of the words that make up this article and put
   them in a bag.
Shake it gently.
Then take out the scraps one after the other in the order in which
   they left the bag.
Copy conscientiously.
The poem will be like you.
And here you are a winner, infinitely original and endowed with a
   sensibility that is charming though beyond the understanding of the
   vulgar.

Robert Motherwell, ed., *The Dada Painters and Poets* (New York: Wittenborn, 1951), p. 92.

77. Sigmund Freud, *Standard Edition*, vol. 18, pp. 263–65. For the Borne text itself, unavailable in English, see Jean Fourton, "Freud avec Borne," *Littoral* (October 1981), 2:151–59.

78. Jack Kerouac, "Essentials of Spontaneous Prose," *Evergreen Review,* 2(5):73.

79. "Growing up Surreal," *Art News* (May 1968), 67(3):41.

80. "They Came from Inner Space," *Art News* (December 1967), 66(8):58.

81. André Breton, *Manifestos of Surrealism,* trans. Richard Seaver and Helen Lane (Ann Arbor: University of Michigan Press, 1969), p. 26.

82. *VW* (June 1942), 1, the frontispiece.

83. Sue Gangel, p. 13.

84. Quoted by Perloff in *The Poetics of Indeterminacy,* pp. 249–50.

85. "Silence d'Or" an unpublished piece in Jean-Louis Bedouin, *André Breton* (Paris: Seghers, 1950), pp. 83–86.

86. Sigmund Freud, "The Interpretation of Dreams," *Standard Edition,* vol. 4, p. 312.

87. See Sigmund Freud, *Standard Edition,* vol. 5, pp. 433–45, for the section on "Absurd Dreams," and also vol. 4, pp. 331–33, on the subject of "clarity" in the dream where "the form of a dream or the form in which it is dreamt is used with quite surprising frequency for representing its concealed subject matter."

88. Christine Brooke-Rose, *A Grammar of Metaphor* (London: Secker & Warburg, 1958), p. 93. "Metaphor is not merely the perception of similarity in dissimilarity, it is the changing of words by one another, and syntax is rich in methods of doing this, each with different effects."

The Failure of Modernism: A Conclusion

1. Charles Bernstein, "Three or Four Things I Know About Him," $L=A=N=G=U=A=G=E$, Supplement no. 3 (October 1981), p. 20 (my pagination).

2. James Breslin, *From Modern to Contemporary: American Poetry 1945–1965* (Chicago: University of Chicago Press, 1984), p. 3. Breslin quotes Randall Jarrell from his essay "The End of the Line" (1942).

3. Breslin does, in fact, go on to support that "the end of mystification, like the end of literature, is infinitely deferred" (p. 58), in arguing that everything that had once been claimed for modernism is now claimed for postmodernism.

4. For an account of these circumstances, and the response of the language poets, as a group, to a corresponding change in the direction of Marxist aesthetics, see my article "The New Sentence and the Commodity Form: Recent American Writing," in Cary Nelson and Lawrence Grossberg, eds., *Marxism and the Interpretation of Culture* (Urbana: University of Illinois Press, 1986).

5. Paul de Man, *Blindness and Insight: Essays in the Rhetoric of Contemporary Criticism* (Minneapolis: University of Minnesota Press, 1983; 2d ed.), p. 144.

6. Ibid., p. 151.

7. The chapters on Joyce and Eliot in Franco Moretti's *Signs Taken for Wonders: Essays in the Sociology of Literary Forms* (London: Verso, 1983) present these traditional issues of Marxist interpretation in a fresh and illuminating way.

8. For many American poets, however, it was the Vietnam War, a concrete series of external events, that revived the modernist anxiety about the relation between poetic form and history, furnishing it with all the fantasmatic trappings of an "American failure." Thus, the Adamic faith in "open" American forms was shaken, perhaps for the last time, by the perception that history had somehow "closed," or surrendered its own formal promise to Americans. See Cary Nelson's *Our Last First Poets: Vision and History in Contemporary American Poetry* (Urbana: University of Illinois Press, 1981).

9. Charles Altieri, *Enlarging the Temple: New Directions in American Poetry During the 1960's* (Lewisburg: Bucknell University Press, 1979), pp. 16–17.

10. The single most important document of American literary modernism is Donald Allen's 1960 anthology, *The New American Poetry*. The original edition boldly sports a flowing flag motif on the cover. The cover of the revised edition, entitled *The Postmoderns*, ed. Donald Allen and George Butterick (New York: Grove Press, 1982) is designed to highlight the artificiality or self-conscious irony of the patriotic gesture; it depicts, instead, Jasper John's *Three Flags*, a canvas with flags superimposed on top of each other, suggesting an illusory three-dimensional construction, as if to invoke the self-prepetuating nature of Americanist ideology. Each cover represents a different reading of these poets' cultural response to American values. Even if one is inclined to reject the former's suggestion that any patriotic complicity on the part of these poets was a relatively unproblematic one, it is even more difficult to accept the revised perception because it seeks to impose its own critical retrospection on the sixties, in replacing a code of spontaneity and immediacy commonly associated with the period with a more contemporary set of parodic and self-reflexive signifiers.

11. Sacvan Bercovitch, *The Puritan Origins of the American Self* (New Haven: Yale University Press, 1975), p. 157.

12. After all, the "truth" of Nature, once the genuinely subversive practice of Romanticism, has long since been a theoretical construction in its own right—even for writers like Emerson. This is what seems to flaw Anthony Easthope's otherwise valuable discussion of the history of English versification in *Poetry as Discourse* (London: Methuen, 1983). His initial acceptance of Althusser's perception of ideology as a subject-constituting agency—which obliges subjects to see themselves as naturally "free" agents—seems to militate against his argument that the modernist espousal of free verse (and thus the liberation of poetry from "inherited discourse and metre") was necessarily a challenge to the "transcendental ego" position that he finds dominant in the "bourgeois" tradition of verse. In effect, Easthope fails to see the continuity between an illusion of "free" agency promoted by ideology, and an illusion of "natural" discourse promoted by theories of free verse.

13. One could, of course, say the same of Bloom's own critical project, which outlines the ways in which a writer Oedipally sidesteps, or resists, the influence of his precursors. The breadth of Bloom's work, straddling his interests in Jewish mysticism and the patrician canon of American poetry, can be seen to fall prey, in exactly the same way, to the patrilinear experience in offering itself up to a less orthodox Kabbalistic origin by "swerving" through the "Americanist" tradition of Orphic transcendentalism which it constructs as its object.

14. "Religion Without Humanism," in Norman Foerster, ed., *Humanism and America* (New York: Farrar & Rinehardt, 1930), p. 112.

15. Theodor W. Adorno, *Aesthetic Theory*, trans. C. Lenhardt, ed. Gretel Adorno and Rolf Tiedemann (London & Boston: Routledge & Kegan Paul, 1984), p. 1.

Index